CALVIN MEMORIAL ADDRESSES

First Presbyterian Church, Savannah, Ga.

CALVIN
MEMORIAL ADDRESSES

Delivered Before the General Assembly
Of the Presbyterian Church in the U.S.
at
First Presbyterian Church, Savannah, GA

Benjamin B. Warfield
Richard Reed
James Orr
R.A. Webb
Thomas Cary Johnson

SOLID GROUND CHRISTIAN BOOKS
BIRMINGHAM, ALABAMA USA

Solid Ground Christian Books
PO Box 660132
Vestavia Hills AL 35266
205-443-0311
www.solid-ground-books.com
sgcb@charter.net

CALVIN MEMORIAL ADDRESSES
Celebrating the 400th Anniversary of Calvin's Birth
Delivered Before the General Assembly
Of the Presbyterian Church in the United States
At the First Presbyterian Church, Savannah, GA, May 1909

Published in 1909 by the Presbyterian Committee of Publication
Richmond, VA

First Solid Ground Edition in July 2007

Cover Image of John Calvin

Cover design by Borgo Design, Tuscaloosa, AL.
Contact them at borgogirl@bellsouth.net

ISBN: 1-59925-122-1

CONTENTS.

	PAGE
Introduction, ...	5

Calvin's Contribution to the Reformation, ... 15
    REV. RICHARD C. REED, D. D., LL. D.

Calvin the Theologian, ... 37
    REV. HENRY COLLIN MINTON, D. D., LL. D.

Calvin's Contributions to Church Polity, ... 57
    REV. THOMAS CARY JOHNSON, D. D., LL. D.

Calvin's Attitude Towards and Exegesis of the
    Scriptures, ... 89
        DR. JAMES ORR.

Calvin's Doctrine of Infant Salvation, ... 107
    REV. R. A. WEBB, D. D., LL. D.

The Relation of Calvin and Calvinism to Missions,.. 127
    REV. S. L. MORRIS, D. D.

Calvin's Influence on Educational Progress, ... 147
    GEORGE H. DENNY.

Calvin's Influence Upon the Political Development
    of the World, ... 175
        FRANK T. GLASGOW.

CONTENTS.
(Continued)

PAGE

How Far Has Original Calvinism been Modified by Time, ... 195
 REV. SAMUEL A. KING, D. D., LL. D.

Present Day Attitude to Calvinism, ... 223
 REV. BENJ. B. WARFIELD, D. D., LL. D.

How May the Principles of Calvinism be Rendered Most Effective Under Modern Conditions, ... 241
 A. M. FRASER.

John Calvin—The Man and His Times, ... 261
 DR. CHARLES MERLE D' AUBIGNE.

INTRODUCTION.

The General Assembly of the Presbyterian Church in the United States in session at Birmingham, Ala., May, 1907, received from the Executive Commission of the Alliance of Reformed Churches throughout the world holding the Presbyterian System, the following communication relative to a general observance of the 400th Anniversary of the birth of John Calvin:

"The Executive Commission draws the attention of the churches in the Alliance and of all lovers of true progress to the approaching Four Hundredth Anniversary of the birth of John Calvin. The Reformer was born at Noyon, Picardy, France, July 10, 1509. His life was lived during one of the most important and crucial epochs of human history. In the providence of God he was one of the most potent forces of his day for human progress, and his influence continues in the present, and will abide in the future, a great power for the welfare of mankind. Men of all classes of thought and of all nations recognize his greatness. Particularly was he influential in setting in motion those forces which have resulted in the formation of the American nation. Great historians speak of him as the founder of the United States. While thus connected, however, with the American Republic, the great Genevan had and has a vital relation to all Christian nations. No man of his age has been more influential in securing civil and religious liberty, the development of popular government, the secular progress of man, the reformation of the Christian Church, the development of religious thought along true lines, and the general advance of the Kingdom of God in the world. It is recommended:

That the Supreme Judicatories of the Churches in the Alliance be requested and urged to take steps for the general observance by all their congregations of the four hundredth anniversary of the birth of John Calvin.

Overtures were received from thirteen presbyteries to the same effect.

In response to these overtures, the following *ad interim* committee was appointed "to consider and report upon a plan for the general celebration of the four hundredth anniversary of the birth of John Calvin throughout our Church": R. F. Campbell, J. W. Stagg, C. M. Richards, D. H. Ogden, W. W. Moore, W. M. McPheeters, Geo. E. Wilson, J. D. Murphy, J. W. Faxon, W. J. Martin, A. G. Hall.

The Assembly of 1908, in session at Greensboro, N. C., took the following action, in accordance with the recommendation of the *ad interim* committee:

"The General Assembly, recognizing the historic significance of this anniversary, and the unusual opportunity afforded thereby for the vindication, propagation and inculcation of the great principles of the Reformed Faith, which lie at the foundation of civil and religious liberty, and earnestly desiring, along with sister churches of the same faith and order throughout the world,

"To take
Occasion by the hand and make
The bounds of freedom wider yet,"

adopts the following plan looking to the general observance of the Calvin Quadricentennial by the Presbyterian Church in the United States:

I. All institutions of learning within the bounds of the Assembly, under Presbyterian auspices, are requested to consider the feasibility of arranging for series of sermons and addresses bearing on the life and work of John Calvin at such time or times during the year 1909 as may be most convenient.

II. The Assembly suggests that the religious papers of the church have prepared and published in their columns at intervals during the year 1909 as many articles as possible relating to Calvin and Calvinism.

III. The Assembly recommends that each Presbytery at its meeting in the fall of 1908 appoint a special committee to arrange for a formal celebration of the Calvin Quadricentennial at its meeting in the spring of 1909, and to plan for appropriate sermons and addresses in the individual churches of the Presbytery at such time as each church may determine, giving preference to dates as near as possible to that of Calvin's birth, July 10.

IV. The Assembly adopts the following program of exercises for the celebration of the Calvin Quadricentennial during the sessions of the General Assembly of 1909."

The program referred to was successfully carried out by the Assembly in session at Savannah, Ga., May 20th to 28th, 1909, and the addresses delivered on that occasion are contained in this volume, which is issued by the Committee of Publication, in accordance with the order of the Assembly.

R. F. CAMPBELL,
Chairman of the *ad interim* Committee.

GAVEL PRESENTED.

Mr. C. S. Wood, who invited the Assembly to Savannah, presented to the Moderator, on behalf of the Session of the First Church, Savannah, a historic gavel, made from a beam taken from the belfry of St. Peter's Cathedral, in Geneva, where John Calvin preached. A picture of this gavel was published in the *Christian Observer* of May 19. The address was as follows:

PRESENTATION ADDRESS BY CHARLES S. WOOD.

Mr. Moderator: The great honor and privilege has been accorded me this morning of investing you with the implement of authority that you may successfully resume your labors and properly transmit the office of Moderator to your successor. The words I must submit have to do with a long and devious pathway of history, even up to this historic occasion. I shall not depart from old or modern methods if some of the threads of my scattered history are spun of fancy; for history, they say, is written from facts and fancy. You will discern the facts and wrestle with the live things of imagination. First, Geneva is my theme.

In the commentaries of Caesar we find the first appearance of Geneva in history, "The most northerly city of the Allabroges." He relates how he cut the bridge over the Rhone in order to prevent the passage of the Helvetes, B. C. 58, intimating that the gods had ordained its favorable destiny—a statement of unconscious Calvinism. This great soldier found then, as it is now, a city beautiful for situation; one side guarded by the undulating pine-clad Jura, another by the verdant ledges of the Saleve, with the snow-clad range of Mt. Blanc thrown into relief against the deep blue sky, and fronting a lake, the matchless beauty of which has never ceased to inspire painters and poets of all lands.

In the fourth century we find this city and state organized into the first kingdom of Burgundy. Subsequently it came under the control of the Franks and Germans successively governed by one or the other or by both directly or indirectly for several hundred years. Early in the sixteenth century it was remarkable for the final struggle between the people and the partisans of the Duke of Savoy, the successes of the former becoming effective finally with the adoption of the Reformation, when the Episcopal authority was abolished.

About this period of unrest, 1536, there came to Geneva John Calvin, a refugee from Picardy, already celebrated for his bold utterances and distinguished for his scholarly accomplishments in letters, law and theology. He was impressed by Farel to abide and lend his wisdom and talents to the emergency. The people accepted him, then exiled him, and at last embraced him; and so the canton of Geneva became a republic, governed by Syndics and Councils elected by the people. The city quickly became famous through Calvin, whose influence now extended over the whole of Europe in Church and State and public instruction. He elaborated civil and sumptuary laws, investing old institutions with a simplicity which attracted the attention and obtained the support of reformers in all countries. He trusted the people to elect a Council, competent to appoint the judges. He founded an academy which in modern times became a university of wide renown. He advocated the necessity of public instruction to children of tender years and upwards.

The great John Knox sat at his feet, and subsequently put the mantle of his intellect over the hills of Scotland. He believed that a child of the Covenant should be a child of the Church, and but for the fact he was only a man, he might have settled the "Infant Clause" with which you are troubled to-day. As was said of the ancient roads, "all leading to Rome," so it may be said of the modern theological roads, they all lead to this modern Protestant Rome, "The court of the Alps." The great Napoleon found in its possession a resource for governmental adaptation and profited by the study of its institutions. The peace of Vienna sanctioned its independence under the present Swiss confederation, whereby it now constitutes the twenty-second canton of Switzerland.

Such is my reference to fact, but now I must refer to fancy and fact and then my history will be spoken. Above the Black Forest on the crest of the mountain, near a wooded villa, where now the iron steeds of modern travel merge from the tunnel of the road from Berne, there stood for parting words a patriot youth and lover, June, 1366. Leagues of confederation had been made for fifty years between the Swiss States and as often broken through alien interference. This youth was the son of Schwyz, the loved was a princess of the House of Hapsburg; then and there was formed a compact known as the "Everlasting League." They melted their mutual sorrows with their mutual joys while they listened to the music of forest anthems and watched the feathered songsters assemble. Why should not this beautiful land respond some day in accord with these happy fixtures of forest, flowers and song! The patriot youth planted there a branch and called it the twig of the dual league and seal of hand and heart, for here will grow a tree, he said, the boughs of which shall shelter soldiers, as these around should have done, but after, its wood shall support the eternal harmony of the music of peace while it looks down upon a soldier of the Cross wielding the effective Sword of the Spirit. From this towering prospect with a vast circumference of vision, these lovers looked around them with a radius of extended area, upon mountain and meadow, forest and field, river and lake, hill and dale, village and farm-land, far off city and shimmering water; and, in the further language of Van Dyke, over all, the westering sun wove a transparent robe of gem-like hues, forming a picture of nature, every feature of which was quivering and pulsating with conscious beauty. With what distinctness did they look into the future! Far out by the distant lake was the castle of Chillon, since made famous by Byron's genius, where Francois de Bonnivard was imprisoned for six cruel years by the Duke of Savoy. And yonder was Vevey, where the weary traveller was wont to sleep the "sleep of the just."

A hundred years and more from that date, in 1470, a sturdy axeman felled a sturdy tree on this spot and workmen placed a strong beam from that tree in the belfry of St. Peter's Cathedral, situated on the central plateau of Geneva, first erected in the tenth century on the site of an ancient pagan temple, nearly destroyed by fire in 1430, finally restored many years afterwards. This timber beam was there when Calvin taught and preached in that famous cathedral and for four hundred years it called the worshippers to the peaceful shelter of the old sanctuary. In recent years, having accomplished its labors there, it gave place to modern beams in the erection of a new tower to conform with ancient design before the fire of 1430. The Administrative Council of Geneva, now controlling this building, through the good offices of Francis B. Keene, the American Consul, presented this congregation with a large section of the beam, and gave orders for its shipment. I need not go further than to say from this wood a beautiful gavel has been carved, designed on the pattern of an altar with Ionic columns. On one side the profile likeness of Calvin, on another the famous Calvin seal, the extended hand and heart, surrounded with the motto "Promte et sincere in orere Domoni," and on the other side a bronze plate bearing this inscription, "Wood from old belfry St. Peter's Cathedral, Geneva, where John Calvin preached. Presented by First Presbyterian Church, Savannah, Ga., to the General Assembly, May, 1909."

In behalf of this congregation and by order of the Church session, I now present you with this gavel with which the deliberations of this Assembly may be conducted. The gavel is rather large, but remember, you have to do with great affairs. If you find that a cunning hand has made its harmony complete, the symbol of united measures makes it a souvenir of a great past, and as you see in its design a symbol of devotion, be reminded that the one whose memory it is intended to perpetuate, laid his heart upon the sacrificial altar.

Gavel Made from Wood from Tower of St. Peter's Cathedral, Geneva, Switzerland.
Presented to the General Assembly at Savannah, Ga., May, 1909.

CALVIN'S CONTRIBUTION TO THE REFORMATION.

Rev. Richard C. Reed, D. D., LL. D.,
Columbia Seminary.

It will hardly be expected of me to answer with perfect precision the question, What was John Calvin's contribution to the Reformation of the 16th Century? That mighty revolution was not the work of one man, nor of a few men, but it was wrought by the combined labors of a multitude of men. Consequently, there was the blending of forces, and it would be impossible to segregate the work of the one from the many, and to weigh with nice accuracy the sum total of influence emanating from the single individual. Every actor in the great drama was acted on. He was at the same time a generator and a transmitter of power. Only an omniscient eye could separate the intermingling currents, and trace each to its true source. Nevertheless, John Calvin stands out with marked distinctness, from his colaborers, and we can specify the most important things which he did, and estimate with some approach to accuracy the value of these as a contribution to the great movement.

Calvin was a mere lad, eight years old, when, on the 31st of October, 1517, Martin Luther struck the blow that marked the birth-throes of the Reformation. While he was growing to man's estate, there followed thick and fast the thrilling events of an ever-expanding struggle. In Germany there was the disputation with

Eck, the excommunication, the burning of the bull, the diet of Worms, the Knight's war, the Peasant's war, the Protest of Spiers, the Augsburg Confession, the Smalcald League; in Switzerland, the eloquent voice of the noble, patriotic Zwingle had stirred the hearts of his fellow-countrymen, and the War with Rome was on in earnest. While Calvin was growing to man's estate, there were fifteen years of noise and tumult, of high and hot debates, of diets and edicts, of terrible anathemas, and bold defiance, with the result that nearly the whole of North Germany, the Scandinavian countries and many of the cantons of Switzerland were hopelessly lost to the Papacy. The Reformed Faith was still spreading. In thousands of hearts the dawn was breaking, fresh life was throbbing, heaven-born hopes were kindling. But the war was still on. Martyr fires were burning in France, in the Netherlands, in England and Scotland. The life-blood of Zwingle had stained the battlefield of Cappell; and nowhere outside of Germany was there a man gifted with powers of leadership, and filled with the spirit of God, who could point the way, and lead these newly emancipated souls out of the wilderness into the promised rest. Such was the condition of affairs when John Calvin, having reached the age of 23, and having been trained in the best schools of France for the role he was to play, was born into the Kingdom of God. It had not yet been determined whether Luther was to be the hero of a great success or the victim of a great failure.

Just when and where and under what circumstances Calvin was converted, the most diligent students of his life have not been able to discover. He is silent touching time, place and circumstance. He is not

silent touching the fact, and that is the great thing—
one of the greatest things of the kind that has happened since Jesus met Saul of Tarsus near the gates
of Damascus. Calvin speaks of his conversion as sudden. However sudden, it was thorough, lifting him
at once and forever out of the superstitions of Popery
into the clear, radiant light of the Gospel. Calvin was
not only certain of his conversion, but he was equally
certain that his conversion was the work of God, and
was an act of His sovereign, electing grace. This constituted both his fitness and his call to service. His
doctrine was that election unto eternal life meant election to eternal obedience.

Immediately he began to make his contribution to
the Reformation. "A year had not elapsed," he says,
"when all who were desirous of purer doctrine were
continually coming to learn of me while as yet but a
novice and a tyro." He tried to hide himself, "but
this was so far from being permitted to me that all of
my retreats were like a public lecture room." "Men
do not light a candle and put it under a bushel." Men
were groping in darkness, yearning for the light, and
God set John Calvin on a candlestick, and constrained
him, however reluctantly, to give light to all who
were in the house.

I feel that I can best serve the demands of this occasion by not attempting too much. I shall select,
therefore, for consideration only the most signal contributions which Calvin made to the Reformation.
I. His Theological and Exegetical Writings. II. His
Church Polity and Genevan Reformation. III. His
Educational Measures and Correspondence.

I. *His Theological and Exegetical Writings*. He was
at Paris when he cast in his lot with those who were

breaking away from the old faith; and consequently in the midst of enemies who were alert to detect and to suppress every outcropping of heresy. His life was soon in danger and he fled in disguise. In 1535, we find him at Basle, Switzerland. The gracious Providence of God could not have done him a greater kindness than to direct his footsteps to this spot. It furnished just the secure retreat and the literary atmosphere which his retiring nature and his scholarly tastes craved. We might expect him to make this his permanent resting place, and we find that he had planned to do this at a later day. For the present he has brought in his heart to this paradise of the scholarly recluse the sorrows of his suffering fellow-countrymen. The King, the Parliament, the University of Paris, the Sorbonne, were roasting some of these over slow fires. Not content with this, they were putting upon their names and memories the most base and unjust accusations. They spread abroad the report that these saintly martyrs were fanatical anabaptists, whose turbulent and disorderly lives were a menace to society. They were especially concerned to have these slanders believed by the Lutherans of Germany, whose friendship the King was courting for political purposes. This was more than Calvin could silently endure. He must speak a word in their defense. Such was the origin of the first edition of his Institutes of the Christian Religion.

It was a brief manual as published at that time, and was published for no other reason, as Calvin avers, than to bear witness to the faith of those whom he saw basely maligned. He was not attempting to do a great thing, nor did he suppose, when he put forth his little book that he had done a great thing. So

Earnestly Pleading with Calvin to Remain in Geneva and Help in the Work.

far was he from seeking fame from it that he slipped away from Basle without anyone's knowing that he was the author of it, and resolved that he would keep it a secret elsewhere, as it was his purpose to avoid taking open part in the fierce religious war that was raging around him. But at once the lovers of evangelical truth saw the value of this book. It met, as no other writing had yet met, the most exigent need of the times. It did for struggling Protestantism what the Council of Trent later did for Rome, defined clearly the issue. It put into lucid, logical and succinct form, with solid scriptural basis, the doctrines over which the tremendous conflict was waging. Friend and foe alike could see just what it was that some men were willing to die for, just what it was that other men were willing to make them die for.

Calvin dedicated the book to the King of France in a preface which for manly frankness, sustained eloquence, directness and pathos, has never been surpassed. If it had been in the power of words to touch the King's heart, and secure for his suffering subjects a fair and just treatment, this appeal would not have been in vain. But the proud monarch had already chosen his ground. Having decided that the safety of his kingdom required that there should be *"un roi, un loi, un foi,"* he turned a deaf ear and held on his ill-starred course. Other ears however heard, other hearts felt, and from the day that the *Institutes of the Christian Religion* saw the light, the champions of Reform knew that a power had been added to their cause which would be felt from one end of Europe to the other.

In respect to the dominance and extent of their influence only two theologians in the history of the

Church can be placed by the side of Calvin—St. Augustine and Thomas Aquinas. By common consent, these three have been lifted to a solitary eminence of fame. Without claiming for Calvin greater genius than the other two, no Protestant can hesitate to claim for him a more intelligent and unbiased devotion to the word of God, the one exclusive source of all true theology. Both Augustine and Aquinas were in slavish subjection to the Church, and it was impossible for them to elaborate a system of doctrine that would not be darkly shaded, and fatally distorted by the great and manifold errors which had been embraced, and consequently hallowed for them by the authority of the Church. In contrast with these, Calvin, with mind freed from the trammels of tradition and superstition, freed from the doctrines and commandments of men, bowed with absolute and undivided reverence before the living oracles, and, discarding speculation, drew from these alone the doctrines out of which he constructed his matchless System. The value of such a gift to the Reformation can not easily be exaggerated. Protestants and Romanists bore equal testimony to its worth. The one hailed it as the greatest boon; the other execrated it with the bitterest curses. It was burnt by order of the Sorbonne at Paris and other places, and everywhere it called forth the fiercest assaults of tongue and pen. Florimond de Raemond, a Roman Catholic theologian, calls it "the Koran, the Talmud of heresy, the foremost cause of our downfall." Kampschulte, another Roman Catholic testifies that "it was the common arsenal from which the opponents of the Old Church borrowed their keenest weapons," and that "no writing of the Reformation era was more feared by Roman Catholics, more zealously fought against, and more hostilely pursued than Calvin's *Institutes.*" Its popularity was evidenced by the fact that edition followed edition in quick succession; it was translated into most of the languages of western Europe; it became the common text-book in the schools of the Reformed Churches, and furnished the material out of which their creeds were made.

Perhaps we should name this book in its final and enlarged form as the greatest contribution that Calvin made to the Reformation. It controlled or colored, moulded or guided, the theological thinking for the next hundred years of all the countries that adopted the Reformed faith. Not yet have the Protestant churches grown away from it, nor will they leave it behind so long as the Pauline conception of the Gospel continues to command the homage of Christian students. Its comprehensive mastery of Biblical and Patristic lore, its logical strength and coherence, its pure and elevated style, its reverend tone, its freedom from scientific technicalities must ever secure for it a prominent place in the regard of all who have a taste for theological studies.

Three years after the first edition of the *Institutes* issued from the press, Calvin published the first volume of his commentaries on the Scriptures. This was on the Epistle to the Romans, and was followed by other volumes from time to time throughout the remainder of his life. The completed series, as published in English translation, comprises forty-five portly volumes and covers nearly the whole of both Old and New Testaments. Viewed in connection with the other labors of Calvin, the magnitude of this work is nothing less than marvellous. It was not the magnitude, however, but the quality of this splendid series which gave it a permanent place in the front rank of exegetical works on the Scriptures. The style which Calvin proposed to himself was comprehensive brevity, transparent clearness and strict adherence to the spirit and letter of the author. The best description of the result is to say that Calvin accomplished what he intended to do.

To estimate the service which he rendered to the Reformation by these commentaries, it must be borne in mind that commentaries based on correct principles of exegesis were rare in that day. Calvin has indeed been called the founder of that method of exegesis which stresses dictionary, grammar and history. He led the way in discarding the custom of allegorizing the Scriptures, a custom which had come down from the earliest centuries of Christianity and which had been sanctioned by the greatest names in the Church, from Origen to Luther, a custom which converts the Bible into a nose of wax, and makes a lively fancy the prime qualification of an exegete. Calvin proceeded on the sound assumption that the writers of the Bible, like all other sensible writers, had in mind one definite thought, and that they used language in its natural, everyday meaning to express this thought. "I acknowledge," he says, "that Scripture is a most rich and inexhaustible fountain of all wisdom, but I deny that its fertility consists in the various meanings which any man at his pleasure may put into it. Let us know, then, that the true meaning of Scripture is the natural and obvious meaning; and let us embrace and abide by it resolutely. Let us not only refuse as doubtful, but boldly set aside as deadly corruption those pretended expositions of Scripture which lead us away from the natural meaning." In addition to correct principles of hermaneutics, Calvin brought to his task ample learning, deep spiritual insight and a heart that delighted in the work. The word of God was to him "more precious than gold, yea, much fine gold, sweeter also than honey and the honeycomb." If he ever did any work *con amore*, it was the work of studying and expounding the Scriptures.

The way in which the commentaries were received, and the influence allowed to them are sufficiently indicated by a statement in a MS. note quoted from Hooker. "The sense of Scripture which Calvin alloweth was held in the Anglican Church to be of more force than if ten thousand Augustines, Jeromes, Chrysostomes, Cyprians were brought forth." If such was the weight allowed to Calvin in the Anglican Church, much given to reverence for the fathers, we can hardly overstate the weight attached to his expositions in the Reformed Churches, made up of those who were altogether willing to be known as his disciples.

I can not dwell upon all the writings of Calvin, but must pass over many that exerted a profound and wide influence—his catechisms, sermons, treatise on the Lord's Supper and many other minor works that did much to fashion the views of his day. I must, however, say a word about some of his polemical writings, aimed directly at Rome. His "Reply to Cardinal Sadolet," his tract "On the Necessity of Reformation," and his sarcastic "Admonition showing the advantages which Christendom might derive from an Inventory of Relics," were merciless exposures of the corrupt and corrupting doctrines and practices of the Romish Church. These not only inspired the friends of Reform, but furnished them their most deadly ammunition. What Luther said of one of these writings might, with truth, have been said of them all: "They had hands and feet"—they could smite and they could travel. Calvin took occasion in all of his writings to uncover the hideous deformities of the Papacy, and he did it with such telling effect as to make himself the most hated man of the Reformation period. It was early recognized that as a controversialist, in which intellectual force, a well-disciplined mind, and keen powers of analysis are supreme requisites, Calvin stood out, the most formidable antagonist with which the enemies of the Reformation had to contend.

II. *His Church Polity and Genevan Reformation.* In 1536, when Calvin set foot in Geneva, he had reached the spot which God had predestined as the field of his life-work. His fellow-countryman, William Farel, had prepared the way for him by battering down the strongholds of Popery and securing freedom for the preaching of the gospel. For two years these earnest fellow-laborers not only preached the pure gospel, but they tried by calling in the aid of Caesar, to make the people of Geneva live the pure gospel. The yoke was found to be too heavy, and so the people deposed the preachers and drove them out. This, however, was but an episode. Calvin's field was Geneva. A brief experience of anarchy, following his expulsion, convinced the Genevese that they had separated what God had joined together. Deeply penitent, they pleaded for his return. The prospect offered to Calvin nothing but a life of prolonged crucifixion, but the call was too manifestly from God for him to resist it.

He entered Geneva a second time in the fall of 1541. He was just 32 years old, when it was recognized by both parties that they belonged by divine appointment to each other. Certainly no young man, standing practically alone, ever confronted a more formidable task than that which now confronted this ardent reformer. He faced "a tottering republic, a wavering faith and a nascent church." His first concern, of course, was with the Church, and his first concern for the Church was to provide for it an organization. Fortunately, during the period of his recent banishment, he found time to mature his views on church government. He had just published these views in the fourth book of the second edition of his *Institutes*. He knew, therefore, as he confronted the situation in Geneva, just what he wanted. At once, on his arrival, he waited on the Civil Council and asked for the appointment of a commission to draft the ordinances for the government of the Church. He was appointed on the commission and the work was his. But before the ordinances were adopted, and put into effect, they were modified, so that we do not see in the Genevan Church an exact realization of the theory set forth in the *Institutes*.

Without going into any analysis of these ordinances, we may say that they embodied the following fundamental principles. First, clear distinction between Church and State; second, as permanent officers of the Church, pastors, ruling elders, and deacons; third, the exercise of ecclesiastical power by a court composed of pastors and ruling elders; fourth, unity of the Church to be realized by placing a number of congregations under the jurisdiction of one court. In the application of these principles, in Geneva, the civil government took a hand and prevented Calvin from realizing his ideal. It must also be said that his ideal was not exactly our ideal. Still, these four fundamental principles are the fundamental principles of

Presbyterianism, and hence this church may rightly be called the mother church of all modern Presbyterian and Reformed churches.

If Calvin's church polity was not his greatest contribution to the Reformation, it was certainly his most original contribution. His system of theology was not new; his church polity was. There was nothing even remotely like it in the bounds of Christendom. It differed radically from the Roman Catholic Church, the Episcopal Church of England, the Lutheran churches of Germany, and the Zwinglian, or Reformed churches of Switzerland. So far was Calvin from copying any existing form that he did not even borrow from any existing form. Where, then, did he get the form of his church organization? He went to the same source from which he drew his system of theology— the word of God. Whatever we may be in this degenerate day, John Calvin was, with all his soul, a *jus divinum* Presbyterian. What he proposed to do, what he believed he did and what I believe he did, was to bring once again to the light of day and make effective those inspired principles of church government, laid down by the apostles, which had for centuries been buried under the colossal structure of Papal despotism. Calvin was a high-churchman in the sense that he cherished a profound reverence for the visible church, as an institution of Christ, endowed with rare prerogatives, and discharging vital functions. "We may learn," he says, "from the title *mother* how useful and even necessary it is for us to know her; since there is no other way of entrance into life unless we are conceived by her, born of her, nourished at her breast, and continually preserved under her care and government till we are divested of this mortal flesh and become like the angels." With such views of the church, he naturally assumed that God had not left the form of its organization to the device of man. He never had any misgivings touching the Scriptural basis, and therefore the divine origin of the church polity which he provided for the city of Geneva. Moreover, he secured from the whole city, through its representatives, an expression of the same conviction. In the preface to the ordinances they say, "We have ordained and established to follow and to keep in our town and territory the ecclesiastical polity following, *which is taken out of the gospel of Christ.*" The convictions of the people were shallow, not so Calvin's conviction. Consequently, to make this church polity effective, he consented to wrestle with the turbulent democracy of Geneva, and for years to live over the thin crust of a rumbling volcano. John Calvin alone of the Reformers found his chief foes, his most relentless foes, to be those of his own household. The reason was that he alone of the Reformers set to work with a resolution "fixed as the stars," to rule his own household according to the law of God.

Certainly it was no slight contribution which John Calvin made to the Reformation when he gave to it a restored Apostolic Presbyterianism. In connection with this, and perhaps we might say as a part of this, he gave to the Reformation a demonstration of the value of ecclesiastical discipline. For a thousand years and more there had been a lamentable divorce of religion from morals. The church had not drifted further away from the doctrinal teachings of the New Testament than from its ethical standards. Piety of heart and purity of life were no longer associated with the Christian profession. It was not enough for the church to grant tolerance to all forms of immorality among the private members, but it went so far as to enthrone iniquity in its highest offices. What sins in the whole history of human depravity, more gross and more offensive than those which soiled the lives of such Popes as John XXIII. and Alexander VI. When, as frequently happened, the head of the church, allowed to be the vicar of Christ, set an example of shameless debauchery, it is not surprising that the general state of morals throughout Catholic Europe was almost intolerable. John Calvin believed that reforming the church meant not merely the restoration of a pure doctrine and a pure worship, but above all and as the end of all, the restoration of the morals enjoined in the Word of God. He purposed to establish a church which should not only glorify orthodoxy by the profession of a true creed, but which should glorify God by the practice of holy living. He determined to draw the line so that all might discern between the righteous and the wicked, between him that serveth God and him that serveth Him not. Moreover he insisted that the church must be the sole judge of the qualification of its own members.

There may seem to us no novelty in such a conception of the church and its functions. Such a conception may commend itself to us as so manifestly just and true as to hardly deserve mention. But this only shows how far we have travelled since Calvin's day. He was the first of the Reformers to demand for the church complete separation from the State, with the right of untrammelled discipline over its members. He was the first of the Reformers who actually inaugurated a system of discipline which was designed to make the church a mighty witness to the ethical purity of the gospel of Christ.

Calvin lived to demonstrate the value of this contribution to the Reformation. When God gave Geneva to Calvin, He gave him a field that would put his reforming principles to a crucial test. "The Genevese," says an eminent writer, "were a light-hearted, joyous people, fond of public amusement, dancing, singings, masquerades, and reveleries. Reckless gambling, drunkenness, adultery, blasphemy, and all sorts of vice abounded. Prostitution was sanctioned by the authority of the State, and superintended by a woman called the *Reine du bordel*. The people were ignorant. The priest had taken no pains to instruct them, and had set them a bad example." Just how bad the example set by the priests, the writer does not tell us, but we learn from other sources. Shortly before Calvin went there, the monks and even the bishop were guilty of crimes, for which in our day, hanging is not adjudged too severe a penalty. In that age of relaxed morals, there were few, if any, cities in Europe more wicked than the one which Calvin set himself, with God's help, to reform. For fifteen years he fought a doubtful battle, the scale of victory frequently inclining against him. In 1547, he wrote to Viret: "Wickedness has now reached such a pitch here that I hardly hope that the church can be upheld much longer, at least by means of my ministry. Believe me, my power is broken, unless God stretch forth His hand." Eight years more of unyielding, unflinching, uncompromising struggle, vibrating between hope and despair, victory and defeat, and then the climax and crisis of the battle was reached. Calvin believed that he was going down, but he harbored not for one moment the thought of striking his colors. He preached his farewell sermon expecting banishment on the morrow. But the trembling scale turned in his favor, and for the short remainder of his life, about nine years, he was left the undisputed master of the city.

If his theology was his greatest contribution, and his church polity his most original contribution, we may safely say that his demonstration of the value of discipline was his most costly contribution to the Reformation. He has been persistently reproached and sometimes maliciously censured for burning Servetus. Grant that he was responsible for the death of Servetus, and that he ought not to have prosecuted him before the civil tribunal, this should not be forgotten, that he was at that time standing in the midst of enemies, numerous and powerful, who would gladly have substituted him for Servetus, because of his unparalleled zeal for righteousness. For years he imperilled his life for no other reason than that he might see the glory of the gospel reflected in the life of Geneva.

Were the results such as to vindicate the wisdom of Calvin and the efficiency of his methods? The answer is that Geneva became more famed for the quiet, orderly and moral lives of its citizens than it had previously been for their wickedness. John Knox, who lived in Geneva for several years, wrote to a friend in 1556: "In my heart I could have wished, yea, I can not cease to wish, that it might please God to guide and conduct yourself to this place, where I neither fear nor am ashamed to say, is the most perfect school of Christ that ever was on the earth since the days of the Apostles. In other places I confess Christ to be truly preached; but manners and religion to be so seriously reformed, I have not yet seen in any other place besides." Dr. Philip Schaff, born and reared in Switzerland, with every qualification for forming a trustworthy judgment says: "If ever in this wicked world, the ideal of Christian society can be realized in a civil community with a mixed population, it was in Geneva, from the middle of the 16th to the middle of the 18th century." Without endorsing the severity of the discipline employed, much less the aid rendered by the State in enforcing with civil pains and penalties the censures of the church, we may assert that Calvin did demonstrate in the eyes of all the world the value of a representative form of church government as a means for purifying public morals, and developing the highest type of Christian character. To show how much this was worth to the Reformation, we should have to write a history of the Reformed churches, and show that in respect to the realization of true Christian ideals, they shone with a glory all their own.

III. *Calvin's Educational Measures and Correspondence.* It was principally through these means that Calvin's influence overflowed the narrow bounds of the little city where he lived and wrought. It has been said, and I think truly said, that with Calvin, Geneva was never an end, but always a means. From the beginning of his ministry Calvin set himself to make Geneva an asylum for the persecuted, and a training school for the Reformed faith. In a large measure his purpose and his hopes were realized. From all the countries of Europe the persecuted fled for safety to this retreat. Many of these refugees were men of great learning and distinguished ability, but none were too eminent to learn from Calvin; and no one returned to his distant home without carrying away knowledge that he was eager to impart.

In 1558, the famous Academy of Geneva was established. This has been called Calvin's crowning work in the field which God had given him to subdue and to cultivate. In this crowning work especially we can see that Calvin's vision was sweeping a wider horizon than that which bounded his little city. No sooner was the Academy opened than it enrolled 900 pupils, representing the same wide range of territory that was represented by the refugees. In addition to these, there were sometimes as many as 1,000 sitting under Calvin's theological lectures. Thus pastors and evangelists were trained to go forth and spread the doctrines which they had learned, and to establish churches after the model which they had seen in Geneva. It is easy for us to see with what good reason this city was called the Rome of Protestantism. It was the center from which emanated the spiritual power, and the educational forces that guided and moulded the Reformation in the surrounding countries. While Calvin soon came to be so bitterly hated that he was never permitted to set foot on the soil of his native France, yet to him the eyes of the Huguenots turned for advice and counsel at every step in their mighty struggle, and when under cover of darkness they met to organize their 2,000 congregations into one united whole, his hand drafted their Confession of Faith, and their form of government. Through France his doctrines invaded the Netherlands, and coming into contact with Lutheranism, which was first on the ground, won the day. John Knox added Scotland to the theological domain of Calvin. The ardent Reformers from England, who rested in Geneva during the reign of Bloody Mary, carried back to their island home the teachings and the spirit of Calvin, and gave to England the Puritanism which proved such a thorn in the side of tyranny, until finally it brought down the Stuart dynasty tumbling in ruins.

There was yet another method by which Calvin propagated his influence. He carried on a voluminous correspondence with all the conspicuous leaders in both church and state throughout Protestant Christendom. We have to-day from Calvin's fertile brain letters addressed to over 300 different persons and bodies, some of them to crowned heads, some to princes and nobles and some to high ecclesiastical dignitaries. As a rule, they are not brief documents designed merely to pass the compliments of the day, but they are carefully prepared treatises discussing in masterly manner the profound and perplexing questions with which statesmen and churchmen had to do. The influence of these in moulding the thought, in guiding the policy of those who were holding the reins of power and shaping the history of those tumultuous times cannot easily be over-stated.

To sum up the aggregate of Calvin's influence outside of Geneva, we may say that all the non-Germanic countries that embraced the Protestant faith, with the one exception of England, enthroned the doctrines of Calvin and set up his church polity. Had not the free development of Protestantism been repressed in England by the iron hand of royal despotism, it is morally certain that England would have been no exception. As it was, Calvinism found its way into the doctrinal system of the Established Church, and into the hearts and creeds of all dissenting bodies.

What shall we say more? Time would fail us to trace in detail the manifold currents of influence that had their source in Geneva, and that were flowing in every direction to carry and deposit the seeds of the new faith. One testimony to the predominant influence that radiated from this center must be mentioned —it is the testimony borne by the great adversary. No spot in Europe was so hated as Geneva. Philip II, than whom the Pope was not more zealous for the old order, wrote to the King of France: "This city is the source of all mischief for France, the most formidable enemy of Rome. At any time, I am ready to assist with all the power of my realm in its overthrow." When the Duke of Alva was to lead his Spanish army near Geneva, Pope Pius V asked him to turn aside and "destroy that nest of devils and apostates." Do we admire Calvin for the friends that he made? Equally may we admire him for the enemies that he made.

I shall close this discussion of John Calvin's contribution to the Reformation of the 16th century with a statement, to which I am sure friend and foe would alike assent. John Calvin contributed to the Reformation all that he could contribute. He put into it all that God put into him; all the resources of his intellect, all the devotion of his heart, all the energies of his will. For 30 years he had but this one interest, and to this be consecrated every moment of his time, every element of his influence, every faculty of body, mind and soul. He toiled for it to the utmost limit of his strength, fought for it with a courage that never quailed, suffered for it with a fortitude that never wavered, and was ready at any moment to die for it. He literally poured every drop of his life into it, unhesitatingly, unsparingly. History will be searched in vain to find a man who gave himself to one definite purpose with more unalterable persistence, and with more lavish self-abandon than Calvin gave himself to the Reformation of the 16th Century. There was a pathos in his position which almost moves to tears. During many weary years when the burden was the heaviest, when the conflict was the fiercest, and when the issue still was doubtful, he stood to his post, an alien in a strange city, without citizenship, without a family, broken in health, and living in the shadow of a desolate home from which he had buried his wife and only child. He toiled on with an utter self-immolation, giving to his personal sorrows no voice, and refusing his physical infirmities the solace of rest and care. He burned the candle to the socket, and at the age of 55 "went to God." They buried him without pomp in an unmarked grave. Buried John Calvin! No, no, they put the frail, wasted body under the ground, but John Calvin has never been buried, nor will be, till all the Reformed churches of two hemispheres have apostatized from the faith once delivered to them by this saint. May God postpone this evil day forever and forever.

CALVIN, THE THEOLOGIAN.

REV. HENRY COLLIN MINTON, D. D., LL. D.,
Trenton, N. J.

It is an interesting fact, more significant, I believe, than appears on the face of it, that the four hundredth anniversary of John Calvin's birth is being so widely and so signally celebrated throughout the Christian world in this year of grace nineteen hundred and nine. Most names, even of those whom their own age calls great, fade out into oblivion within the limits of a single century. It is allowed to but few to outlive a dozen generations of mankind. The secret of such enduring fame must be looked for elsewhere than in the merely personal qualities or in the contemporary appreciation of its possessor. The great name of John Calvin is embalmed in the immortal doctrines of Calvinism. It is not linked, like that of Luther, with any great branch of the Christian Church; it is more appropriately associated with a great system of thought, and that system is so comprehensive, so pervasive, and so polygonal that, from one point of view, it is a solid body of doctrine embracing all the great truths of religion and of life, while from another point of view it is scarcely more than a frame of mind, an attitude of the intellect, affecting every possible condition and relation of man.

Psychologically, Calvinism is Calvin writ large. There is an element of truth, however exaggerated, in the remark once made to me in San Francisco by a scholarly Jewish Rabbi, to the effect that theology is nine-tenths temperament. It has been said that John Calvin's God was John Wesley's devil; this, too, of course, is over-stated; but whatever difference there was in their conceptions was not owing to the difference between God and the devil but to the difference between the two sainted Johns. Both accepted the same Scripture as true, both prayed to be guided by the same Spirit of Truth; both devoutly subordinated their own reason to the supreme voice of Revelation—and yet how great the difference! John Calvin and Ignatius Loyola were schoolmates at the same college, De Montague, in Paris; what was it that developed the one into the great intellectual organizer of the Reformation and the other into the indefatigable founder of the Order of Jesus?

No man can understand Calvinism who is not in some measure acquainted with the life of John Calvin. The same conditions that developed the one produced the other, and although it is true that he was in a remarkable degree unresponsive to the external conditions of his life, yet when we say that he was, under God, a creature of the historical conditions of his age, we are only saying that John Calvin was human, not more and not less.

Any man's theology is his thought concerning God and the world; and that thought must depend of course in large measure upon his ability to think and the conditions of his thinking. Calvin, as theologian, was Calvin looking Godward and turning to tell the world what he saw. His eyes were keener than most men's. His vision was more telescopic in its range and more microscopic in its accuracy; but his eyes were still his own. We must remember the mists that hung low and heavy in his time, as well as the clouds of ignorance that ever darken man's upward look. We must not forget Calvin's inherited gifts of head and heart, the circumstances of his home and school and early life, the strange and fitful career that finally landed him most unexpectedly in Geneva; the innumerable cares, the exacting tasks, the irritating antagonisms, the ever enlarging responsibilities of his public life and the generally belligerent conditions existing in Europe at the age in which he lived; we must bear in mind the intellectual awakening and consequent unrest which characterized the era of the Renaissance, and the loud call in all this for a master spirit to organize the social forces and to co-ordinate the intellectual elements which were in utter confusion after the frontier skirmishes of the Reformation. These were among the thousand and one things which, under God, entered into that mighty and majestic composite which all the world acknowledges to have been not only historic, but also history making, in John Calvin, the great thinker and theologian of the 16th century.

All theology should relate itself in some way to human experience. Every truth in the confession should have its place in the life of the confessor. It may not be explicit in his consciousness but it should be implicit in his life. Few can fully state their faith in the Trinity or the Atonement or the gracious work of the Holy Spirit but, if their faith is deep and their life sincere, a full analysis of that faith and a thorough explication of that life will bring out into the open the elements that lie dormant and hidden in their breasts.

The story of Calvin's life is too familiar to need repeating. His birth, unlike Luther's, was into a home of gentle life and easy comfort. He enjoyed the best educational advantages which the universities of his time afforded. Both in taste and in attainments, he was an accomplished humanist. His first literary production was a commentary upon Seneca's *De Clementia*, and this purely classical essay has almost no reference to scripture teaching or religious interest. In the preface to his Commentary on the Psalms, he tells us of his sudden conversion, and his biographers have discussed, with differing conclusions, what Calvin's conversion at this time was. Less spectacular than that of Saul of Tarsus, less protracted than that of Augustine of Hippo, less violent than that of Luther, we are inclined to believe that it was a sudden reversal of intellectual attitude toward the momentous issues, so profoundly spiritual in their essence and ethical in their import, which were at that moment at stake between the people and the Pope. This is not to disparage the genuineness of his personal spiritual experience, or to slur over the importance of regeneration; but Calvin was nothing if not intellectual, and such a change of allegiance involved both convictions and courage, which gave splendid play to all the spiritual graces and heroic virtues of the true man of God.

His *Institutes*, appearing at the early age of twenty-six, were at once accepted as the product of a master spirit. In its immediate intention it was an appeal, a defense and a challenge; while in its larger references it was at the same time an Evangel, a Dogmatic, an Apologetic, and a Polemic. The historic dedication to Francis the First, is one of the immortal bits of the world's literature. Calvin wrote the *Institutes*, he somewhere tells us, with an evangelistic purpose first of all, but we may sum up its object as three-fold: first, to state the doctrines of the Reformation; second, to disabuse the mind of Francis of certain misconceptions; and, third, to disclaim and refute the wild vagaries of the Anabaptists. When we remember that the Pope and the Emperor were in front of him, and the pestiferous Anabaptists and Libertines in his rear, it is remarkable that Calvin was able to develop the profound theology of the Institutes with such calm spirit and such complete mental poise and, if at times an unseemly harshness smites upon our ears, we have no need to forget that this was but the mark of a universal weakness in theological controversy at that time, and that the provocations to impatience were very numerous and grievous to be borne.

Calvin's literary labors were wonderfully prolific. If Luther was the great Bible translator of the Reformation, Calvin was its great Bible commentator. His tasks of administration were very heavy and never to his liking. He was a preacher of singular clearness and power, and yet he longed for the quiet life of the student. Driven from place to place in his native France, sojourning for a time in the south country of Italy, he finally made his way back to the north, tarrying in Geneva but for a single night. William Farel laid almost violent hands upon him and, under the spell of this fiery Frenchman's anathema if he should not heed his call to remain, Calvin found in Geneva not a night's lodging only but the scene of his great life work. He was seeking Strasburg for quiet study; he finds the seething caldron of Geneva. He fain would shun all noisy conflicts and bitter controversy; he finds the great battle-ground of the Reformation. No man was ever thrust into an unsought place of prominence more suddenly and more reluctantly than was

Calvin thrust into the midst of the ferments of Geneva. This is but one of a most remarkable series of such personal experiences in the life of the great reformer. "Man proposes, God disposes." This means Divine Providence in human affairs; it means a "Divinity shaping man's end"; it means an over-ruling, ever-living, sovereign God.

If we are to succeed in our search for the fundamental and formative principle of Calvin's teaching, we must remember that his mental make-up was such as required that all his thinking should group itself into a complete and systematic unit. His mind demanded some truth large enough for all other truths to stand on. His logic was sharp and severe, but his logic was only formal; the material for his thinking he found in the Word of God. His dialectic was as keen as that of a Plato, but we see its magnificent display only as it is at work on the rich treasures of Divine Revelation. To him any truth that was not related or relatable to every other truth in the field of vision would have been fatal. We sweetly sing with Tennyson:

> "Our little systems have their day,
> They have their day and cease to be;
> They are but broken lights of Thee,
> And Thou, O Lord, art more than they."

Yes, "our little systems"—if they are only ours, conceived by us, created by us! But if the system be either found in or founded upon eternal truth, then why is that system not as eternal as the truth itself? "God's thoughts are not as our thoughts"—not because His thoughts are essentially different from ours, but because they are "higher" than ours. To think at all is to think systematically, and if there be no system, no order, no self-consistent harmony in God's thinking, then there can be no such thing as thinking God's thoughts over again after Him, and Agnosticism, with its cruel hand, has forever closed the door against all human knowledge of things Divine.

The sweep of Calvin's mind found only one basal truth broad enough on which to build his theology and his theodicy. "In the beginning, God." Calvin took the scripture at its word. The Divine must underlie the human; the eternal is presupposed in the temporal; the Creator is, both in the order of thought and of time, antecedent to the creation.

Here we find the *principium*, the organizing principle of Calvin's system. His theology is fundamentally theistic. "He has God in all his thoughts." Not the sovereignty of God, as is so often affirmed, not His justice or His power, or His governmental authority— "In the beginning, God." Let the scripture develop its own conception of what God is. Let reason judge and experience interpret; only let him be God. Every theology waits upon its definition of God. Many people, in explicitly defining God, implicitly deny Him. They reverently repeat the words of the Creed, "I believe in God, the Father Almighty," and then proceed to strip Him of the very attributes in the possession of which alone He can be either God or Father or Almighty.

A God who is not holy is no God. A God who is not just or good or true is no God. A God who does not satisfy and surpass our highest conception of ethical ideal is no God. A God who is not supreme over all, who shares the throne of His rule and glory with angel or man or devil, who does not know all things, who does not control all things, whose eyes are closed to any scene of tragedy or distress, whose ears are stopped to any cry of suffering or of need, whose love is quenched by any offense against His holy will, whose arm is bound by any force or fate or law—this is no God. When we hear any one declare that he believes in God, it is necessary to wait until he tells us what kind of a God he believes in that we may be sure that he believes in God at all. Many a qualified theism is, at bottom, an unqualified atheism.

Here is the seed thought of Calvinism. Once grasp and grant its conception of God and many of its far-reaching and battle-scared doctrines stand forth as inevitable and indisputable corollaries. Not less than Spinoza of Amsterdam, only profoundly more sane and ever loyal to Holy Scripture, was Calvin of Geneva "the God-intoxicated man." He had not touched the meaning of a single fact in time, he had not reached to the hem of the garment of any great principle in philosophy, until he had related it to God. No plan back in the eternity that was, no end in the eternity that is to be, is beyond the purview and control of the eternal God. Man's place and part in time, his portion and destiny in eternity are ordained in the vast panoramic program of his Creator. Calvin hesitated at no barrier or challenge. If the thought of Calvin the dogmatician seems harsh and *a'priori,* let us not forget that it was at the same time Calvin, the greatest inductive Scripture commentator of his age, and one of the greatest of any age, that propounded that thought. Grant Calvin's theism and only the adroitness of the sophist or the inconsistency of the weakling will balk at his theology.

But if we find the seed of Calvin's system here it is here also that we find its very crux. It is not the question whether the celebrated five points of the Calvinistic star shall fade out or endure; their brilliancy or their extinction will depend upon the constancy of the mother light at the centre. The only way to extinguish the sunlight from the world is to blot out the disc of the sun itself from the sky. The only way to stop the scintillations of the star is to drown out the star itself in the blackness of the surrounding night. It is child's play to talk of surrendering certain principles of essential Calvinism and holding on to others. Whatever we may think of Calvinism, it has this merit, that it is a unit and that unit is a vital organism, not a dead mechanism. There are Calvinists and Calvinists, to be sure. Some one has pointed out for us the varying grades of Calvinistic loyalty. There is John Calvin himself and there are those to-day who doubtless are worthy to bear the name of their theological patronymic; there are Calvinists, loyal disciples of the great teacher of Geneva; then there are those who are honestly and in a healthy sense Calvinistic, then there are those who are Calvinistical; next, there are those whose homeopathic adherence to the faith may be characterized as Calvinisticalish; and last of all, there are those, standing far out on the circumference, who are slightly tinged with *Calvinisticalishness.* But, whether the dye be deep or dim, the great fundamental truth of God at the centre and God at the circumference, and God everywhere between, can never be abandoned.

You have all, of course, heard of the memorable and classical definition of a crab in which the crab is defined as "A red fish which crawls backward." This has, upon very good authority, been pronounced to be a highly scientific and essentially correct definition, with three incidental corrections, however, which are deemed worthy to be noted. These are, first, a crab is not a fish; second, it is not red; and, third, it does not crawl backward. It is to be feared that there is not a little which passes for Calvinism in the world to-day which calls for just such incidental criticisms as this learned and scientific definition of the crab.

Of course the test of Calvin's theology must always be upon the absolute universality of this first postulate. He placed at the foundation of his thought not the sovereignty of God but a God who is sovereign. He never stood exclusively for the transcendence of God any more than did his great teacher, St. Augustine, before him. He sets forth the Immanence of God as clearly, far more clearly, than do the writers of our own day who fain would have us believe that this is one of the great finds of modern philosophy.

But can the teachings of Scripture, can the facts of experience, can the common consciousness of men, be fairly construed so as to support Calvin's views? I am not here to defend Calvinism or to refute its critics. We are only striving to find the characteristic intellectual animus, the bed-rock truth of his teaching.

That objections were forthcoming, that marvelously acute and comprehensive intellect knew very well. It is safe to say that no argument has been hurled at Geneva which Calvin himself did not carefully consider and discuss with more or less fullness in his writings. He knew that men said that he made God the author of sin; he knew that men said that he left no place for the actual freedom of man; he knew that men shrank back from believing that God's predestination positively contemplated the eschatological penalties and endless miseries of the finally impenitent—a thing which he himself, with humble awe, called the *"Decretum horribile."*

Nevertheless, based on Scripture, he could find no other *rationalé* that met the demands of his all-comprehending thought. These objections all melted down, in the mighty alembic of his master mind, into one, and that one had for its fatal weakness that it contradicted his first fundamental Bible-buttressed conception of God.

His notions of freedom were fearless and frankly stated. He did not scruple to affirm that, although he was created free, yet man in a state of sin is not free, and that he and he himself alone is responsible for his lack of freedom. He regarded sin as a self-imposed handicap upon man's spiritual freedom and life, which is adequately characterized only in the Scripture term which calls it spiritual death. That sin means death, that death means alienation from God and forfeiture of His favor, this he found in Holy Scripture; that sin introduced a wholly abnormal order—a disastrous disorder—into the natural and moral world, and that this abnormality entailed a curse not only on man but also on the cosmos of which man is the crowning part,—this he found in Holy Scripture; that the grace of God in Jesus Christ was manifested in the incarnation of His only begotten Son and was consummated in the historical Atonement which was accomplished on the heights of Calvary, sufficient for all mankind and certainly efficient for all those who will believe upon him,—this also he found in Holy Scripture; that the number of those who will thus believe and be redeemed unto holiness and eternal life was ordered and known in the mind of the Eternal before the foundation of the world,—this, too, he found in Holy Scripture; and that in the progress of His kingdom, in the development of His redemptive purpose, God sent forth His Holy Spirit into the world who, with or without Papal prerogatives and Sacerdotal or sacramental functions, can and does work when and where and how He pleases in gathering the innumerable body of the elect of God out of every land and age and nation into the comprehensive fold,—this also he found in Holy Scripture. On this broad ground Calvin took his unalterable position. That God had foreordained man's course in time and goal in eternity was not to be denied because man's consciousness tells him that he is free. However this may be, refusing to cast a shadow upon the veracity of its testimony, yet even granting that consciousness is a trustworthy witness to a man that the man himself is free, even so, it does not follow that that inner witness has a single word of competent or relevant testimony either for or against the inscrutable purposes of the Divine, or the unchangeable decrees of the Eternal.

Calvin's defense was based in part upon the inevitable limitations of human knowledge. That he was in any fair sense an Agnostic is a base libel upon his fame. Agnosticism is essentially the dogmatic affirmation of man's constitutional inability to know. The verb "to know" is a transitive verb, but agnosticism persists in denying it any object, from things celestial or things terrestrial, from things infinite or things finite; and when a transitive verb is defrauded of the object of its action, the verb itself lapses and shrinks into a nonentity; accordingly, agnosticism would fain wipe the words "knowledge" and "to know" from the dictionaries of human speech. Hume, and Hamilton, and Mansell, and Spencer, and Huxley base their doctrine of nescience upon man's integral and inherent incapacity to know anything. That tree or this book is as inscrutable as the infinite God and his eternal purposes. Calvin was no agnostic. He did hold that there are truths that reach beyond our finite faculties. He stood in awe in the presence of the solemn and unyielding mysteries of God. God's control and man's freedom are the opposite poles of a mystery, and we call it mystery because we are not able to trace the invisible line which connects the obvious truths which stand at each emerging end. Mystery is not contradiction, for, as Jonathan Edwards said long ago, "A contradiction is not a thing," whereas the very crux of a mystery is in the fact that though we cannot comprehend it fully it is nevertheless an existing truth. *Homo mensura rerum* is the discredited dictum of a rationalizing agnosticism. We are always afraid of a philosophy which leaves nothing to be explained. Calvin did not hesitate to accept what seemed to him to be true, and baffling difficulties, stubborn antinomies, though they might embarrass him, did not cause him to waver in his allegiance to his underlying theistic postulate.

Whatever may be men's verdict upon the rational integrity or the moral merits of Calvin, we have here its essential strength and its reputed or its imputed weakness. His notion of God is large enough to embrace all things that are. Ascribing only infinite perfection to Him, he nevertheless maintained that in His all-sweeping purpose He contemplated the evil as well as the good, the bitter as well as the sweet, the sinner as well as the saint, the deepest depths of hell as well as the highest heights of heaven. If men said that in this he was bringing an indictment against the Divine holiness and the Divine love, he replied that the mystery is there; but it is a mystery less abhorrent, both to Scripture and to reason, than the mystery which we are bound to face if we dethrone God or limit the scope of His rule. A broken scepter, a mutilated crown, a restricted rule, undeifies God. Only God rules. No force or fate or fact disproves that bottom truth. If there be unsolved problems, locate them elsewhere, let God be God and the developments of history the bodying forth in time of His eternal purposes.

The magnificence, the audacity, the reverential awe of this conception, who can gainsay? John Calvin's system was, in a sense that is true to the etymology of the word, a genuine *theology.* Not yet had the degenerate days arrived when men study the objective facts of men's life and history and gravely christen the result "theology." He made theology inductive, but the sources whence he drew his inductions were not the fitful and fleeting scenes of human history but, first of all, the Divinely given and devoutly accepted teachings of the inspired Word of God. He would have repudiated with abhorrence the crude modern notion that theology is only the science of religion. Like the beloved disciple, the Theologos of the New Testament, he studied history in the light of God and afterward God in the light of history. He first drew his light from higher sources and then made that light interpretative of scientific and historical truth; and while, of course, the sunburst of modern scientific discovery had not yet broken upon the world, yet his attitude toward the whole field of empirical truth was typical and unaffected, in principle, by the multitude or the magnitude of the conquests of recent scientific research.

That essential Calvinism is out of date to-day, who that keeps an eye upon the drift of twentieth century thought will presume to affirm? It is safe to say that if he were with us to-day John Calvin would be a vigorous reactionary against the extreme Determinism of many of our scientific and philosophical thinkers. Calvin never reduced man's freedom to a farce. There is a scientific fatalism in vogue to-day that out-Mohammets Mohammet, and while singing to men the sweet songs of freedom it would rob them of the last shreds of the real thing. The apostle of selection has usurped the place of the apostle of election, and many are eager to accept Darwin's natural selection who hold up their hands in horror at Calvin's divine election. The one does not know or care whether there is intelligence and will back the selecting process; while the other insists that behind the electing act is the true and living God "Whose judgments are unsearchable, and whose ways are past finding out."

Neither can the spirit of modern metaphysics wage war upon the theological citadels of Geneva. The last word of the best philosophy of to-day, the ultimate category of a sane metaphysics, is Personality. All knowable truth is knowable because a knowing mind has foreknown it. History can be scientifically studied and rationally stated because it embodies a rational plan. Geology is a science because it finds, first concealed and then revealed in its rocks and hills, the records of a science-like order. Keplar traced the stars and thought God's thoughts over again after Him; not more did Keplar, than does every other man who finds truth knowable because it bears upon its face or hides within its folds the ordering purpose of Another. Plato's "Eternal Geometer of the Universe" is none other than Calvin's Eternal Foreordainer "of whatsoever comes to pass."

That the course of Calvinism, like that of true love, "has not run smooth" all the world knows right well. That it is a bankrupt system of thought to-day, that it was at best only a crude seventeenth century report of theological progress, that the succeeding ages have been sifting out its modicum of truth and have thrown forever into the scrap-heap the great bulk of its offensive dogmatisms, this is affirmed by the few and echoed by the many until legion is the name of those who, innocent if not incapable of a single independent conception in their own right of what John Calvin really did think or teach, are ready to accept the howling chorus of condemnation as unchallenged and conclusive. Let us not forget that whoever calls Calvin infallible is as false to Protestantism and to the great Protestant of Geneva as he who locates infallibility on the banks of the Tiber; let us remember that it has been given to no saint or sage in all the course of time to formulate into a finality the great truths of Divine revelation; let us not forget that with the developments of the Kingdom of God in the world, under the gracious tuition of the Spirit of all Turth, new light may from time to time be expected to break forth from the treasures of Divine truth; let us remember, too, that every age has its peculiar difficulties for him who would perform the colossal task of constructive creed building, and that the war-like tactics of self-defense which were forced upon the reformer by the tyrannies of King and Pope on the one side and by the vagaries of Anabaptist and Libertine on the other, caused their utterances to bristle with antagonisms, and sometimes to exhibit the unhappy blemishes of unwarranted exaggeration. Calvinism was Calvin's view of God and the world. The sources of his thinking were higher than the tops of his unstained Alps; his guidance was surer than his own frail thought; his vision was far out toward the fugitive horizons of the infinite. The fields of time were to his gaze outlined and bounded only by the purpose of eternity. Men think and choose and act; they ponder and decide and go forth to the doing of the deed; they rise up in the morning and after their little day's work is done they lie down to sleep through the long hours of the approaching night. They are unconscious of millions of their fellows who are living the same life, doing the same tasks, and walking the same way; with mistaken and egoistic pride they imagine that they are all alone in choosing their own ways and ordering their own steps. But the vision is as yet partial and incomplete. This is chaos, not cosmos; this is confusion, not order. Every toiler has his task assigned him, though he know it not. Every traveler finds his path opening out before him, and a voice, not his own, though he recognize it not, calling him down along that way. His lot is measured out; his days are numbered out before him. The sphere within which he moves is large enough for the widest, wildest wanderings of his weary feet, and that sphere is of another's ordering. His choices are to himself entirely free, for they are his very own; his determinations are spontaneous, for they are unforced, and yet, far down in the subsoil of his subliminal self, beneath the surface gaze of his superficial consciousness, forces are at work, forces sent forth and controlled by the hand of the Eternal, forces which men call heredity and environment and nature and Providence and the mysteries of Divine grace, forces which in their own time, in their own silent and subtle but ever effective way, quietly swing those free choices and effectually bring those free actions around to the accomplishment of the end eternally in view. And each end in turn becomes a means to a higher end until the ultimate end is merged and lost in the effulgent glory of Him whose wisdom foreordained the course and whose power caused those Heaven-born forces to go forth upon their prescribed orbits in space and appointed errands in time.

If men call this sophistry, then only sophistry can defend the crown rights of the Creator. If men deny that this is genuine freedom, then the Calvinist is quick to make reply that any other freedom means anarchy in history and as many little deities each supreme in his own petty sphere, as there are free agents in the wide world of being. This "untenants Heaven of its God," this breaks up every possible philosophy of history into a wreckage of dismembered fragments; this turns into "the dream of a dreamer who dreams that he has been dreaming" the splendid vision of the poet.

"And I doubt not through the ages one increasing purpose runs
And the thoughts of men are widened with the process of the
  suns."

In estimating the gross theological assets of John Calvin's short life, how appalling is the magnitude of the task! Certainly no one can read history and be blind to the greatness of his work. He was neither prince nor pope, and yet his work outshines that of both. Denying and defying the Divine right of kings, he established a magistracy at Geneva more enduring than any crown, more potent than any scepter, while he touched with the magic wand of his theological faith and genius the rock from which flowed out over all the broad plains of modern history the life-giving streams of equality before God and democracy among men.

Historians argue whether he was greater as theologian or as magistrate. We believe that his theological thought pre-determined his views of civil as well as of ecclesiastical government. We believe that his work was great and his fame enduring because, first of all, he held to his Biblical conception of God, and with relentless perseverance he carried it, with its implications and applications, into his work as preacher, as educator, as statesman, and as reformer.

Let men say what they will, Calvin's niche in the pantheon of the world's few immortals is forever assured. The record is wanting that he was ever formally ordained, either as Roman Catholic priest or as Protestant preacher, and yet the same living God who could use Saul of Tarsus, unordained of man, in the first century of the Christian era, and Dwight L. Moody, unordained of man, in the nineteenth century of the Christian era, used John Calvin, the pale, frail layman of Geneva, to turn a new and mighty page in the history of intellectual and spiritual Christianity, and of civil and religious liberty. His work was not creative, it was constructive. He did not originate, he organized. His name has been "scarred with calumny"; his work has been traduced with ridicule and slander; his thinking has been combated, but it has never been belittled except by little and impoverished spirits. His intellectual powers have been conceded by all to have been of the very highest order, and they were unselfishly consecrated with the best light his age afforded to the God that gave them to him and to the Lord whose service he espoused.

He dwelt aloft amid the cold and placid peaks of God's eternal truth. In a most unusual way, he combined the contemplative genius of the philosopher with the practical genius of the man of affairs. He loved and longed for quiet and yet he lived his life in constant scenes of civil strife and theological controversy. He was human with all his greatness, and his faults and weaknesses, like those of every other great man, seem all the greater because he was himself so great.

We devoutly believe that it was because he held the theology which he taught that he was, under God, the force he was, and that, under God, he did the work he did; and we devoutly believe that the truths of that same logic-ribbed, bible-based, crimson-stained theology will, under God, continue to produce, as it has been for these four hundred years producing, men of giant stature, men of heroic mould, men of stalwart thought, men of genuine Christian faith and culture and conduct and character, who, learning God's truth in God's book, led by God's spirit in God's service, will do well and faithfully their appointed work, and will leave a beneficent legacy to the generations that come after.

CALVIN'S CONTRIBUTIONS TO CHURCH POLITY.

Thomas Cary Johnson, D. D., LL. D.
Richmond, Virginia.

Calvin did not originate the principles of ecclesiastical polity which he describes in his writings and which he endeavored to establish in Geneva. Having repudiated utterly the whole man-made polity of Rome, he carried men back to the New Testament for the God-given polity of the Church. He tried to draw from the apostolic writings the divinely given principles of church government, and to apply these principles in the government of the church of Geneva.

Accordingly, in order to have clearness in the treatment of the subject assigned us, we shall attempt, first, to indicate, very briefly, the nature of the government given of God to the church in the apostolic age; second, to show, very briefly again, how far the church apostatized from the divinely-given type of government; and third, to set forth the part of Calvin in exposing the apostasy and in leading back the church toward the pattern shown in the mount of New Testament teaching.

First, then, of the nature of the government given to the New Testament Church.

The government of the New Testament church is easily distinguished from civil government. They differ in their instruments, aims, and ways of regarding God. The instruments of civil government include amongst them physical force, the sword being the emblem of its power. The aim of civil government is to conserve justice between man and man and to secure the temporal well-being of the governed. God, as regarded by civil government, is regarded in the aspects and relations of Creator and moral Governor of the universe. The instrument of New Testament church government, on the other hand, was not the material sword, not physical force, but the sword of the Spirit, the word of God. The aim of the New Testament church government was to further the spiritual, and, chiefly, the eternal welfare of the governed. It aimed not at the conservation of justice, but at the moral and spiritual improvement of the governed. It regarded God as Redeemer as well as Creator and Governor of the universe.

The distinction between the two kinds of government had long been before God's people in a more or less vague way; but was clearly developed by our Lord and His apostles. Not only was the distinction between them clearly developed; the separation of the two governments, in fact as in law, was brought about by the teaching and providence in the apostolic age. An independent and self-governing church, under God, came to stand out over against the civil power as embodied in the Graeco-Roman Empire. Christian people found themselves in actual relations to two commonwealths, one ecclesiastical and spiritual, the other, the world power of Rome; the one using the word of God, the other using the sword material; the one seeking spiritual harmony with God and eternal well-being, the other seeking temporal order and temporal well-being; the one regarding God as in Christ redeeming and saving His own, the other regarding God, if at all, merely as the Creator and moral Governor of the universe. At the end of the apostolic age and during the next two centuries, Christian people found these governments struggling with one another —found the civil government trying to destroy all the representatives of the ecclesiastical commonwealth; found the ecclesiastical commonwealth trying to win the heart's allegiance of all men, while leaving them to become better citizens of a state rendered inhostile to the church.

The peculiar power with which the church was dowered, was, in part, that of bearing witness to Christ and to His teaching, and, in part, that of authoritatively governing its members from the smallest to the greatest, by the application of the Scriptures which are the rightful constitution of the ecclesiastical commonwealth. According to the New Testament, the members of the church severally are to bear witness to the truth of the Gospel, and severally are to rule themselves and others, so far as they can, by teaching and admonition, in consonance with the same truth; but the church as a whole is to govern itself with all its members through chosen and ordained organs—through a "plurality of chosen representatives," officers organized into the form of courts or parliaments. It is also to teach through such courts, but generally through certain of these representative officers acting singly. These representative rulers, in the New Testament, are called indifferently elders or bishops. In the apostolic writings every elder is a bishop and every bishop is an elder. These scriptural representative church rulers—presbyter-bishops—existed in the later years of Paul in two classes, viz.: a class of bishops called to rule only, and a class of bishops called to labor in word and doctrine as well as to rule —the passing away of the apostles having necessitated the development of representative teachers, and that development having taken place naturally within the sphere of the eldership.

A plurality of these representative rulers was to be elected by every local church; and they, after organization under a moderator, or president, were to govern that church on the principles set forth in God's word. When a matter of general concern should come before them, they were to convene with representatives of the church elsewhere, and with them deliberate and conclude concerning the matter; as may be seen from the example of the presbyter-bishops of Antioch carrying the question, whether or not the Gentile converts should be circumcised, to the synod at Jerusalem. Thus the church was to govern itself, under God, and in the light of His word by a graded series of courts, made up of chosen representatives of two classes.

To summarize still more briefly: Ecclesiastical government, according to the New Testament, is a government in which the power is purely spiritual— a power of interpreting, declaring, and applying the will of Christ, the Head of the church, as that will is revealed in the Scriptures. This power is used by the members of the church in choosing their representative officers. It is applied in governing by pluralities of chosen representatives of two classes, teaching elders, or teaching bishops, and ruling elders, as they may be called indifferently, organized into courts, or parliaments, or congresses, or synods, or assemblies, or presbyteries, and these courts so related as to realize the idea of unity. There is neither democracy nor monarchy in the New Testament church government. The principles of that polity are those of the spiritual republic—the principles of perfect representative government according to a divine constitution.

Second, of the Church's Apostatizing from the type of government set up by the Lord Jesus Christ and His apostles.

Unhappily the church did not long maintain its divinely given type of government. Churchmen thought they could improve on the divine plan. Under the influence of the current civil government—that of the empire—which had displaced the old Roman republic to the seeming advantage of the governed; and in the presence of many foes, internal and external, it was deemed best to have rule by one strong presbyter-bishop rather than by a body of presbyter-bishops. It was thought that one man—a dictator—could act with more dispatch than a collective body; and that he could more easily and effectively stifle heresy in its first outcroppings, or throttle schism in its nascency. Accordingly, here and there, even before the end of the second century, the prerogatives of the presbytery, in certain congregations, in part were concentrated in the hands of one presbyter; and to him the name of bishop was more and more restricted. Thus came into existence congregational monarchs—the bishops of the Middle Ages in the first stage of their evolution. A little later, some congregational bishops, partly by the cession of further prerogatives on the part of the presbytery, and partly by usurpation of still other parliamentary functions, grew into diocesan stature. Toward the end of the third century, certain diocesans grew by similar means into the stature of archbishops. In the early part of the fourth century, a few of the greater archbishops approached the patriarchal rank. During the Middle Ages, the Pope of Rome came to be, according to the papal theory, of right the absolute monarch of the whole church. Actually he ruled as an oppressive tyrant over the whole of western Christendom for centuries prior to the Reformation, though not without various rebellions and insurrections against his rule, some of which seriously threatened his overthrow.

Meanwhile, along with the centralizing drift into monarchy, the people were stripped by degrees of the elective franchise. They had chosen their officers in the apostolic church. After the development of the old catholic bishop into his full-grown diocesan maturity, he began, in the west, to appoint presbyters and deacons who should labor in his bounds, taking the right of electing them out of the people's hands. Mindful of their ancient privilege of electing their officers, the people sometimes anticipated action by the clergy on occasion of a vacancy in the bishopric, by a more or less tumultuous calling of the man of their choice. But such popular action became rarer with the passing centuries; and, ere the depths of the Middle Ages had altogether ceased. A vacancy in the episcopate was filled by the choice of the cathedral clergy. The bishop elect after obtaining the sanction of the pope, might be ordained by the other bishops of the province. Powerful civil rulers, throughout many decades and over wide regions, bent this papal mode of filling offices in the church, so as to place therein their favorites; but, in general, after 1073, and thence down to the

Reformation, the papal theory found widespread application.

Not only did the church forsake the representative type of government for the monarchical, and the elective rights of the people for the papal method of filling offices, but it essentially changed the nature of ecclesiastical power. According to the New Testament, church power is, as has appeared, declarative and ministerial. The church has the power only to find out, declare, and do, the will of Christ. But in the Middle Ages the church claimed a power magisterial and legislative. It not only claimed the right; it assumed to exercise the power of sole authoritative interpreter of Scripture, and forced its faulty interpretations as the truth of God on the protesting consciences of multitudes. Moreover, to Scriptures it added traditions, which it made of superior authority to Scripture, since it bent the word of God by the superimposed traditional rubbish.

Not only so; the church of the Middle Ages joined to the magisterial and legislative power, which it had substituted for the ministerial and declarative power of the New Testament church, the power of state—physical force. It merged its peculiar character as a kingdom whose one weapon is truth.

Once more; amongst these changes, the ministry of the New Testament, mere officials in the spiritual commonwealth, had given place to a special priesthood, whose functions were not primarily to teach, to rule, or to serve tables, but to offer sacrifice and administer sacraments.

Thus, while still retaining the names of the officers of the New Testament church—bishops, elders, and deacons,—the church of Rome had changed the genius of her government from representative to monarchial, stripped the covenant people of the right of electing their officers, perverted the nature of ecclesiastical power and joined to it the power of state; and substituted a special priesthood for the simple officers of the New Testament church.

In the remarks just made, we have given only the meagerest sketch of the apostasy of the Romish church, from the type of government set up by our Lord and His apostles; but the limits of our time allow nothing more; and the sketch clears the way for,

Third, the discussion of our real subject, *Calvin's contributions to the church polity, or, the part of Calvin in exposing Rome's apostasy and in expounding a type of church government closely approximating the New Testament type, and in leading a portion of the church back to it.*

That member of a farmer's household contributes not a little to the production of a good crop, who does the most to clear the ground in which it is to be grown, of obnoxious growths, breaks it up and makes it ready for the reception of good seed; and that one of the great reformers whose exposition of the falsity of the Romish system was most radical and effectively published did not least to contribute to the correct polity. It is to be doubted whether any reformer really contributed more by this sort of preparatory work, toward a rectified church polity, than Calvin. Calvin's abilities to gather the facts of Scripture teaching and to throw them into system was so pre-eminent that we ordinarily think of him as an incarnation of constructive genius. His genius for the destruction of the false and vicious was not less great. The work of demolition had been done, in part, indeed, in the generation before Calvin. Luther had been stalking among the fabrications of Rome. He had shattered the columns and the walls. But it was given to Calvin to crush into fine dust the foundations. Luther with the flail of a Titan, had bruised, crushed and beaten down many noxious Roman growths. It was left to Calvin, with mattock keen as a scimitar, to uproot them. Luther had swept off the huge tubercular ulcers which bespoke the vanishing spirituality of the Romish body,—had swept them off as if with a great two-handed sword. It was left to Calvin to go after the roots and the rootlets of the ulcers with a scalpel.

As far as men would submit to his surgery, Calvin could take out the uttermost rootlets of these putrid and cancerous ulcers. What he could do, he did. His exposition of the unscriptural character of the Romish church was thoroughgoing, complete and effective with all the lovers of the truth who pondered it. The warfare which he made against the Roman scheme of church government was, indeed, incidental to his establishment of his own system. Naturally, therefore, he attacked the Roman scheme now in one of its aspects and now in another of them, the point of attack being determined in every case by the corresponding truth, of his own system, which he was just then inculcating. But if his attacks were incidental, and against peculiar tenets, they were nevertheless radical, reaching to the innermost springs of the open sores.

Hear this impeachment of the Romish church government of his day—an impeachment which he, by previous exposition, had justified: "Now if anyone will closely observe and strictly examine this whole form of ecclesiastical government, which exists at the present day under the Papacy, he will find it a nest of the most lawless and ferocious banditti in the world. Everything in it is clearly so dissimilar and repugnant to the institution of Christ, so degenerated from the ancient regulations and usages of the church, so at variance with nature and reason, that no greater injury can be done to Christ than by pleading his name in defense of such a disorderly government. We (they say) are the pillars of the church, the prelates of religion, the vicars of Christ, the heads of the faithful, because we have succeeded to the power and authority of the apostles. They are perpetually vaunting these fooleries as if they were talking to blocks of wood; but whenever they repeat these boasts, I will ask them in return, what they have in common with the apostles. . . . So when we assert that their kingdom is the tyranny of Antichrist, they immediately reply, that it is that venerable hierarchy, which has been so often commended by great and holy men. As though the holy fathers, when they praise the ecclesiastical hierarchy, or spiritual government, as it had been delivered to them by the hand of the apostles, ever dreamed of this chaos of deformity and desolation, where the bishops, for the most part, are illiterate asses, unacquainted with the first and plainest rudiments of the faith, or, in some instances, are children just out of leading strings; and if any be more learned—which, however, is a rare case—they consider a bishopric to be nothing but a title of splendor and magnificence; where rectors of churches think no more of feeding the flock, than a shoe-maker does of ploughing; where all things are confounded with a dispersion worse than that of Babel, so that there can no longer be seen any clear vestige of the administration practiced in the time of the fathers." Thus speaks Calvin in Book

Calvin Refusing the Lord's Supper to the "Libertines."

IV, Chapter 5, Section 13 of the Institutes, a chapter under the heading: "The Ancient Form of Government Entirely Subverted by the Papal Tyranny,"—a chapter in which he has shown that all the "rights of the people had been entirely taken away,"—"Their suffrages, assent, subscriptions, and everything of this kind"; a chapter in which he shows that the electors of the clergy, whether canons of the cathedrals, as in the case of bishops, or bishops in the case of lower clergy, are governed by considerations far different from those held forth in I Timothy iii. 2-7, since, instead of choosing to office persons, "blameless in character, monogamous, . . . apt to teach, . . . not brawlers," they chose, commonly drunkards, fornicators, gamblers, Simoniacs,—persons who force "themselves into the possession of a church, as into an enemy's farm," who obtain it "by a legal process, who purchase it with money, who gain it by dishonorable services, who, while infants just beginning to lisp, succeed to it as an inheritance transmitted by their uncles and cousins, and sometimes even by fathers to their illegitimate children,"† and persons who cannot be present with the flock to which they are chosen even if they would, having already many benefices,—canonries, abbacies, bishoprics, it may be.

In Chapters VIII, X, and XI, of Book IV of the Institutes, he shows in the same thorough way the papal and prelatic, licentious and cruel perversion of church power; that the hierarchy, throwing off the role of teachers and ministers of the divine will as revealed in God's word, have assumed to make and impose laws of their own. Having exposed the per-

---

† Institutes, Book IV., Chapter 5, Section VI.

version and contemplated the fruits of this usurped legislative power, he asks: "How can they vindicate themselves, while they esteem it infinitely more criminal to have omitted auricular confession at a stated time of the year than to have lived a most iniquitous life for a whole year together; to have infected the tongue with the least taste of animal food on Friday, than to have polluted the body by committing fornication every day; to have put a hand to any honest labor on a day consecrated to any pretended saint, than to have continually employed all the members in the most flagitious actions; for a priest to be connected in one lawful marriage, than to be defiled with a thousand adulteries; to have failed of performing one vow of pilgrimage, than to violate every other promise; not to have lavished anything on the enormous, superfluous, and useless magnificence of churches, than to have failed of relieving the most pressing necessities of the poor; to have passed by an idol without some token of honor, than to have insulted all the men in the world; not to have muttered over, at certain seasons, a multitude of words without any meaning, than to have never offered a genuine prayer from the heart? What is it for men to make the commandment of God of none effect, if this be not?"*

Calvin was not less careful in his criticism of the church because of its having joined the power of the sword with the power of the church and the Pope's having become an earthly sovereign. In Book IV, Chapter 10, of Institutes, sweeping back over his previous teaching, he says:

"While the Romanists boast of their spiritual juris-

---

* Institutes, Book IV., Chapter 1c, Section X.

diction, it is easy to show that nothing is more contrary to the order appointed by Christ, and that it has no more resemblance to the ancient practice than darkness has to light.

"Though we have not said all that might be adduced for this purpose, and what we have said has been condensed within small compass, yet I trust we have so confuted our adversaries as to leave no room for anyone to doubt that the spiritual power arrogated by the Pope and all his hierarchy, is a tyrannical usurpation, chargeable with impious opposition to the word of God, and injustice to his people. Under the term spiritual power, I include their audacity in fabricating new doctrines by which they have seduced the unhappy people from the native purity of the word of God, the iniquitous traditions by which they have ensnared them, and the pretended ecclesiastical jurisdiction which they exercise by their suffragans, vicars, penitentiaries, and officials. For if we allow Christ any kingdom among us, all this kind of domination must immediately fall to the ground. The power of the sword, which they also claim, as that is not exercised over consciences, but operates on property, is irrelevant to our subject; though in this it is worth while to remark, that they are all consistent with themselves, and are at the greatest possible distance from the character they would be thought to sustain to the church. Here I am not censuring the particular vices cf individuals, but the general wickedness and common pest of the whole order, which they would consider as degraded, if it were not distinguished by wealth and lofty titles. If we consult the authority of Christ on this subject, there is no doubt that He intended to exclude the ministers of His word from civil dominion and secular sovereignty, when He said: "The kings of the earth exercise dominion over them; but it shall not be so among you."* His criticism is a demonstration that the ecclesiastic, as such, should not wield the power of the sword. On a kindred subject, the proper relation of church and state, Calvin was not indeed prepared for an adequate criticism, as will appear in the sequel. Believing that the church should not possess the power of civil coercion, he believed, nevertheless, that it was "the part of pious kings and princes to support religion by laws, edicts, and judicial sentences."†

In irrefutable fashion, he showed that the Romish church had substituted for the officers of the New Testament church, a special priesthood; showed that the monkish priests,—the mendicants and a few others excepted,—spent their time in the cloister either in chanting or muttering over masses, as if it were the design of Jesus Christ that the presbyters should be appointed for this purpose, or as if the nature of their office admitted it; he showed that they did not administer sacraments or execute any other branch of public duty, whereas the New Testament presbyter must tend his flock. He showed, also, that many of the secular priests were mere mercenaries, who hired themselves to labor by the day in singing and saying masses; and that the vast majority of the priests were not at all doing what God requires of the presbyter, viz., feeding the church and administering the spiritual kingdom of Christ. He showed that, in his day, there was in point of character, no body of men more infamous for

---

* Book, IV., Chapter 11, Sections VII and VIII.
† Book IV., Chapter 11, Section XVI.

profusion, delicacy, luxury and profligacy of every kind; that no class of men contained more apt or expert masters of every species of imposture, fraud, treachery and perfidy; that nowhere could be found equal cunning and audacity in the commission of crime; that there was scarcely one bishop and not one in a hundred of their parochial clergy who, if sentence were passed upon his conduct, according to the ancient canons, would not be excommunicated, or, at the very least, deposed from his office.

Thus Calvin showed the world of his day, so far as it had eyes to see, that the government of the Romish church was wholly unscriptural and not only unscriptural but morally nasty and against reason and nature.

In all his criticism of Rome, in revealing her cancerous growths, he was controlled by intensest honesty, desire for correspondence with the objective facts. And in this criticism he did great service to the cause of true ecclesiology. Men who are not aware that they have putrid organs are not inclined energetically to seek surgical aid. Men who do not feel the rottenness in the political life around them are not wont to seek its cleansing. Recognition of the evil of the Romish polity—a clear vision of it,—was needed, that men might turn with adequate energy and persistence to a nobler form of church government.

But his work nowhere stopped with the destruction of the false, the vicious and the monstrous. His was pre-eminently a constructive genius. From his very nature he must take the elements of truth accepted by him and throw them into a system. Accordingly, as early as the summer of 1536, he expressed his wish that preachers, bishops, and elders should be chosen according to scriptural method and given their scriptural functions; and by the year 1542 he had the system fully developed and in partial application in Geneva. It is but just to observe here that it was in the sphere of church polity that he did his constructive work with least of aid from previous teachers this side the apostolic age. When building his doctrine of trinity, he wrought in the light of Athanasius and Augustine. In setting up his doctrine of Christology, he worked in the light of Leo I, and of the Chalcedon council. In the realm of anthropology, Augustine had laid out and graded the way. On the doctrine of the atonement, Anselm had thrown a great light. On the doctrine of the Lord's Supper, Ratramnus and Berengar. On justification by faith, Lefevre and Luther. But if Calvin got suggestions touching the Biblical form of church polity from Lambert, and Oecolampadius, he got little more. With little help, he derived his system of ecclesiastical government, for the most part, from the scriptures of the New Testament,—a system forming the approximately Biblical counterpart of his theological system and helping to conserve that system whenever adopted by a body of God's people, an ecclesiastical system which insures the largest individual liberty compatible with order and common well-being, suggests analogous civil governments and has been a powerful factor making for free representative government in the state.

In this was his greatest contribution to church polity, his eduction from the scripture of so many elements of the New Testament plan of church government.

To appreciate this contribution we must bring before ourselves the main features of the plan of government which he constructed, and which, with modifications he applied in the Genevan church, viz.: The self-government of the church under the headship of Christ; the stress laid upon the ecclesiastical discipline of all the members from the smallest to the greatest; the exercise of the power of governing by a consistory, or parliamentary court, consisting of elders of two classes, viz.: ruling elders and elders who not only rule but also labor in word and doctrine; and the restoration of the bishop, presbyter, and deacon, to New Testament dimensions and functions.

Taking up these features in their order:

First. *The self-government of the Church under the headship of Christ.*

Calvin taught that men may not "enjoin upon the observance of the church anything that they have invented themselves, independently of the word of God"; that "this power was unknown to the apostles and so frequently interdicted to the ministers of the church by the mouth of the Lord, that it was a marvel that they have dared to usurp it, and still dare to maintain it, contrary to the example of the apostles and in defiance of the express prohibitions of God's word." He taught that everything pertaining to the perfect rule of a holy life, the Lord has comprehended in His law, so that there remains nothing for men to add to that summary; and that He has done this, firstly, that since all rectitude of life consists in the conformity of all our actions to His will, as their standard, we might consider Him as the sole master and director of our conduct; and secondly, to show that He requires of us nothing more than obedience"—obedience to the divine will. Turning, in heaven-born wrath from the pernicious and impious ecclesiastical constitutions, the traditions of men, "after the rudiments of the world," "which were making the commandments of God of none effect,"—constitutions, which as he said, "absolved in adultery and condemned in meat, that allowed a harlot and interdicted a wife,"—and that were so contrived as to have a "show of wisdom in will-worship, and humility, and neglecting of the body," petty inventions fitted to lead the minds of the vulgar, the weak and the worldly-wise, captive,—turning from these, Calvin taught that Jesus is King in Zion; that He gives the spiritual kingdom a complete constitution in accord with which it is to govern itself; that that law, once given to the church, remains forever in force,—that law which reads "Whatsoever thing I command you, observe to do it; thou shalt not add thereto nor diminish therefrom"; that the Lord's kingdom is not to be taken away from Him, which is done when He is worshipped with laws of human invention, as when the church teaches, "for doctrine, the commandments of men," or binds burdens on their backs by rule not of Him; that church order, indeed, includes a variable element, as well as a fixed, the variable to be determined by the power in the church to make regulations; but that in regard to such regulations care must be taken that they be not considered necessary to salvation, and so imposing a religious obligation on the conscience, or applied to the worship of God, and so represented as essential to piety that this power of making regulations only about circumstances so standing around enjoined actions that the divinely enjoined actions cannot be separated from them, or at least cannot be separated from them without loss of decorum or order,—that this power is limited to making such regulations, for example, as, that certain hours shall be appointed for public worship, quietness and silence shall be observed under sermons, days shall be fixed for the observance of the Lord's Supper, and decorum observed in the administration of it, and regulations for the preservation of discipline, as catechising, ecclesiastical censures, fasting and everything else that can be referred to the same class,—regulations touching *ceremonies, rites,* or *discipline and peace;* and that in making of these the church must conform to the general rules divinely given.* He teaches that these regulations are to be regarded for the sake of order and decorum and not for God's authority in them. He thus teaches that the government of the church is to be by divinely given constitution; that it is the Lord's kingdom and to be governed by His law.

As is implied in what has been said, Calvin distinguished sharply between civil government and ecclesiastical government. He taught that the church has no power of the sword to punish or to coerce, no authority to compel, no prisons, no fines, or other punishments, like those inflicted by the civil magistrate; that the object of ecclesiastical power is not that he who has transgressed may be punished against his will; but that he may profess his repentance by a voluntary submission to chastisement; that the difference between church and state is very great, the church not assuming to itself what belongs to the magistrate, and the magistrate being unable to execute that which is executed by the church. This particular he illustrates by the following example: "Is any man intoxicated? In a well regulated city he will be punished by im-

---

* Book IV., Chapter 10, Sections XXIX, XXX, XXXI.

prisonment. . . . With this the laws, the magistrate, and the civil judgment will be satisfied; though it may happen that he will give no sign of repentance but will rather murmur and repine against his judgment. Will the church stop here? Such persons cannot be admitted to the sacred Supper without doing an injury to Christ and His holy institution. And reason requires that he who has offended the church with an evil example, should remove by a solemn declaration of repentance the offence which he has excited."

But, while Calvin distinguished thus clearly and sharply between church and state, holding that they were independent of one another, each in its domain, he saw no propriety in their separation. On the contrary, he believed that every civil government should profess the true religion; that *it should* "by punishment and corporeal coercion, purge the church from offences;" and that it should support and further its good work as the first object of its own existence.

Here was a mistake of Calvin's. He believed that God in Christ is head both of church and state; that the office of civil government extends to both tables of the Decalogue. This was a conception of his age, inherited from the ages back to Constantine the Great, which he was not able to shake off. But the logic of the position is persecution by the state for that which it esteems to be religious heresy. If the state has the right to profess Christ as its head and to propagate His religion, then it has the right to protect it from heresy, the right to punish heresy with the forces at its command. Duties are correlated with rights. Naturally we find the Geneva state punishing with fine, imprisonment, banishment or death, such men as Gruet, Bolsec and Servetus. God has given to no

Christian state such a right—the right of corporeally "punishing for heretical opinion."

Calvin and his age were wrong in holding that it was a concern of the state to enforce the observance of the first table of the Decalogue; that the state properly could become Christian and make the protection, support and advancement of the church its highest aim; and that in the outworking of this aim it could use physical coercion.

But we have him to thank for distinguishing between the civil and ecclesiastical powers and governments so clearly; and showing that ecclesiastical government is of right only by the God-given constitution. We have him to thank, too, for the emphasis he laid on the duty of the church to *govern itself*. For while he believed in the propriety of the union of church and state, he was so convinced that the church should govern itself that he taught that it should do this at the cost of self-support, if necessary. That is, he taught that while the state should support the church, and allow the church to govern itself in accord with its divine constitution, yet, if it will not give this support while conceding freedom, then the church should forego state support that it may govern itself.

The first main feature, then, of Calvin's plan of ecclesiastical government was the self government of the church under the headship of Christ. In this teaching he was vastly superior to the earlier reformers; he planted seed that had fruited in the weakening of the connection between the church and the state throughout all reformed christendom; he is making to-day for the separation of the two powers in whatsoever quarters his influence has reached; he is developing the reformed churches by the process of self government; and should more and more enthrone Christ as King *de facto* as he is King *de jure*, in the universal church.

The *second main feature* was the *emphasis laid upon ecclesiastical discipline, the ecclesiastical discipline of all the members of the church from the smallest to the greatest.*

Calvin valued discipline as second only to teaching. The effort to introduce discipline was the primary occasion of his expulsion from Geneva in 1538. He was hardly settled comfortably in the church of the strangers in Strasburg before he introduced it there. When recalled to Geneva in 1541, he proceeded at once to the work of establishing it firmly there. The importance of discipline he formally sets forth as follows (Book IV., Chap. XII., Section 2):

"As some have such a hatred of discipline as to abhor the very name they should attend to the following consideration, that if no society and even no house, though containing only a small family, can be preserved in a proper state without discipline, this is far more necessary in the church, the state of which ought to be the most orderly of all. As the saving doctrine of Christ is the soul of the church, so discipline forms the ligaments which connects the members together, and keeps each in its proper place. Whoever, therefore, either desire the abolition of all discipline or obstruct its restoration, whether they act from design or inadvertency, they certainly promote the entire dissolution of the church. For what will be the consequence, if every man be at liberty to follow his own inclinations? But such would be the case, unless the preaching of the doctrine were accompanied with private admonitions, reproofs, and other means to enforce the doctrine, and prevent it from being altogether ineffectual. Discipline, therefore, serves as a bridle to curb and to restrain the refractory, who resist the doctrine of Christ; or as a spur to stimulate the inactive; and sometimes as a father's rod, with which those who have grievously fallen may be chastised in mercy, and with the gentleness of the spirit of Christ. Now when we see the approach of certain beginnings of a dreadful dissolution in the church, since there is no solicitude or means to keep the people in obedience to our Lord, necessity itself proclaims the want of a remedy; and this is the only remedy which has been commanded by Christ, or which has ever been adopted among believers."

In accordance with the teachings of Christ, Calvin made three degrees of discipline, viz.: private admonition, admonition in the presence of witnesses, or before the church, and excommunication. Private admonition is to be employed universally when occasion demands, and by all. But pastors and presbyters, beyond all others should be vigilant in the discharge of this duty; being called by their office not only to preach to the congregation, but also to admonish and exhort in private houses, if in any instances their public instructions may not have been sufficiently efficacious, as Paul inculcates, when he says that he taught "publicly and from house to house" and protests himself to be "free from the blood of all men" having "ceased not to warn every man night and day with tears." Admonition in the presence of witnesses is to be employed against public offences of less heinousness and against private offences of an inferior sort when private admonition fails. Excommunication is to be employed only "for the correcting of atrocious crimes," such as "adultery, fornication, theft, robbery, sedition, perjury, false witness, and other similar crimes, together with obstinate persons, who after having been admonished even of smaller faults, contemn God and his judgments."

He represents the ends of discipline as: First, that those who lead scandalous and flagitious lives may not, to the dishonour of God, be numbered among Christians . . . for as the church is the body of Christ, it cannot be contaminated with such foul and putrid members without some ignominy being reflected upon the head." The second is, "that the good may not be corrupted, as is often the case, by constant association with the wicked; for such is our propensity to err, that nothing is more easy than for evil example to seduce us from rectitude of conduct." "A little leaven leaveneth the whole lump." The third end is, "that those who are censured, or excommunicated, confounded with the shame of their turpitude, may be led to repentance."

On no point does Calvin lay more emphasis than that discipline should be administered "with a spirit of gentleness," "For there is," he says, "constant need of the greatest caution, according to the injunction of Paul, respecting a person who may have been censured," "lest perhaps such an one should be swallowed up with over much sorrow; for thus a remedy would become a poison, but the rule of moderation may be better deduced from the end intended to be accomplished; for as the design of excommunication is that the sinner may be brought to repentance, and evil examples taken away, to prevent the name of Christ from being blasphemed and other persons tempted to imitation; if we keep these things in view, it will be very easy to judge how far severity ought to proceed and where it ought to be stopped."

He inculcates earnestly the duty of trying to win to a holy life the excommunicated. He made it the church's duty to receive into communion again, upon his repentance, one who had been excommunicated; and this also although the repentance were after a second excommunication. "Such," he says, "as are expelled from the church therefore, it is not for us to expunge from the number of the elect, or to despair of them as already lost. It is proper to consider them as strangers to the church, and consequently from Christ, but this only as long as they remain in a state of exclusion." He thought that the Anathema, or devotion of a person to eternal perdition, ought to be very rarely or never resorted to.* It was a principle of his that correction should be tempered with such moderation, as to be salutary rather than injurious to the body.

He endeavored to make the discipline of the minister of the gospel more severe than that of the people. Against the Romish church he vindicated, indeed, the minister's right to marriage, on the one hand, but on the other, denied his right to exemption from the civil courts, and taught that he should be afflicted with the same civil penalties as laymen for misdemeanors. And he held that as ensamples to the flock ministers were under special obligations to live an approvable life.

He proposed, in short, to realize as far as possible, the ideal of the church, without spot or wrinkle,"—to glorify God by the dominion of His word in the life of the church—by the application of the power of God,

---

*Book IV., Chapter XII, Section X.

as well as the truth of God; although he knew that the church, while on earth, is mixed with good and bad, and will never be free from impurity."

Touching Calvin's views of the importance of discipline, its proper ends, and the spirit with which it should be administered, it would be hard to speak too praisefully. They have done not a little to develop the peculiar fibre of Calvinistic character.

Owing to the unhappy union of church and state in which he and all his age believed, he was not entirely happy in locating the power to be used in discipline; but this brings us to the *third* distinctive feature of his policy.

That this power for discipline and for all the functions of government, is to be exercised by a consistory, or parliamentary court, consisting of elders of two classes, viz., ruling elders and elders who not only rule but labor in word and doctrine.

Calvin teaches that, in order to the preservation of the spiritual polity, God institutes a certain order; that for this end, there were from the beginning judiciaries appointed in the churches to take cognizance of matters, to pass censures on vices, and to preside over the use of the keys in excommunication," that "this order Paul designates in his first Epistle to the Corinthians, when he mentions "government," and in the Epistle to the Romans, when he says "he that ruleth, let him do it with diligence"; that Paul is not here "speaking of magistrates, or civil governors, for there were at this time no Christian magistrates, but of those who were associated with the pastor in spiritual government of the church; that in the First Epistle to Timothy, also, he mentions two kinds of presbyters, or elders, some who labor in the word and doctrine," others who have nothing to do with preaching the word, and yet, "rule well"; that "by the latter class, there can be no doubt that he intended those who were appointed to the cognizance of manners and the whole exercise of the keys;" for that this power of government "entirely depends on the keys, which Christ has conferred upon the church in the eighteenth chapter of Matthew, where He commands that those who shall have despised private admonition shall be severely admonished in the name of the whole church, and that if they persist in their obstinacy, they are to be excluded from the society of believers. He argues that since the admonitions and corrections cannot take place without an examination of the cause, there is necessity of some judicature and order."

Men can to-day demonstrate, and more compactly than Calvin did, that the local church of the apostolic church was governed by a parliamentary court of elders, and that two or more churches united under a superior presbytery. But it was Calvin's part to open the way for this, and that way he opened.

In accord with these views, Calvin established consistorial (or presbyterial) government in the Genevan church. The Genevan consistory (or presbytery, as we may call it) embraced, in Calvin's day, five pastors and twelve elders. The duty of this body was to overwatch, and to apply the power of God to, every member of the Genevese church, from the least to the greatest, according to individual need. It was never to assume any of the rights of the civil power. In cases of discovered crimes against the state, of such enormity as to make corporal punishment necessary, it was simply to lay the circumstances before the civil government. "it belonging unto God to determine the powers of both." The severest punishment which could be inflicted by the presbytery was excommunication from the communion of the faithful.

The civil government was long indisposed to concede the right of excommunication to the church court; and there were numerous appeals from the church court to the civil government; but after 1555 the church enjoyed, without opposition, the right to inflict this penalty.

Calvin's presbytery in Geneva was not, however, in all respects, a close approximation to the New Testament presbytery. He knew very clearly the Bible mode of inducting man into ecclesiastical office; and taught that the apostles ordained men to office in the church according to the suffrages of the members of the church to be served by them.* But in Geneva, owing to the connection of church and state, the members of the presbytery were not elected in the Biblical way. Of the twelve ruling elders, two were taken from the Little Council of the State, four from the Council of sixty, and six from that of the two hundred. They were chosen to their ecclesiastical functions by the Little Council of the State, and confirmed by the preachers.

The preachers were always elected first by the body of preachers already in existence; their election was then submitted to the Little Council for confirmation. In case the congregation had anything to object, it was made its duty to state its objection to the syndics that all might be satisfied with the choice.

It thus appears that the state had much to do with the appointments of the members of the presbytery.

---

* Commentary on Matt. 13: 47.

Under the circumstances this was natural. The state had adopted the church. The court of the church was, in one of its aspects, the state's court to handle its ecclesiastical business, and the state was exercising its prerogatives in electing these, its own, officers. Practically, however, this mode of filling ecclesiastical offices was an infringement on the autonomy of the church—a principle of which Calvin made much in theory; and it was out of harmony with Calvin's own representation of the mode of filling offices in the apostolic church. For he teaches, as has already appeared, that in the apostolic church the apostles ordained those whom the whole multitude of believers, "according to the customs observed in elections among the Greeks, declared by the elevation of their hands "to be the object of their choice." *

The moderator of the Genevan presbytery was a syndic, an executive officer of the state, an arrangement which helped to express and to further the union between the church and the state.

The dependence of the church upon the state for support prevented the full development of the great beneficent functions of the church court, in maturing and supporting plans for the church's expansion.

A sort of subsidiary organ of ecclesiastical rule was the Venerable Company, constituted of all the ministers of the city and district of Geneva. It took the general supervision of all strictly ecclesiastical affairs, especially of the education, ordination, and installation of ministers of the gospel; but as has appeared, no one could be admitted to the ministry and installed without the co-operation of the civil government and the assent of the citizens.

---

* Book IV., Chapter III, Section XV.

In regard to this presbyterial feature of Calvin's polity, it must be said, that in both theory and practice, he gave to the communicant church members, too little power in the choice of their rulers. He gave too much power to the state.

He did not develop all the several functions of the church court. Had he gotten rid of the belief in the propriety of the connection of church and state, or had he been forced to make a practical separation of the church from the state, he would probably have followed the Biblical plan in bringing into being the organ for the government of the church—the presbytery composed of representatives of God's people chosen by the people, and consisting of two classes, elders who rule only, and elders who also labor in word and doctrine.

The fourth main feature of Calvin's polity is his *restoration of the bishop, the presbyter, and the deacon, to New Testament dimensions, and functions.* He saw clearly, with the reformers generally and with leading Catholic and Anglican doctors, that the New Testament bishop is the New Testament elder, and that the New Testament elder is the New Testament bishop; and he stripped the bishop of all diocesan functions and made him an elder in his theory of him. He also saw what many reformers did sot see, that of the bishops or elders in the apostolic age, there are two classes,—elders that rule only and elders that not only rule but also labor in word and doctrine.

For centuries previous to Calvin's day, the ruling elder had been extinct. Calvin brought him back into existence and vindicated, as has appeared, his place in the presbytery. He also showed that the mediaeval deacon,—who was a priest in the tadpole stage of his development,—was not a Biblical officer; and restored the deaconate of the New Testament church—the organ of the communion of the saints in things temporal,—an administrative office under the general oversight of the presbytery.

In this constructive work of Calvin—in his exhibition of the church as of right self-governing under its head, Christ; in his exposition of its right to govern in accord with its divinely given constitution, all the members from the smallest to the greatest; in his exposition of the aims, means and proper spirit of discipline; in his restoration of the presbytery,—the divinely appointed organ of church rule, according to the New Testament; in his reduction of ecclesiastical offices "to their New Testament character"—we have a contribution to church polity not equalled since the days of Paul. The errors in his system, including union of church and state and the incoherencies in his system springing from this error about the proper relation of the church and state, were to be expelled from his system by the truth in it.

To occasional successors, such as James Henley Thornwell, it has been given to deepen and broaden Calvin's correct ecclesiastical teachings in certain aspects; but for the most part, it has been necessary for them to walk in paths blazed by Calvin, unless they would abandon God's word when diverging from Calvin's track. His poineer work in the sphere of polity was so ably done, that the direction has been fixed for the unbiased student of God's word.

One thing more should be said: Though Calvin had done work of such value in the sphere of polity, he did not overrate the work or the sphere. He believed in a God-given polity as in a God-given doctrine; but he did not regard doctrine and polity as of equal value. He recognized as a church of God every society claiming to be a church, which held the essential doctrines taught in the scriptures, whether the body had a presbyterian organization or not. He saw in the Lutheran bodies, with or without bishops, churches of God, and in the Anglican church, with its bishops, a true church of Christ. He would have recognized our Baptist and Methodist churches as true churches of Christ, notwithstanding their imperfect forms of polity.

In speaking thus, we must not be understood to represent Calvin as rating church polity as of small value. He considered it necessary for the well being of the church, though not to the bare being of the church. The cart-horse is a horse; he has all the essential marks of a horse; but the Arabian courser, worth two, three or four, ten thousands of dollars, has, we know, other marks, not essential to the bare being of a horse, but of capital value nevertheless. Calvin believed that the Arabian courser among the churches must have representative government,—government by courts of presbyter bishops.

He not only gave to polity an approximately Biblical form, but estimated its relative value Biblically.

In his masterly exhibition and deadly criticisms of the mediaeval Roman Catholic polity, he served the church well. In his discovery in the Bible, and deduction therefrom, of the principles of representative church government, he made practical the realization of "The noblest, the manliest, the equalist, the justest government on earth,"—a government through the best,—the true governmental counterpart to the most humbling and exhalting, the most gracious and most ethical theology, ever drawn from nature or revelation.

CALVIN'S ATTITUDE TOWARDS AND EXEGESIS OF THE SCRIPTURES.

Dr. James Orr,
Glasgow, Scotland.

Few men have been more misunderstood than John Calvin. His name, with multitudes to the present hour, is a synonym for everything hard, gloomy, and repellent, in religious thought. It is the fate of a great personality to call forth strong antagonisms, as well as to inspire intense attachments. Calvin could not have been the man he was—massive in intellect, uncompromising in principle, fixed and resolute in will—and could not have done the work he did in Geneva and in Europe, without evoking fiercest opposition, and drawing upon himself storms of personal hatred. Yet without these qualities he would not have sowered above his fellows as, next to Luther, if ever next to him, the greatest moral force of the sixteenth century, or have achieved the unspeakable service he did to the cause of Protestantism. The man of whom one of the most recent and ablest liberal theologians of Germany, P. Werule, writes: "It is not so easy to be done with the man who was the clearest, acutest theologian of his age and the founder of the power of Protestantism in Scotland, France, England and Holland. . . . Rigorously as he ruled Geneva, as heroically did he lead half the Protestantism of Europe to a unity of purpose, the power of which nothing could break;" of whom Mark Pattison said: "The Protestant movement was saved from being sunk in the quicksand of doctrinal dispute chiefly by the new moral direction given to it in Geneva. . . . Calvinism saved Europe;" of whom John Morley declares that, in comparison with him, the men included in the Positwist "New Calendar of Great Men" are "hardly more than names wet in water;" of whom Motley, the historian testified: "It would be ridiculous to deny that the aggressive, uncompromising, self-sacrificing, intensely believing, perfectly fearless spirit of Calvinism, had been the animating soul, the motive power, of the great revolt. For the provinces to have encumbered Spain and Rome without Calvinism, and relying on municipal enthusiasm only, would have been to throw away the sword, and fight with the scabbard only." Is not a man the modern world can afford to despise.

It is entrusted to others to show how Calvin has been misunderstood in his personal character and his theological teachings. One can afford to smile at the picture some times drawn of Calvinism when one thinks of Calvin's own *Institutes,* and recalls how one finds him there entailing the paternal tenderness of God, recognizing as a work of God's Spirit the truth and wisdom that shone in the minds of heathen says, exalting the love of God in giving His Son for the reconciliation of the world, and setting forth in glowing language the ideals of Christian characters. Calvin went deep, indeed, into the spiritual need of man through sin, and high in his attribution of everything in salvation to the immediate grace of God; looked at human life and salvation ever in the light of the eternal purpose on which everything that is or happens rests as on an immovable rock—for what, after all, is Calvin's doctrine of predestination but simply the actual process of salvation viewed *sub specie oeternitatis*; refused to give the name of true freedom to acts of the soul enslaved by sin, or the name of true goodness to character or deeds that lacked the genuine spring of goodness. But it was because his theology ploughed thus into the depths that it was able to lay so strong a foundation for individual and national character; because it soared thus into the heights that it was able to elevate and strengthen as it did the intellect and will of those who accepted it. The tree is known by its fruits, and it may well be asked, with Froude, "how it came to pass that if Calvinism is indeed the hard and unreasonable creed which modern enlightenment declares it to be, it has possessed such singular attractions in past times for some of the greatest men that ever lived. And how—being, as we are told, fatal to morality, because it denies free will—the first symptom of its operation, wherever it established itself, was to obliterate the distinction between sins and crimes, and to make the moral law the rule of life for States as well as persons."

My immediate object is Calvin as an exegete of Scripture, and here, whatever debates may have arisen as to Calvin's merits in other relations, I am happy in having allotted to me a department of his work in regard to which almost unbroken unanimity reigns. Calvin's theology may be challanged, his character and work may be adversely criticised, but a chorus of testimony from well-nigh every school and shade of opinion in Christendom could be produced to the remarkable gifts of mind and heart displayed in his exposition of Scripture—to his breadth, moderation, fairness, and modernness of spirit, in exhibiting the sense and inward genius of holy writ. Reuss, one of the editors of his works, pronounces him "beyond all question the greatest exegete of the sixteenth century;" and Tholuck, in an appreciation regarded as classical, extols "his simple, elegant style, his dogmatic freedom, the fact with which he treats his subject, his multifarious learning and profound Christian piety." I shall not detain you by quoting opinions of others, but will rather endeavor to show from the works themselves how justly Calvin is entitled to the eulogies passed upon him in this connection:

One testimony, however, I think I should not omit, on account of the source from which it comes. The theological antithesis to Calvinism is Arminianism, and it is interesting to hear what Arminius himself had to say of Calvin as an exegete. Here are the words of this certainly unbiased witness: "Next to the perusal of the Scriptures," he says, "I exhort my pupils to peruse Calvin's commentaries, which I extol in loftier terms than Helmick himself [Helmick was a Dutch divine]; for I affirm that he excels beyond comparison in the interpretation of Scripture, and that his commentaries ought to be more highly valued than all that is handed down to us by the library of the fathers; so that I acknowledge him to those possessed above most others, as rather above all men, what may be called an eminent gift of prophecy." Let us see whether this judgment is not merited.

First, with respect to Calvin's qualifications for the work of interpreter, let me remind you that he was *a ripe scholar.* His early education at leading universities, of chiefly classical and legal, was very thorough. He had a splendid command of Latin and of his own tongue, French; and at Bourges, in addition to his legal studies, he acquired from Wolmar a knowledge of Greek. His knowledge of Hebrew, acquired from Grynoeus, is attested not only by his numerous references to and comments on Hebrew words, but by the fact that he assisted his kinsman Olivetan in the production in 1535 (the year before he went to Geneva) of a French translation of the Scriptures from the Hebrew. In 1540 there appeared at Geneva in Calvin's own name a translation of the whole Bible into French. Patristic and scholastic learning he was master of. Few men of his age, if any, had a nobler equipment.

What was even more important than learning for his task, Calvin had a *deep and rich Christian experience.* After sore spiritual struggle, he had been brought to God, as he tells us in the preface to his Commentary on the Psalms, by "a sudden conversion"; and his life thereafter was one of habitual devotion and prayer, and earnest endeavor to know and to do God's will. Werule, before quoted, writes of him: "Does anyone desire to know the man as he lived with God and the world, let him read the chapter in the *Institutes* on 'The Life of the Christian Man.' That is the portrait of himself."

But next, one observes that Calvin of set purpose made the Scriptures from the first his *constant study, and the text-book and basis* of his work. We have seen him assisting in translating the Scriptures. His labors in Geneva began with expository lectures on the Epistles of Paul and other New Testament books, and exposition of Scripture was a principal feature of his work all through. His mind was steeped in the Word of God, not as a dead letter, but as a living spirit. His *Institutes*—a work wrought in glowing heat of spirit on the anvil of an intense conviction for the practical purpose of vindicating his persecuted brethren in France—is based on sound Scriptural exegesis. It is penetrated with the language, the spirit, the ideas of Scripture. Calvin's treatment is as far as may be from a dogmatic handling of texts. Scripture is apprehended in the organic connection of its truths. But Calvin has no use for anything in theology which cannot be established by *broad* and fair appeal to the written Word. This was the reason why for a time he shrank from using the terms "Trinity" and "Person" in the doctrine of the Godhead, while holding the truths which these terms denote.

Approaching nearer, one must take into account, and cannot fail to be impressed by, the *immense range* of Calvin's work in Scriptural exposition. It is not the case, indeed, that his Commentaries cover the whole of Scripture. They do not, nor were they produced in the order of the books of Scripture. He began with the Epistle to the Romans in 1540, while at Frankfort. Then followed, at intervals, the remaining Pauline and other Epistles of the New Testament. Acts belong to this period; the Gospels are later the only book of the New Testament not commented on is Revelation, which Calvin frankly declared he did not understand. He lectured, however, on Daniel, which was nearly as difficult, and possibly felt that this superseded the necessity of a second work of the kind of his Old Testament commentaries, the earliest were those on Isaiah, on Genesis, and on Psalms. The remaining books of the Pentateuch appear in the form of a "Harmony," as also do the first three Gospels. Calvin here shows a quite modern instinct in separating the Synoptic Gospels from John for treatment by themselves. The principal Commentaries appear in both Latin and French versions. The latest was the Commentary on Joshua, published shortly before

Calvin Writing His Commentaries.

his death. A good many books of the Old Testament are left untouched, viz.: Judges, Ruth, Samuel and Kings, Esther, Ezra and Nehemiah, Proverbs, Ecclesiastes, and the Song of Solomon.

In so wide a field of achievement it would be unreasonable to look for an equal level of excellence. Some of the expositions, as on Job, the Minor Prophets, Jeremiah, Daniel, were taken down from Calvin's extempore pulpit discourses, and in their character and style bear traces of this popular origin. The Commentaries prepared by Calvin himself are works of great thoroughness. His chief repute rests on the Commentaries on the Pauline Epistles and on the Psalms. The Apostle of the Gentiles never had a more sympathetic expounder, and the Commentary on the Psalms, with its wonderful biographical Preface, is a masterpiece, into which Calvin's whole soul is poured. His own trials, as he says, helped him to understand David's. He calls the Psalms "an anatomy of all parts of the soul, for no one will discover in himself a single feeling, whereof the image is not reflected in this mirror." Bishop Horsley speaks of Calvin as "a man of great piety, great talents, and great learning," yet thinks that, by his want of taste and poverty of imagination, he was "a most wretched expositor of the prophecies." The modern exegete will probably much prefer Calvin's sobriety to the worthy bishop's elegance. Meanwhile, it may be suggested that a man who could so excellently expound the Psalms was hardly likely to be wholly unfitted to expound the prophets.

I ought perhaps to remark at this point, on the singular testimony which Calvin's Commentaries afford to the *wide range and potency of his influence in the highest circles.* The Dedications to the Commentaries are here instructive. They reveal Calvin as a European power.

Already, when yet unknown, he had addressed his *Institutes* to the French King, Frances I., in a Preface which is recognized as one of the finest things in literature. Now, in maturer years, he dedicates his Commentary on Isaiah, and again that on the Catholic Epistles, to the youthful Edward VI. of England. His Commentary on the Epistles to Timothy had been dedicated to the Duke of Somerset, the Protector during Edward's minority. With both Somerset and Edward he had correspondence, and Cramner was in regular communication with him. His Commentary on the Hebrews was dedicated to King Sigismund Augustus of Poland; the first part of his commentary on the Acts, to Christian I. of Denmark, and the second part to the son of that monarch. His Commentary on Hosea was dedicated to Gustavus Vasa of Sweden. His Commentary on the last four books of Moses was dedicated to Henry IV. of France, then a boy, with noble admonitions. His Harmony of the Gospels was dedicated to the Council of Frankfort, which received it with thanks; and so with nearly all. The language in these Dedications is marked by a dignity, courtesy, and elevation of tone, an absence of the customary flattery of the great, and a seriousness and directness of purpose, which give the compositions a character all their own. Calvin wrote as one who sought nothing for himself, and knew that what he gave was not unworthy of those to whom he gave it. His words were not platitudes, but earnest exhortations, intended to produce an effect.

I pass to the qualities of the works themselves, which give them their permanent value for the Church and for mankind. Here, naturally, we have to recognize that, with all his gifts, and depth of insight, Calvin was yet a *man of his own age*. He had not at command the elaborate critical apparatus which modern scholars rejoice in. Textual criticism had scarcely commenced; the religions and civilizations of antiquity were known only through the imperfect accounts of classical authors. It was a time when the modern science of nature was yet unborn (Calvin was ignorant, *e. g.,* of the Copernican astronomy); when "Higher Criticism," with its marvelous feats of analysis, disintegration, and reconstruction of of books, history, and legislations, was still undreamt of; when the wonders disclosed by Egyptian, Assyrian and Babylonian exploration, lay yet centuries in the future, the seals of the book of modern knowledge were yet unbroken. What is to be said for Calvin is that he worked with the classical, patristic, philological and other materials he *did* possess—and they were not slight—as faithfully and successfully as any man in his generation could do; but far better, that his exegetical labors were mainly concerned with those ideas and teachings of the books of Scripture which are largely unaffected by the changes introduced by modern knowledge and discovery,—which belong to the abiding and unalterable side of the message of the Bible. This is a lesson which our modern age has perhaps yet to learn. For, if knowledge grows from less to more; if theology, too, in its human apprehension of divine truths, necessarily becomes wider in its processes and outlook; it is not less certain that the foundation of God standeth, and that the great truths of God's character, man's nature, sin's ruin, Christ's Person and redemption, the Spirit's work in renewal—those truths which are the living substance, the very warp and woof of Bible teaching,—remain what they are as surely as before science or criticism were heard of,—abide as truly as do the great constellations in the mighty sky amidst the changes of theoretical astronomy.

This, specially, is Calvin's greatness as an expositor, that it is ever the primary, not the secondary, matters that interest him—that he deals with the *eternal* in Scripture, with the living word that abideth. How small a thing, after all, the ability to divide up a verse or chapter into its supposed critical constituents, or to throw new light on a historical statement or prophetic allusion from philological knowledge or some Babylonian or Assyrian parallel, compared with the insight that penetrates into the very heart of divine revelation; the skill which expends itself on the shape and chasings of the vessel which contains the water of life, compared with the hand which ministers the living water itself!

With these inevitable limitations which belong to his time, it is now to be remarked that Calvin exhibits many of the qualities characteristic of the *best modern exegesis*. The principles that guided him are laid down in his admirable prefatory "Epistle" to the Commentary on the Romans, and nothing could be sounder. He agreed with his friend Grynoeus that "the principal point of an interpreter is a perspicuous brevity." This, he says, is in a manner his whole charge, "to show forth the mind of the writer whom he has taken upon him to expound." All critics give him credit for a studious endeavor to adhere to the historical and grammatical meaning of the text. His mind is not overburdened by his learning or over-ridden—or this only rarely—by theological prejudices. He starts, as the good commentator always should, from the text itself, from the meaning of the author in his own place and time, and displays an acumen and sobriety in his judgments as refreshing as it is rare. There is no padding with Calvin. He knows what he has to do, and sets about his work in a thoroughly practical and business-like fashion. His feet are ever on the ground, however loftily his thoughts may soar. "It is sacrilegious boldness," he says, "to use the Scriptures at our pleasure, and to play them as with a tennis-ball."

The result in Calvin is a singular ballance and moderation in judgment, and a note of modernness in his work, which impresses one the more the more closely he is studied. He refuses what he thinks a weak argument, even to support a sound doctrine, *e. g.,* he will not allow the Trinity to be deduced from the plural name, "Elohim." He will admit Maccabean psalms, *e. g.,* Ps. lxxiv. He interprets Ps. xlv. of the marriage of Solomon, though he thinks there is a typical reference to Christ. His prophetic interpretations start from the historical situation. A few illustrations will set these characteristics of Calvin's work more clearly before the mind than any general statement can do.

In his Commentaries on Genesis and on the last four books of Moses we find, of course, nothing of modern critical learning. We hear nothing of J, E, D, and P; nothing about legends. The day for that kind of wisdom had not yet come. Moses is unhesitatingly assumed to be the author. There is not even a suggestion of explanation of the fact, which one might suppose would have struck him, of the alternating use of "Jehovah" and "Elohim." In other respects his comments are singularly opposite and correct. In his "Argument" to Genesis he excellently shows that the main subject of the book is not physical matters, but the purpose of redemption in Christ. In speaking of the creation narrative, how true a note does he strike in insisting that the language used is popular, and that scientific exactitude is not to be looked for! "He who would learn astronomy, and other recondite arts," he says, "let him go elsewhere." "Moses wrote in a popular style things which, without instruction, all ordinary persons, imbued with common sense, are able to understand. . . . Had he spoken of things generally unknown, the uneducated might have pleaded in excuse that such subjects were beyond their capacity. . . . If the astronomer inquires respecting the actual dimensions of the stars, he will find the moon to be less than Saturn; but this is something abstruse, for to the sight it appears differently. . . . He does not call us up into heaven, he only proposes things that lie open before our eyes." He justly denies the distinction of "image" and "likeness" in man's creation, and dwells on the dignity of human nature as evinced by God's counselling with Himself regarding him. "Truly," he says, "there are many things in this corrupted nature which may induce contempt; but if you hightly weigh all circumstances, man is, among other creatures, a certian pre-eminent specimen of divine wisdom, justice and goodness, so that he is deservedly called by the ancients *microcosm*—a world in miniature."

Or take the laws of Moses. It is a great merit of Calvin that he perceives so clearly the relation of the ceremonial and political laws of Moses to the moral law of the Ten Commandments, in which lay the real basis of the nation's covenant with God. "It is not a little important," he says, "that we should understand that the ceremonies and the judicial ordinances neither change nor detract from the rule laid down in the Ten Commandments; but are only helps, which, as it were lead us by the hand to the due worship of God, and to the promotion of justice towards men." "We are aware," he adds, "that of old there was a constant controversy of the prophets against the Jewish people, because whilst strenuously devoting themselves to ceremonies, as if true religion and holiness were comprised in them, they neglected real righteousness. Therefore God protests that He never enjoined anything with respect to the sacrifices; and He pronounces all external rites but vain and trifling, if the very least value be assigned to them apart from the Ten Commandments. Whence we more certainly arrive at the conclusion to which I have adverted, viz., that they are not, to speak correctly, of the substance of the law, nor avail of themselves in the worship of God, nor are required by the lawgiver Himself as necessary, or even as useful, unless they sink into this inferior position." Calvin, evidently, had no difficulty in understanding Jeremiah in Ch. vii. 22: "For I spake not unto your fathers," etc.

As Calvin's views on the Sabbath are sometimes misrepresented, it may be observed that in his comments both on Genesis and on the laws, he takes the Sabbath to be as old as the creation, and regards it as continuing to the end of the world. It was probable (in the French edition he thinks certain that it was observed by the patriarchs, but "I am unwilling," he says, "to make this a matter of contention."

As a New Testament illustration, I take his Judiciaries remarks on the difficult question of Christ's human knowledge. He discusses this in commenting on Luke ii. 40: "And the child grew, and waxed strong, filled with wisdom, and the grace of God was upon Him," and v. 52: "Jesus advanced in wisdom and stature, and in favor with God and man." "If it takes nothing from His glory," Calvin says, "that He was altogether 'emptied' (Phil. ii. 6), neither does it degrade Him, that He chose not only to grow in body, but to make progress in mind"; and maintains that Christ's humiliation "no doubt includes, that His soul was subject to ignorance." He rejects the view of timid persons that this progress was only in appearance, and declares: "We are not at liberty to suppose, that knowledge lay concealed in Christ, and made its appearance in Him in progress of time. . . . If we do not choose to deny, that Christ was made a real man, we ought not to be ashamed to acknowledge that He voluntarily took upon Him everything that is inseparable from human nature." He guards himself from the inference that ignorance implies sin. "We ascribe to Christ," he says, " no other ignorance than what may fall upon a man who is pure from every taint of sin."

I have already referred to the rigor with which Calvin insists on an historical interpretation of psalms and prophecies. Even the psalms, as the 2nd, the 45th, the 110th, which are interpreted typically of Christ, are held in their historical meaning to apply to David or other kings. "To whom is that voice addressed?" he asks on Is. xl. 3, "Prepare ye the way of the Lord." "Is it to believers? No, but to Cyrus, to the Persians, and to the Medes, who held that people in captivity." But this group of prophecies, he thinks, "ought not to be limited to the captivity in Babylon; for they have a very extensive meaning, and include the doctrine of the Gospel, in which chiefly lies the power of 'comforting.'" The story of Hosea's wife, with other passages, he interprets parabolically.

It is sometimes said that Calvin held free views on the inspiration of Scripture, and did not scruple to admit errors and discrepancies in the sacred text. I do not think this is a correct statement. To Calvin, Scripture is throughout the inspired word of God, and seeming discrepancies are, as a rule, treated by him as seeming only, and he has generally some sensible remarks to offer for their reconciliation. This is seen in his comments on the laws of Moses, or in his treatment of the discrepancies alleged in such cases as the census of Quirinius, the cure of Bartimeus, and the narratives of the ressurection.

Yet he does not overstrain, and acknowledges difficulty where it exists. In regard to the genealogies in Matthew and Luke, he gives what he thinks to be the best solutions, and warns those who desire more to remember Paul's injunction to avoid disputing about geanealogies. Referring to the mention of Jeremiah instead of Zechariah in the quotation in Matt. xxvii. 9, he says: "How the name of Jeremiah crept in, I do not know, nor do I give myself much trouble to inquire. The passage itself plainly shows that the name of Jeremiah has been put down by mistake, instead of Zechariah (xi. 13); for in Jeremiah we find nothing of the sort, nor anything that even approaches to it." On the discrepancy in Stephen's speech, Acts vii. 16, with Genesis, as to the purchase of a burial-place, he suggests that Stephen or Luke drew on uncertain tradition rather than on Moses, and made "a mistake in the name of Abraham." With reference to New Testament divergencies from the Hebrew in quotations from Ch. lxx. he remarks: "We know that, in such a matter, the Apostles were not very scrupulous. In the thing itself, however, there is but little difference." He gives considerable latitude to the formula, "that it might be fulfilled." The critical acumen of Calvin is seen in his refusal to acknowledge Paul as the author of Hebrews, and in his hesitation about 2 Peter.

A few words may be said in conclusion on Calvin's view of Holy Scripture as a whole, as growing out of his insight into it, and experience of it. The subject is discussed in several chapters of the first book of his *Institutes*, and the authority of Scripture is there placed, as it came to be in many of the Reformed creeds, in the inward witness of the Spirit. It is incontestable to Calvin that, to the spiritually illuminated mind, the Scriptures bear internal evidence of their divine origin and authority. "Scripture bears upon the face of it," he says, "as clear evidence of its truth, as white and black do of their color, sweet and bitter of their taste." Again, "Scripture, carrying its own evidence along with it, deigns not to submit to proofs and arguments, but owes the full conviction with which we ought to receive it to the testimony of Spirit." This is strong language. In explanation, it should be said that it is not to be understood as implying the rejection of historical evidences—Calvin proceeds to devote a chapter to these under the name of "secondary helps"—or as suggestion that such evidence should be made light of, or dispensed with. The meaning is that the ultimate conviction of the credit of God's word in the Scripture must spring from that experience of its truth and power which the Holy Spirit alone can give. There is profound truth in this, and it is well it is so, for some of the historical arguments by which Calvin supports the credibility of Scriptures are now a little outworn.

The real criticism to be made on this resting of the authority of Scripture *exclusively* on the internal witness of the Spirit is that, at best, it can apply only to Scripture taken as a whole, or in its general teaching, and can hardly be employed for the settlement of critical and exegetical questions, or the determination even of the canonicity of disputed books—of such books, *e. g.*, as Esther, or Ecclesiastes, or Song of Solomon; and Calvin himself does not so employ it. He brings his full exegetical power to bear on every passage, and freely uses what critical or historical aids he possesses to determine points of difficulty. What he would perhaps say—what at least we may now say for him—is, that, if Scripture be attested by the subject-matter of its teaching, by its inward harmony, light, power, and holiness, to be, or contain, the word of God, we may then listen with deference to the further claims it makes of itself and its authors, which extend its inspiration to the whole Book. In practice there can be no doubt that Calvin treated the Bible as through and through inspired—the word of God in all its parts. His own words in his exposition of 2 Tim. iii. 16, with which I conclude, are decisive on that point. "This is a principle," he says, "which distinguishes our religion from all others, that we know that God hath spoken to us, and are fully convinced that the prophets did not speak at their own suggestion, but that, being organs of the Holy Spirit, they only uttered what they have been commissioned to declare. Whoever, then, wishes to profit in the Scriptures, let him, first of all, lay this down as a settled point, that the law and the prophets are not a doctirne delivered according to the will and pleasure of men, but dictated by the Holy Spirit. . . . This is the [purport of] the first clause, that we owe to the Scripture the same reverence which we owe to God, because it has proceeded from Him alone, and has nothing belonging to man mixed with it." Those who seek countenance for a lowering of the authority of Scripture must seek it else where than in John Calvin.

CALVIN'S DOCTRINE OF INFANT SALVATION.

Rev. R. A. Webb, D. D. LL. D,
Kentucky Theological Seminary.

By appointment of the last Assembly, I appear with a brief in defence of Calvin against the charge of teaching the actual damnation of some infants who die in their infancy.

The accusation has been so widely and industriously circulated that its truthfulness, with many, passes as a matter of course, too well known to be disputed, too obvious to be contradicted.

While Luther was essentially a "breaker," and Protestantism is an everlasting debtor to him for shivering ecclesiastical medievalism, and emancipating the religious mind; it was devolved by Providence upon Calvin to indoctrinate the Reformation, and give to the movement that system of evangelical truth—those principles and convictions—necessary to sustain it and save it from final collapse. Protestantism is no stronger than Calvinism, and the Reformation will last no longer than Calvinism endures.

If, therefore, the name of the great Genevan—the theologian of the Reformation—can be cleansed of any aspersion, by what rises only to the rank of a plausible exculpation, one would naturally expect a grateful Protestant world to accept it with joy, and acclaim it with delight. The spirit which could be pleased with a cloud upon his great and serviceable name is nothing short of inscrutible.

It is sought to sustain this charge against Calvin in two ways. It is held, first, that certain quotations from his writings warrant the charge that the consciously and avowedly held that some infants, dying in infancy, are finally lost. Then it is held, in the second place, that infant damnation is a logical and necessary implicate of his theological system.

Now Calvin certainly taught the doctrine of Predestination, and with it classified all mankind as elect and reprobate. From such a conclusion he did not shrink, but boldly avowed it and defended it.

It is also indisputable that Calvin held that Predestination determined destiny, and that there was no way by which any person could escape the fate fixed for him by divine decree.

And it is equally certain that he taught that Predestination was eternal, antedating the birth of every human being; and consequently that all infants make their advent into the world, either as elect infants or as non-elect infants. From such a conclusion neither he nor his disciples recoil.

We are compelled then to consider his views, first as to elect infants, and then as to non-elect infants.

Elect Infants.

Concerning elect infants, dying in infancy, it is undeniable that Calvin taught two things: (1) the fact of their salvation, and (2) the mode of their salvation.

As to the *fact* of their salvation we have this explicit assertion in his own language:

"Now, it is certain that some infants are saved; and that they are previously regenerated by the Lord is beyond all doubt."—*Institutes*, Book IV., Chap. XVI., Sec. 17.

There are other supplementary quotations which could be made just as explicit upon this point; but this is categorical enough to satisfy any fair mind, and there is nothing in his writings which any one adduces in support of the contention that Calvin taught the damnation of any elect infant. Indeed no one has the hardihood to bring such an accusation against him.

But Calvin not only taught the fact of the salvation of all elect infants; he also showed the *mode* in which they are saved; and thus differentiated himself from the theology of his day, and laid down immortal principles for all Protestant theology. He says:

"But, however this may be, we consider it as clear, beyond all controversy, that not one of the elect is called out of the present life, without having been previously regenerated and sanctified by the Spirit of God. . . . We deny that it ought to be concluded from this (that the word is in the instrument of conversion), that infants cannot be regenerated by the power of God, which it is as easy to him as it is wonderful and mysterious to us. Besides, it would not be safe to affirm, that the Lord cannot reveal Himself in any way so as to make himself known to them."—*Institutes*, Book IV., Chap. XVI., Sec. 18.

"If any of those who are the objects of divine election, after having received the sign of regeneration, depart out of this life before they have attained years of discretion, the Lord renevates them by the power of His Spirit, incomprehensible to us, in such a manner as He alone foresees will be necessary."—*Institutes*, Book IV., Chapter XVI., Sec. 21.

In these quotations, and in other places, he distinctly rejects the Pelagian view, which, denying original sin, grounded the salvation of dead children in their supposed innocency and sinlessness; and he also rejects the prevailing Romish view which grounded it in the baptism of such as had received that ordinance.

As against both Pelagians and Romanists, Calvin predicated infant salvation upon their election by the Father, their redemption by the Son, and their regeneration and sanctification of the Spirit. Such a program made the salvation of the infant, *as an infant*, possible. Calvin is entitled to the praise of having shown this originally and clearly.

Non-Elect Infants.

While it is thus indisputably true that Calvin did thus avow and explain the salvation of all elect infants, dying in infancy, what did he hold concerning the fate of non-elect infants? Did he hold that there were any such infants? Did he hold that any such infants die in infancy? Did he hold that any such infants are finally damned? These are the questions over which there is debate and controversy.

Concerning the first of these questions, Calvin certainly held that there were reprobate infants, for he distinctly taught that reprobation was eternal and antenatal, and consequently that all reprobate persons make their advent into this life as reprobate.

He certainly taught that all reprobate persons are finally lost. But he did not teach that any reprobate persons are lost *as infants*. He did not teach that any reprobate persons die in infancy. He did explicitly teach that some elect infants die in infancy and are saved as infants; but he did not teach that any reprobate infants die in infancy and are damned *as infants.*

But his accusers charge that this is precisely what he did teach, namely, *that some reprobate infants die in infancy and are damned as infants.* To prove this accusation they undertake to quote his language, and then to support the quotations by showing that the doctrine is a logical implicate of his system of theology.

I shall undertake to show that neither the quotations, nor the system, warrant this accusation of the most illustrious genius Protestantism has ever produced.

Concerning non-elect infants. To appreciate Calvin's position a distinction must be drawn between *condemnation* and *damnation.*

Condemnation is the pronouncement of sentence; damnation is the execution of that sentence. It is the office of the judge to condemn—to pronounce the criminal worthy of death; it is the office of the sheriff to carry that sentence into execution—to inflict the penalty assessed by the court. A longer or shorter time may intervene between the imposition of the sentence and the execution of the same.

Now Calvin taught, unmistakably, that a judgment of condemnation, predicated upon their original sin, was passed upon all non-elect infants; but he does not teach that that sentence was executed upon any non-elect infant while in its infancy, during the period of its moral minority.

They are condemned when infants; they are executed only as adults. They are condemned on account of original, or Adamic, sin; they actually perish only on account of actual, or personal, sin.

This is the distinction which many of his critics overlook. They hear him say that this class of infants are guilty, depraved, condemned, and reprobate; and then, unwarrantably, leap to the conclusion that he must have held that the judgment of death is executed upon some non-elect infants *while infants.*

Calvin teaches infant condemnation, but he nowhere teaches infant damnation.

He asserts that all persons who are not the subjects of God's saving grace will finally be lost, but he explicitly, and throughout, teaches that all the reprobate "procure"—(that is his own word)—*"procure"* their own destruction; and they procure their destruction by their own personal and conscious acts of "impiety," "wickedness," and "rebellion."

Now reprobate infants, though guilty of original sin and under condemnation, cannot, while they are infants, thus "procure" their own destruction by their personal acts of impiety, wickedness, and rebellion. They must, therefore, live to the years of moral responsibility in order to perpetrate the acts of impiety, wickedness and rebellion, which Calvin defines as the *mode* through which they procure their destruction.

While, therefore, Calvin teaches that there are reprobate infants, and that these will be finally lost, he nowhere teaches that they will be lost *as infants,* and *while they are infants;* but, on the contrary, he declares that all the reprobate "procure" their own destruction by personal acts of impiety, wickedness and rebellion. Consequently, his own reasoning compels him to hold (to be consistent with himself), that no reprobate child can die in its infancy; but all such must live to the age of moral accountability, and translate original sin into actual sin.

Calvin's critics seek to fasten the charge of infant damnation upon him in two ways: (1) By quoting certain detached sentences from his writings, and (2) and chiefly, by charging that it is a logical implicate of his theology.

QUOTATIONS.

Concerning all these citations, I make the following general remarks:

(1) They are relatively few in number; too few to justify the conclusion that Calvin consciously avowed the dogma of infant damnation. Calvin's writings number more than fifty volumes, some of them dogmatic, some exegetical, some controversial, some epistolary. His critics have searched his multitudinous pages for language which could be quoted in proof of the charge that he taught the doctrine of the damnation of infants. With all their diligence and zeal they have been able to point out less than a dozen sentences, or parts of sentences, in the thousands of pages which he wrote, which even seem to support their charge.

(2) They were all passing utterances; mere *obiter dicta;* made while addressing himself to other topics; not one of them was written for the purpose of revealing his mind on the dogma of infant damnation. It is therefore unfair and illegitimate to hold him to a construction of language which he employed in the development of other subjects, and wrote when the fate of infants was not present to his mind.

(3) All these citations have a context; and when they are taken in connection with their immediate contexts,

and also in connection with the whole system of truth which he was inculcating, they are susceptible of a different interpretation from that which his opponents' put upon them.

When, therefore, we consider the relative fewness of these quotations, their purpose, occasion and contexts, it is clearly improper to hold Calvin responsible for the construction which his critics force upon them.

To test the charge that the doctrine of the damnation of infants, *as infants,* is inferable from the language which Calvin employed, I select a few of the most pronounced and oft-quoted passages for examination.

The first of these passages is taken from his *Institutes,* Book II, Chap. I., Sec. 7, as follows:

"And therefore infants themselves, as they bring their condemnation into the world with them, are rendered obnoxious to punishment by their own sinfulness, not by the sinfulness of another. For though they have not yet produced the fruits of their iniquity, yet they have the seed of it within them; even their whole nature is as it were a seed of sin, and therefore cannot but be odious and abominable to God. Whence it follows, that is properly accounted sin in the sight of God, because there could be no guilt without crime."

The subjects of these predications are not some infants, but all infants, elect and reprobate alike and co-equally. All mankind having sinned in Adam and fell with him in the first transgression, all infants "bring their condemnation into the world with them," "are rendered obnoxious to punishment by their own sinfulness," and "their whole nature is a seed of sin." This is but the assertion of the well known doctrine of original sin—the doctrine of the universal guilt and native depravity of the entire race. It is but saying of all infants what David specifically said of himself. But surely the predication of the guilt and corruption of the entire race is not synonymous with the actual damnation of the entire human family, for he has asserted over and over again the salvation of some of the race. It is a *non sequitur* to reason from the universal condemnation of mankind to the actual damnation of some infants. Calvin does say, with Paul, that all are "by nature the children of wrath"—that all are guilty and corrupt and obnoxious to God—but he does not here say that any reprobate child dies in this state of condemnation and perishes as an infant in hell before the "seed" that is within him "produces the fruits of iniquity"—conscious actual sins.

A second favorite quotation of his accusers is made from his *Institutes*, Book IV., Chap. XVI., Sec. 17:

"It is certain that some infants are saved."

It is argued herefrom that if Calvin so explicitly said that "some infants are saved," he must have intended to indicate that some other infants are not saved. An affirmation about some is held to be equal to an antithetical denial about others.

In the place quoted, Calvin is arguing for the rite of infant baptism. He is replying to the objection that the ordinance ought not to be administered to babies because they cannot understand its import. He says: It is perfectly certain and undeniable that some infants are regenerated; neither we nor they understand how they are regenerated; but our ignorance of the *modus operandi* does not obliterate the fact; and, consequently, if they can be regenerated without their understanding the process, it would be legitimate to give them the baptismal sign of their regeneration, although they are unable to understand and appreciate the ordinance. The whole context renders it perfectly certain that Calvin was not here saying that some infants are saved in order to imply that some are not.

Then Calvin's accusers bring forward his comment upon Ezek. xviii.: "As to infants they seem to perish not by their own fault but by the fault of another; but there is a double solution. Though sin does not yet appear in them, yet it is latent; for they bear corruption shut up in the soul, so that before God they are damnable." And to this they add a comment of like import upon Isa. xiv. 21: "When the Lord rejects the godless man with his offspring, there is certainly no expostulation which we can make with God. . . . This therefore is to be held for certain, that all who are destitute of the grace of God are included under the sentence of eternal death; whence it follows that the children of the reprobate, whom the curse of God follows, are subject to the same sentence."

There is a distinction perfectly obvious between *damnability* and *damnation*. One is a liability and the other is an actual execution. Calvin does say in these comments that all infants, elect and reprobate, are justly "damnable," not only because of their Adamic connection, but also because sin is "latent" in them, because of "the corruption shut up in the soul." But he does not say that any child, as a child and while a child, is actually *damned* before what is "latent" becomes manifest. Such an inference is a clear reading into his words what he did not say, and forcing his language to yield a meaning which he did not put into it.

It is literally and evangelically true that "all who are destitute of the grace of God are included under the sentence of eternal death;" and it is likewise true that "the children of the reprobate," who are also destitute of grace, are subject to the "same sentence" of eternal death. But surely there is a distinction between the pronouncement of a sentence and the execution of that sentence; and Calvin does not here say, directly or by good and necessary consequence, that this sentence of eternal death is executed upon reprobate children while they are children. We need to be carrying this distinction with us all the while when reading the great Reformer—the distinction between the pronouncement of a sentence and the execution of that sentence. That sentence is pronounced upon all indiscriminately; it certainly is not, Calvin being the expositor, executed upon all universally and indiscriminately.

Another favorite passage which Calvin's accusers quote with great confidence is the famous one which he uttered in his controversy with Pighius: "If Pighius holds that original sin is not sufficient to damn men, and that the secret counsel of God is not to be admitted, what will he do with children and infants, who, before they have reached an age at which they can give any such specimens (of good and evil deeds) are snatched from this life? When the conditions of birth and death were alike to those who die in Sodom and Jerusalem, and there was no difference in their works, why will Christ, at the last day, with some standing at his right hand, separate others at his left? Who will not adore the wonderful decision of God whereby it comes to pass that some are born at Jerusalem, whence soon they pass to a better life, while Sodom, the entrance to the lower region, receives others at their birth. Moreover, I by no means deny that Christ awards the meed of righteousness to the elect, so the reprobate will then suffer for their impiety and crimes."—*De Aeterna Dei Predestinatione. Tom* VIII.

This passage gives me more trouble than any which I have encountered. Pighius has denied that original sin, by itself, is sufficient to damn any man. Calvin asserts against his opponent that original sin is intrinsically so heinous as to be, by itself, a just ground of damnation. To make good his contention he points to children and infants who are snatched away from this life before they come to the years of moral responsibility. Some of these dead children, he seems to say, will, at the last day, stand on the right hand of Christ and some on his left. Some of them, he seems to say, will go from Jerusalem to a better life, and some from Sodom to the regions below. This is the interpretation which his critics put upon his language.

But let us remember that Calvin is in controversy with Pighius over a very serious matter—whether original sin is sin in a strict and proper sense, or only misfortune and moral blemish. His contention is that original sin is so heinous as to be intrinsically worthy of damnation. This is his point—the *sufficiency of original sin,* unsupplemented by actual sin, *to damn men.* He will not tolerate the doctrine that original sin is a trifling, blameless blemish. The proof of its malignity is that children die in Jerusalem as well as in Sodom. Now he adds, that, while I hold that original sin in sufficient to damn men, I by no means deny that it is Christ who bestows righteousness upon the elect, while the reprobate "suffer for their impiety and crimes." But infants cannot be guilty of *impiety* and *crimes,* while they are infants; and yet the reprobate suffer for their *impiety* and *crimes;* so we must conclude that Calvin did not here mean to convey the idea that reprobate infants stand on the left of Christ as infants, or that they go down to death through the gates of Sodom while they are still in the irresponsible infant stage of life. In short, to make him teach infant damnation in this place is to make him clearly inconsistent with himself. It would be fairer to construe the language as strong words, not sufficiently guarded, in the emergencies of fierce and vital debate.

But the passage most confidently relied upon to prove that Calvin held the doctrine of infant damnation is the following from his *Institutes,* Book III., Chap. XXXIII., Sec. 7: "I inquire again, how it came to pass that the fall of Adam, independent of any remedy, should involve so many nations with their infant children in eternal death, but because such was the will of God."

Here the predication is that the fall of Adam, when the gracious remedy is thought out of sight, involved many nations, with their infant children, in eternal death. This, say his critics, settles it; for he distinctly says, "infant children in eternal death," and that by "the will of God."

But the context eliminates from the passage the whole idea of infant damnation. The quotation is made from that chapter of the *Institutes* in which Calvin answers objections to Predestination.

The first objection is: *God precludes Himself from finding fault because reprobation antedates the actual sinning of His creatures.* To this, Calvin makes the sublapsarian reply, that, while chronologically reprobation precedes sinning, logically—at the moment of forming the decree in the divine mind—mankind was conceived as created and fallen. "If all whom the Lord predestinates to death are in their natural condition liable to the sentence of death, what injustice do they complain of receiving from him? . . . If they have all been taken from a corrupt mass, it is no wonder that they are subject to condemnation. Let them not, therefore, accuse God of injustice."

The second objection he gives his attention to is the following: *Reprobation necessitates the very sin for which the reprobate are condemned.* To this objection he makes the following effective reply: God having determined to pass by a corrupt and guilty sinner and leave him in his natural state unregenerated by divine grace, does thus doom him by the negative act of letting him alone and leaving him to himself for the destiny of his own making.

But to this resolution of this objection, some of his critics took the ground that God made no decree concerning the lost of any kind; that is, denied the decree of reprobation outright. To this Calvin replied: If God made no decree, concerning the lost, of one kind or another—if the divine will was only negative and the divine attitude neutral and non-committal—then, in that case, under that supposition, how can his opponents explain the fact that the fall of Adam involved not only Adam himself, but also many nations with their infant children in eternal death?"

It is a Biblical fact that the fall of Adam did involve not only Adam himself, but all his posterity, in a ruin, independent of any remedy, would be eternal. Now this consequence, he argues, was either (1) by nature, or (2) by the will of God. He denies that the involvement of the race in the fall of Adam was a naturalistic result, and affirms that it was a judicial judgment of God. His express language is: "This (the race's participation in the sin of Adam), not being attributable to nature, it is evident must have proceeded from the wonderful counsel of God."

This is the purpose and the connection of the famous sentence in which Calvin called the decree of reprobation an "horrible decree." Think, says Calvin, the remedy out the way—think the whole scheme of saving grace as non-existent—then how could you explain the fact that the fall of Adam involved "nations and their infant children" in a death which would have otherwise been eternal, except you say it was because God so willed it?

It is clear that Calvin has not asserted in this place, said to be the strongest passage on the subject which can be quoted, the doctrine of infant damnation. He has said here that God has passed by some "nations with their infant children" and left them to the doom of "eternal death," but he has not here said that any reprobate infant dies in its infancy and is consigned to "eternal death" while it is an infant.

INFERENCES.

But the main reliance of Calvin's accusers is upon their logical deductions from his theological system. Their interpretation of certain isolated passages from his writings are made plausible because of their inferences from his doctrine of Predestination.

He did hold that all mankind were united to Adam by divine ordination; that they sinned in him and fell with him in his first transgression; that all the race did thus become guilty and depraved; that God did pronounce upon the entire human family therefor a sentence of eternal death; that children are consequently born into the world under guilt and condemnation; that out of this "corrupt mass" God did elect some to everlasting life and pass by others with His saving mercy and leave them in their estate of sin and misery; that this Predestination was eternal and antenatal; that all infants consequently make their appearance in the world either as elect or reprobate, with final destiny determined; but he no where taught, by direction or by indirection, that this sentence of eternal death is executed upon any non-elect infant while in its infantile state.

There are two reasons why his theology would require him to hold, in order to be consistent with himself, that no reprobate infant can perish in its infancy.

1. He everywhere taught that the reprobate "procure" their own destruction. That is, they are the active, conscious agents in bringing about their own doom.

In his last chapter on Predestination, in which he closes and dismisses the subject, he contrasts the mode in which the elect actually attain their predestined end, and the mode in which the reprobate realize their predestined death. The elect come to heaven by the effectual operation of the grace of the Spirit, but the reprobate come to their dreadful doom by the effectual operation of their own will. The elect are patients and the Spirit is the agent of their salvation; but the reprobate are agents and the Spirit is patient in their actual damnation.

He heads this last chapter: "Election confirmed by the divine call. The destined destruction of the reprobate procured by themselves" (Book III., Chapter XXIV.). This is his final thesis and last contention: *The benefits of election are procured for the elect by divine vocation; but the destined destruction of the reprobate is procured by themselves.*

How are these two decrees—election and reprobation—executed in time and made manifest in experience? Calvin answers: Election is made manifest, revealed, declared, developed in conscious experience by the divine call; the other decree—reprobation—is translated into history and experience by the reprobate themselves through their own personal and conscious acts of sin—the destined destruction of the reprobate is procured by themselves."

He says: "The destined destruction of the reprobate is procured by themselves" (Book III., Chapter XXIV.). Again: God does what He does to the reprobate because of "their impiety, wickedness, and ingratitude" (Book III., Chapter XXIV., Section 14). Again: "They can do nothing but what is deserving of his curse" (Book III., Chapter XXIV., Section 17).

In the execution of the decree of election, Calvin predicates the divine causality; but in the execution of the decree of reprobation he predicates the causality of the reprobate themselves. In other words: while *original sin* was the ground of a universal, race-wide condemnation, *actual sin* is the necessary premise of actual damnation.

This being true, it is a logical implicate of his premises that no reprobate child could die in its infancy, but must be kept alive by the providence of God to the years of moral discretion, so that it could "procure" its own destruction by translating the corruption which is "latent" into sin of omission and commission.

2. A second premise of Calvin which precludes the idea of his holding infant damnation is his doctrine of resurrection and punishment.

He says: "It would be as light punishment to be destroyed by death, if they (the reprobate) were not to be brought before the Judge whose infinite and endless vengeance they have incurred, to receive the punishment due to their rebellion" (Book III., Chapter XXV., Section 9).

There is something incongruous and absurd in an infant being "brought" before a Judge to answer for his "rebellion"! Yet this must be charged upon the great Genevan, if we make him teach that any non-elect infants die in infancy. That an infant eight days of age should be engaged in a rebellion against God is something unthinkable.

The whole idea of *punishment* cannot be associated with infants without shocking the very genius of Calvin's theological system. Punishment, strictly speaking, is that suffering which is inflicted upon a person because of his guilt. For suffering to be punishment the subject must be aware in conscience of the moral reason for the infliction. A horse can be made to suffer because he has a nervous system, but he cannot be punished because he has no conscience. An infant can be made to suffer, because it has a sentiment nature; but it cannot be punished, because its conscience has not been developed to the degree where it can appreciate the moral reason for its suffering.

But the death of an infant must be either *penal* or *disciplinary*. The death of a reprobate infant cannot be *disciplinary*, because it is non-elect and outside the pale of the scheme of grace; and its death cannot be *penal*, because it cannot in conscience appreciate the moral meaning of death.

Therefore, we must conclude from Calvin's general premises, that a reprobate infant cannot die as an infant.

On the contrary we must conclude from his general teaching about the justice and judgment of God, that the divine providence must keep all reprobate children alive until they can reach the years of their moral majority, and translate their original sin into actual sin, so as to create a ground, in conscience and consciousness, for their actual punishment.

It is a fair inference from his whole theology, that he predicated *actual damnation* only upon *actual transgression*.

I. Calvin did, explicitly and avowedly, teach the salvation of all elect infants which die in their infancy.

II. He taught, contrary to the Romanism and Pelagianism of his day, that the mode of the salvation of infants was (1) by the election of the Father, (2) by the atonement of the Son, and (3) by the vocation of the Spirit. He said that the Spirit could regenerate, and sanctify, and communicate, with infants in a manner inscrutible to us.

III. Concerning reprobate infants, he taught that there were such infants; that they were involved, with their parents, in the Adamic fall and curse; and that they are all born into the world guilty, depraved, and condemned.

IV. He did not teach that any reprobate infants die in their infancy, and so have executed upon them the sentence of eternal death while at an infantile and irresponsible age.

V. He did teach that all the reprobate "procure their own destined destruction" by their overt and conscious acts of disobedience; and that their final damnation would be predicated upon their evil deeds.

VI. He did teach that all the reprobate must appear before God as a Judge, and receive the judicial punishment due to their sins, which requires us to infer that every one so dealt with must be morally full-grown.

VII. Wherefore we must conclude that Calvin, to be consistent with the ruling principles of his theology, must have held that no reprobate child died in infancy; but that, on the contrary, all such infants live to the age of moral maturity, and "procure their destined destruction" by "their impiety and crimes" and by their "rebellion" against God.

THE RELATION OF CALVIN AND CALVINISM TO MISSIONS.

By Rev. S. L. Morris, D. D.,
*Secretary of Home Missions of the
Presbyterian Church, U. S.*

In its halls of fame, the world enshrines chiefly its warriors, men whose glory is written in characters of blood. In striking contrast with the world's ideals, the grandest of all conquerors was the Prince of Peace, who triumphed by the shedding of His own blood, who rules the thought of men by the scepter of Truth, who wins the allegiance of His subjects by the power of Love. As a consequence, He alone will sway the scepter of universal dominion. To Him every knee shall bow, and every tongue make confession. The means by which He shall eventually be crowned Lord of All and "His glory spread from pole to pole," through the agency of the church is missions—the world-wide proclamation of the Gospel.

In keeping with its ideals are the heroes adjudged by the world worthy of monuments at its hands. I have stood by the equestrian statue of Charles II, near St. Giles Cathedral, Edinburgh, while scarcely ten paces distant, the only tablet to John Knox was a flat stone in the pavement, marked "J. K.," over which rattle the wheels of traffic, and resounds the tread of the passer by. Geneva has erected monuments to Servetus and Rousseau, while even the reputed grave of

Calvin, marked by a modest stone, engraved "J. C.," is at best only a guess at the last resting-place of the great Reformer who sleeps in an unknown grave. Nevertheless, Scotland is the real monument of John Knox, and John Calvin's is every Republican Government of earth, the public school system of all nations and "The Reformed Churches throughout the world holding the Presbyterian System."

The personality and glory of Calvin suffer by any attempt at eulogy. His cotemporaries vie with each other in an effort to do him honor. Even his enemies, by the closest scrutiny, reveal no glaring defects of character. Ernest Renan, who unconsciously awards him apostolic succession by saying, "Paul begat Augustine, and Augustine begat John Calvin," exalts Calvin himself as "the most Christian man of his generation."

I. In discussing our appointed theme, "The Relation of Calvin and Calvinism to Missions," we shall invite attention first of all to Calvin and missions.

The times of Calvin were polemic, rather than evangelistic. It was the great Reformation period of Church History, which afforded not so much the opportunity of evangelistic crusades for the conversion of the world, as it required the heroic spirit of the martyr in witnessing to the truth of God, exemplifying the fundamental root-meaning of witness (martyr) in the original tongue. Not in the sense of sealing his faith with his blood, but in the higher significance of suffering mentally and spiritually for the faith, John Calvin was a martyr to the truth.

Banished from Geneva at one period, persecuted, his life in constant danger, and even when at the zenith of his power and influence, unloved by Geneva, but merely tolerated for the sake of his presiding genius in affairs of statecraft, he suffered not the momentary pangs of a dying martyr, but the long-drawn-out agony of life-martyrdom; as widely removed from the other as anguish of soul exceeds the pangs of physical pain.

The spirit of evangelist and polemic alike is service and sacrifice. The missionary, subjecting himself to the hardships of heathenism, displays no higher type of sacrifice and engages in no nobler service than the soldier of the Cross, who stands for the defense of the citadel of truth. The latter may even demand a severer type of moral courage. Unquestionably the maintenance of the truth is as important to the life of the Church as the propagation of the faith in the extension of the Kingdom.

The choice of God for Calvin's sphere of service fell in the direction of polemics. The battle he waged, and the victory he won for the truth was more than the winning of a heathen continent for Christ. It affected the destiny of all nations, and stretches in its far-reaching consequences unto all the generations of the coming ages.

Still, at the same time, it was also permitted him to exhibit the missionary spirit of Christianity. Occupied by affairs of state, burdened with the responsibilities of civic righteousness, charged with the duty of theological instruction, yet he found occasion to undertake a campaign for the conversion of South America. In the Christian Retrospect and Register, Robert Baird, upon the authority of the "Histoire Universelle," gives the following account of the first mission undertaken by Protestantism:

"To Calvin, the Reformer of Geneva, belongs the credit of having first attempted, in the Protestant churches, to excite interest in behalf of a heathen nation. An expedition was fitted out in the year 1555 by Villegagnon, a Knight of Malta, under the patronage of Henry II. of France, with the view of establishing a French colony in the New World. The approbation of the monarch was secured through the medium of the excellent Admiral De Coligny, whose favor Villegagnon propitiated by the secret understanding that the projected colony should protect the Reformed religion. Accordingly, Calvin was applied to, in order to obtain ministers to embark with the expedition.

"After consultation with the other pastors of Geneva, he sent two—Guillaume Chartier and Pierre Richier,—who were afterward joined by several others. Their object was, at once, to labor among the colonists and to evangelize the heathen aborigines. The expedition reached Fort Coligny, as it was named, on the Rio De Janeiro, Brazil, in March, 1556. On their arrival, the Genevan ministers proceeded to constitute a church, according to the forms and rites of the Reformed churches, and celebrated the Lord's Supper. But Villegagnon soon betrayed his true character and disposition, and after cruelly maltreating the missionaries, forced them to re-embark and return to France."

One can scarcely avoid speculation as to what "might have been," if the unfortunate mission had not been thus prematurely wrecked. As Calvin's name is associated with Augustine, the great theologian, might it not also have been linked with Augustine the missionary in the conversion of a continent? If the seeds of Protestant Christianity planted by him in South America had germinated, who can say if the glory of that misguided continent might not have shone with all the lustre of Protestant North America? But, alas!

his missionary venture served no useful purpose, except to exhibit his Christian spirit and benevolent attitude toward world-wide evangelization in obedience to the Great Commission.

Just as a premature blossom in the treacherous Indian summer, though nipped by the early frosts ot winter, is nevertheless a prophecy of the coming spring; so Calvin's ill-timed evangelism was but the guarantee of the evangelistic spirit of Calvinism, when the springtime of favorable seasons should furnish opportunity to flower out in the glorious harvest of the world's conversion.

In the providence of God, his missionary zeal was confined to the task of laying foundations in practical home mission work, while foreign missions was rather the future outcome of his spirit and principles. Though the foundation of an edifice may not be as ornate and attractive as the superstructure, yet it must be even more substantial by reason of its supreme importance. The glory of Calvin in the sphere of missions is the glory of laying foundations; and he must also share the glory of the magnificent superstructure, supported by so substantial a basis. If some twentieth century Apostle Paul should convert South America to Protestantism, and place a new continent in the galaxy of evangelical Christianity, would that be more glorious than the transcendent work of Calvin, whose well-nigh inspired genius laid the foundations of North America's future greatness, and made it such a potent factor in the evangelization of the world as to justify the rallying cry, "As goes America, so goes the world"?

II. This opens the way for the consideration of the second part of our subject, "The Relation of Calvinism to Missions."

It might be pertinent to inquire first of all, What is Calvinism? The system of Calvinism, by taking the name of Calvin, introduces confusion into the thought of men; for Calvinism has a two-fold significance. From its theological side, it is a misnomer. The Five Points of Calvinism reach back to Augustine and to Paul. Renan was substantially right: "Paul begat Augustine, and Augustine begat John Calvin"; but a profounder thinker than Renan traces Calvinism back to Christ, and indeed to the prophets of Israel, and to the tents of the patriarchs. Consequently, in its theological aspect, Calvinism is older than Calvin; just as Christianity is older than Christ. In the sense that Calvin was a Christian, Christ himself was a Calvinist. It was Christ who affirmed, that "Many are called, but few are chosen"; and unhesitatingly declared that the divine providence affecting individuals and nations was determined and conditioned for "the elect's sake."
No Calvinist ever uttered stronger Calvinism than One who said: "No man can come unto me except it were given unto him of my Father." "All that the Father giveth me shall come to me." "And I give unto them eternal life, and they shall never perish, neither shall any man pluck them out of my hand."

Only on its scientific side, as a Life System, is Calvinism distinctly Calvinistic. The distinctive work of Calvin was to bequeath to the world as his legacy of thought that virile and logical system, which is the creator of the modern world; or, as the English historian Green expresses it: "It is in Calvinism that the modern world strikes its roots; for it was Calvinism that first revealed to the world the dignity and worth of man." The keynote of his religious philosophy was the individuality of the human soul in direct contact and immediate communion with God.

In the sweep of its mighty movement, it affected alike the individual soul, the ecclesiastical system, and the polity of the state. In religion, it swept aside priests and intermediaries with their confessionals and dispensaries of divine grace, and placed the soul in immediate and direct touch with God, in its own individual responsibility. The logical result in church government was to sweep aside bishops and prelates as obstacles and rubbish, and place the people, through their elective representatives, in charge of the church as sole rulers in the house of God.

James I. was astute enough to see the bearing upon civil government of Calvin's system, when he stated: "Presbytery agreeth as well with monarchy as God with the devil"; and we will not presume to take issue with so eminent authority as His Majesty, King James. History has since justified his foresight; for Calvinism has swept aside scepters and thrones, and substituted for autocratic monarchy popular republicanism in its varying forms.

Bancroft, the greatest American historian, was eminently justified in crowning John Calvin as the "father of America"; while D'Aubigne, the historian of the Reformation, supports his position by declaring: "Calvin was the founder of the greatest of republics. The Pilgrims, who left their country in the reign of James I., and, landing on the barren soil of New England, founded populous and mighty colonies, were his sons; and that American nation which we have seen growing so rapidly boasts as its father the humble Reformer on the shores of Lake Leman."

Four considerations will be urged to justify our contention that Calvinism is the most potent agency in the evangelization of the world.

1. In its theological aspect, Calvinism, existing ages before Calvin, had its influence in the early days of Christianity on the life and activity of the church. In character it made men conspicuous in their differentiation from other classes. In heroism and endurance, it gave the world startling exhibitions of martyrdom in men who could kiss the chains binding them to the stake, and sing hallelujahs as their souls departed in chariots of flame. In zeal and activity, it enlisted the rank and file of the church in a religious enthusiasm, which went from house to house, and carried the Gospel "To the uttermost parts of the earth."

The Apostle Paul is the classical illustration of the spirit of the ancient church. Is it a mere coincidence that Paul, recognized as the profoundest exponent of Calvinism, is at the same time regarded next to the Master himself, as the type and model of all missionary effort? Opponents of Calvinism have not hesitated to charge Paul with the responsibility of giving the Calvinistic cast to the theological thought of the church. Yet this same Paul is always exalted as the greatest and grandest of all missionaries. How did these elements in his character stand related as cause and effect? Was it his thorough Calvinism that created his intense missionary fervor, or vice versa? The question answers itself.

The Calvinism of the first century was as unquestionable as that of Paul himself, who gave cast to the thinking of the first century. Sacred history, ere closing, itself gives significant glimpses of the missionary spirit of the church while under the dominating influence of Calvinism. That was an exquisite touch which records in the language of the Church's enemies, the estimate of apostolic success, complaining: "These that have turned the world upside down have come hither also." It was not an ardent admirer of Paul who testified to his credit, "That not alone at Ephesus, but almost throughout all Asia, this Paul hath persuaded and turned away much people" from idolatry. Paul himself gives a suggestive hint of the missionary propaganda of the age by asserting, that they had preached the Gospel "to every creature which is under heaven." (Col. i. 23.)

The remarkable characteristic of the evangelism of ancient Christianity was its propaganda in the face of persecution, and even at the cost of martyrdom. The twentieth century Christianity, "holding the wealth of the world in its hands," propagates the faith by putting a conservative percentage of its wealth into the enterprise of evangelizing the world. The first century Christianity, conspicuous for its poverty, put its soul into the task, and poured its blood more freely than to-day the Church, rolling in wealth, pours its money. It was proverbial: "The blood of the martyrs is the seed of the Church."

In the spirit of Paul, the church of that Calvinistic age "Counted not its life dear unto itself." James Anthony Froude could not be accused of partiality to Calvinism, and yet his statement remains unchallenged that Calvinism, as long as it was the creed of the Church, made the grandest heroes of men, and gives as illustrations, William the Silent, Luther, Knox, Andrew Melville, the Regent Murray, Coligny, Cromwell, Milton and Bunyan. The Calvinism which made heroes and martyrs of men gave also through them such an exhibition of missionary zeal and successful propagation of the Gospel in those early days of Christianity as has never since been paralleled in the history of the world.

2. In its scientific aspect as a Life System, the influence of Calvinism on governments and society has largely produced our modern Christian civilization, whose chief glory is not the marvelous material development, nor the dazzling scientific achievements of the age, but the revival of a missionary zeal, which seeks to rival the apostolic triumphs of Calvinistic Christianity.

Bartholdi's Statue of Liberty Enlightening the World is essentially a false conception in point of fact; but nearly always the false has some basis in truth. Calvin moulded the thought of the Renaissance, which in the political hemisphere of the state manifested itself in the largest freedom of life and action through the operation of modern republicanism. This liberty, thus the product of Calvinistic thought and ideals, reaching its highest development in republican government, has in removing the bonds and shackles by which the Church has been held in more or less restraint, furnished the opportunity for the Gospel of Christ to fulfil its divine mission in enlightening the world. It was not liberty itself, but the Gospel which was given its liberty, that is enlightening the world.

The torch lighted by John Calvin gave to the world the twin-product of republicanism in the state and the free Christian commonwealth in the Church. On its political side, it found expression in the republicanism of Geneva, Switzerland, Holland, Great Britain and America, and in its ever-widening influence is being felt to-day even in autocratic Russia and despotic Turkey. On its ecclesiastical side, it reaches its full stature in "the Reformed Churches throughout the world holding the Presbyterian System," which, however, in its indirect influence modifies alike the independency of Congregationalism and the despotism of Prelacy, attracting each to itself as the golden mean.

It was Calvinism which lifted Geneva from the depths of civic and moral degradation, and placed it, as a glittering gem of civil and religious liberty, on the brow of Europe, the first-fruits of a new philosophy destined to revolutionize society and human governments. It was Calvinism which, through the instrumentality of John Knox, awakened Scotland to a higher life; which hurled the stool of Jennie Geddes at tyrannical encroachments upon religious liberty, and made the sturdy Scotch character the staunchest and grandest national life the world has ever produced. It was Calvinism which took off the head of Charles I. and gave England in the Protectorate of Oliver Cromwell the first full breath of constitutional liberty, and at the same time furnished that larger protectorate to struggling Protestantism throughout Europe, making that era the brightest chapter in English history. It was Calvinism which waged successfully under William the Silent, the unequal contest of Holland with Spain, and created the Dutch Republic, which eventually hurled the Stuarts from the throne of England, and guaranteed constitutional and religious liberty to the English-speaking world. It was Calvinism which founded in America the greatest of Republics, and made it the Liberator of Cuba and the Philippines, and the protector of the weaker members in the family of nations. It is Calvinism which, through the agency of Robert College on the Bosphorus and Presbyterian missions in the East, is leavening the Ottoman Empire, and giving even the Turk a taste of constitutional liberty.

In the historic conflict of the ages, Calvinism was vanquished in France, in the defeat of the Huguenots; and as a consequence France, the fatherland of John Calvin, descended almost to the level of Spain. If Spain had triumphed in Holland, in all human probability Calvinism would have perished from the earth, and Holland would also have joined France and Spain in a trio of degenerate nations. In that case, William of Orange would never have turned the scale against the Stuarts in Britain, and North America would read its fate to-day in the stagnation of South America. So that the glory of North America is due chiefly to the triumph of Calvinism, justifying Ranke, the historian, in speaking of Calvin as "virtual founder of America."

Here the question arises, What bearing has all this on Missions? "Much every way," chiefly because Calvinism created the modern Anglo-Saxon world, and the Anglo-Saxon is the greatest evangelistic force of Christendom. The Anglo-Saxon has created an empire of missions—world-wide, on whose dominion the sun never sets. The statistics of 1908 reveal a total gift to foreign missions last year of $22,846,465, and of this amount, the Anglo-Saxon contingent contributed $19,266,880, nearly 90 per cent., leaving only $3,578,588 for the remainder of the world. If this were not demonstration sufficient of the influence of Calvinism, as an evangelizing force, it could also be further demonstrated by statistics that the Calvinistic churches lead the world in their gifts to missions.

3. The essential principles of Calvinism would lead us *a priori* to infer that it would furnish the strongest incentives to successful missionary effort. Nothing is more reassuring and better calculated to arouse the supremest effort for the advancement of the Kingdom

than a profound belief in the divine sovereignty of God, who "sits on no precarious throne" and sends his servants on no uncertain mission. In human governments, that army will struggle most valiantly which has implicit confidence in the competency of the government to direct its affairs, and its ability to execute its purposes. Calvinism enthrones God in his sovereign omnipotence, controlling alike the worlds which revolve in their orbits and the mote which floats in the sunbeam, directing all the events of the universe according to a divinely appointed plan, arranged in the councils of eternity.

Is it any wonder that His subjects, persuaded that they are executing the designs of God himself, toil in the strength born of the conviction that though their immediate designs may fail, and they themselves perish, yet God himself lives and reigns, and will in His own sovereign wisdom and appointed time bring to pass His purposes of grace? Missions may challenge their faith, and make unrelenting draughts on their resources and activities; but what matters it, if it be the sovereign purpose of God?

Distrust of self would ordinarily weaken and paralyze all effort, were it not for the fact that such distrust flings the soul back upon God in its weakness, and by an abiding faith in Him, obtains a strength that is invincible. "When I am weak, then am I strong," is the paradox of Calvinism. Will the impulsive, spasmodic zeal, springing from self-confidence and reliance on human means, stand the strain of long-continued effort so well as one who makes God his confidence, and "endures as seeing Him who is invisible"? The firm conviction, that we rest not on human but divine efficiency, gives stability to our vacillating efforts, and makes us strong by the mighty hands of the God of Jacob. These "shall mount up on wings as eagles, they shall run and not be weary, and they shall walk and not faint," in the Herculean task of bringing the world to Christ.

Not simply viewed from the standpoint of belief in the divine sovereignty, does Calvinism thus evince its superiority as a potent influence in world-wide evangelization, but it is equally evident from the human standpoint of the perseverance of the saints. If the stereotyped objection to Calvinism were true, that it is cold, calculating, lacking in fervor, it would be more than counterbalanced by the steady, persistent, unflinching, perseverance of an undaunted faith, which holds on the even tenor of its way in the face of opposition, despite difficulties and discouragements, till it wrings victory out of defeat. The fevered brain may produce momentarily an unnatural strength, born of delirium; but will it endure the trials and press on in the race with the steady gait of one in the full possession of robust health?

Calvinism finds its analogy, not in the whirlwind of impetuosity, not in the fire of religious fanaticism, nor in the earthquake of spasmodic upheavals, but in the "still small voice" that speaks conviction in the silent depths of the soul. If, in the sphere of missions, failure and disaster overtake his best efforts, and success be long delayed, the Calvinist undeterred sees in the analogy of nature how slowly and silently she elaborates the best and grandest results of her mighty plan by gradual processes and takes comfort in the thought, that in the Kingdom of Grace, God works by the same methods and executes His largest purposes by the steady, irresistible perseverance of the saints, remembering that though "the Kingdom of God cometh not with observation," it comes none the less surely.

Tested by practical results, will an appeal to the history of missions justify this contention, that the principles of Calvinism pre-eminently qualify its adherents for leadership in evangelizing the world?

Among the Reformers, who led the way of Protestantism in the first missionary venture, but the Calvinists of Geneva? Who penetrated first the trackless forests of the New World, carrying the Gospel to its untamed savages, but Brainerd and Eliot? Who led the modern missionary movement, which is awakening all Christendom to the task of making Christ known throughout the wide world? If the roll were called of the Calvinists who have led the advancing hosts of the Church, in its attack on heathenism, it would include well-nigh all the great names of history conspicuous for missionary enthusiasm and achievement. Time would fail to enumerate William Carey, Henry Martyn, David Livingstone, Robert Moffatt, Alexander Duff, Adoniram Judson, Robert Morrison, John G. Paton, John Leighton Wilson, William H. Sheppard, and a vast host of others, who "through faith subdued kingdoms, wrought righteousness, obtained promises, stopped the mouths of lions, quenched the violence of fire, escaped the edge of the sword, out of weakness were made strong, waxed valiant in fight", etc.

According to Dr. Moses D. Hoge, "the first missionary since the Reformation sent forth by any church in its corporate capacity, and ordained to labor in the foreign field, was Alexander Duff (commissioned by the Presbyterian Church of Scotland), whose name stands as a synonym of whatever is heroic, self-sacrificing and saintly in missionary character and achievement."

At the meeting of the Alliance in Glasgow, Prof. Lindsay informed that august and venerable body, representing the larger part of the Calvinistic forces of the world, that, "The Presbyterian churches do more than a fourth of the whole mission work among the heathen that is done by all the Protestant churches together," and mentioning three of the greatest denominations, asserted that, "The Presbyterian Church is doing more in the foreign field than all of them combined."

At the same meeting of the Presbyterian Alliance, representatives of the Eastern Section of the Ecumenical Methodist Conference appeared and made a most cordial and pleasing address, expressing their fraternal good will and appreciation of our principles and work in the following complimentary language:

"Taking the world over, Presbyterianism in the future must be looked to as one of the greatest and most beneficent forces for the conversion and evangelization of the generations of mankind on every continent. We do unfeignedly rejoice as we behold your goodly array of churches, giving the noblest of their sons, and consecrating their vast resources of learning and wealth to the greatest, the mightiest of all enterprises, the conversion of the world to Christ," and the address closes with the prayer that our "cherished ideal of 'a free church in a free state' shall in every nation under heaven be an accomplished fact, and every citizen be taught that the chief end of man is to glorify God and enjoy Him forever."

Is not the wisdom of Calvinism justified by the missionary achievements of its children?

4. In conclusion, it is Calvinism which furnishes the only guarantee of the ultimate triumph of the

Gospel in extending the sceptre of Christ, till "The kingdoms of the world shall become the Kingdoms of our Lord and of his Christ." Others may indulge a well-grounded hope based upon an abiding faith; but Calvinism plants itself on "The sure word of prophesy," and maintains that the conversion of the world is one of "The eternal decrees of God," revealed as "Foreordained for his own glory," and must therefore surely "come to pass." It has been prophesied, "that at the name of Jesus every knee should bow . . . and every tongue should confess that Jesus Christ is Lord to the glory of God the Father," and it could not be prophesied unless it had been predestinated; for contingent and doubtful events cannot be prophesied. Prophecy is always and everywhere based on predestination, and not upon mere fore-knowledge; for prophecy is fore-knowledge revealed, which presupposes the event, as a fixed and unchangeable decree.

The Son of God, in the 2nd Psalm, encourages himself in the predestined triumph of His Kingdom: "I will declare the decree, the Lord said unto me, Thou art my Son, this day have I begotten Thee. Ask of me, and I will give Thee the heathen for Thine inheritance, and the uttermost parts of the earth for Thy possession." Let the heathen rage, and the world in arms combine; let the evil powers of the Kingdom of Darkness assault the Citadel of Faith; let all worlds join in a universal rebellion against the Lord of Glory; nevertheless the eternal decree shall stand; for "He that sitteth in the heavens shall laugh; the Lord shall have them in derison." The Lord God Omnipotent proclaims from His eternal throne in the heavens: "Yet have I set my King on my holy hill of Zion," and that King, though still uncrowned and at the moment in the weakness of the flesh, even with the cross confronting Him, could yet declare, "Upon this Rock I will build my Church, and the gates of hell shall not prevail against it."

One of the ablest bishops of America recently published, over his own signature, in the daily press, this statement: "The world will either be all pagan or all Christian; I believe it will be all Christian." A thorough Calvinist could not have consistently indicted that statement. Planting himself on the sure word of Prophesy, which grounds itself in predestination, he would have announced: "I know whom I have believed." "He shall have dominion also from sea to sea, and from the river unto the ends of the earth."

No one will dispute the assertion of the author of "The Creed of Presbyterians," "That friends and foes alike award to the Presbyterian Church as its wreath of thorns, or its diadem of glory, the distinction of being the world's historic and leading representative of the creed of Calvinism." Is that the explanation also of the fact that in missions, "It has always led the van of the advancing hosts of God?"

After quotations showing that, "The largest Protestant family in the world is the Presbyterian," in eloquent language Dr. Smith gives a grand summary of her missionary achievements: "More catholic and imposing even than the Presbyterian numbers is the world-wide range of the Presbyterian empire. While the adherents of other Protestant communions are more or less massed in single countries, the Lutherans in Germany, the Episcopalians in England, the Methodists and Baptists in the United States, the line of the Presbyterian Church is gone out through all the earth. She thrives this hour in more continents, among a greater number of nations, and peoples, and languages, than any other evangelical church in the world. As her witnesses in Continental Europe, she has the historic Presbyterian Reformed Churches of Austria, Bohemia, Galacia, Moravia, Hungary, Belgium, France, Germany, Italy, Greece, the Netherlands, of Russia, and Switzerland, and Spain. She is rooted and fruitful in Africa, in Australia, in Asia, in Great Britain, in North America, in South America, in the West Indies, in New Zealand, in Melanesia,—the people of this faith and order gird the earth. Presbyterianism possesses a power of adaptation unparalleled by any other system. It holds in steadfast array a great part of the intelligence and moral vigor of the Christian world, and from its abounding spiritual life are going forth the mighty forces of Christian missions into all the heathen world."

That was not a vain-glorious boast of the American Presbyterian Church in its report to the Alliance of Reformed Churches: "The missionary heralds of our Pan-American Presbyterianism alone, which is but a branch of the catholic Presbyterian Church, are scattered from British Columbia to Ucatan; they are in Central America, and in Columbia; Venezuela, British Guiana, and Brazil; they on the African Coast, from Liberia to the Ogowe, and in the heart of the great Congo Basin; they are strong in Syria and Persia, and side by side in India our separate columns are advancing under one Captain; we are proclaiming glad tidings in Siam and Laos, in Hainan and the Philippines, in Cuba and Formosa; we have long since 'partitioned China,' not for political spoil, but for her own salvation; our united forces are teaching the Hermit Nation that, as no man, so no nation, liveth to itself; we have proclaimed to the Sunrise Kingdom the Sun of Righteousness, whose rising shall know no setting. Our strategic points are taken, our stations occupied, our watch towers girdle the globe."

This is the 400th anniversary of the birth of John Calvin—scholar, author, teacher, philosopher, statesman, theologian, reformer, and, according to Ernest Renan, "the most Christian man of his generation." No man has been more misunderstood, misrepresented, villified. What is to be the outcome of this world-wide, quadricentennial celebration? Will the thought of mankind re-examine his teaching and spirit, and yet accord him substantial though tardy justice? Will he at last come into his own? Will the world of thought revivify a system, which turned' the current of centuries out of its channel, destroyed despotism, broke the yoke of oppression, created modern civilization, and rescued the Church from dead forms and ushered in the largest spiritual life?

Is there to be a revival of Calvinism under the life-giving breath of the Spirit of God? Will the Calvinism of the first century, which triumphed over paganism backed by the power of the Roman Empire, and "turned the world upside down," be paralleled in a twentieth century evangelism rivaling apostolic times? Will the revival of Calvinism be the signal for the ultimate triumph of the Gospel? Will the renewal of its youth and virile power manifest itself in the dream of present-day Christianity, "The evangelization of the world in this generation"?

May the glad shout of a redeemed world speedily resound to the embattlements of heaven: "Hallelujah, for the Lord God Omnipotent reigneth"; and may heaven and earth unite in "bringing forth the royal diadem to crown Him Lord of All." Amen and Amen.

CALVIN'S INFLUENCE ON EDUCATIONAL PROGRESS.

By President George H. Denny,
Washington and Lee University, Lexington, Va.

John Calvin was an organizing genius of the first rank. Upon the altar of that kind of genius, provided it is devoted to great ends, fame is apt to burn its incense. That the genius of Calvin was devoted to great ends is no longer a question of debate among thinking men. It is true, however, that the modern world in estimating his fame is inclined to picture him chiefly, if not solely, as the organizer of a great system of theology or as the apostle of a great movement that was destined to give to a weary world civil and religious freedom. But this myriad-minded and myriad-hearted man did more than that. His organizing genius grappled with another vital problem upon which human gratitude has failed to lay the emphasis that it deserves. I refer to his contribution to educational progress. Indeed, so little emphasis has been placed upon this phase of his work that it is difficult to find any literature* at all that even attempts to deal with it. So far as I know, no elaborate

---

*Special assistance has been secured from the following sources: Kuper's *Lectures on Calvanism;* Walker's *John Calvin;* Smith's *Creed of Presbyterians; Westminster Addresses,* Charlotte, 1897; McPherson, *Presbyterianism and Education in the Centennial Addresses,* Philadelphia, 1888; Morris, *Presbyterianism and Education in the Proceedings Second General Council,* Philadelphia, 1880.

and exhaustive discussion of Calvin's relation to modern education has yet been undertaken. It will, therefore, be understood that I approach my task with the utmost hesitation. Surely, I do not claim to speak with final authority.

That Calvinism and education are intimately associated in fact, as well as in theory, is to be the thesis of our present argument. Indeed, this intimacy of association is such that it has long been true that the mere mention of the one has served to bring to mind the other. The church of Calvin has taken high rank as the church of education. Wherever Calvinism has gone, it has carried the school with it. It has been the sturdy champion of intellectual, moral, and religious training in all its phases,—from early childhood to mature manhood,—in the home, in the Sabbath-school, in the grammar school, in the high school, in the college, in the university, and in the great training school of mature life and experience. Its critics have charged that it has emphasized a partial and particular training, with special reference to theology. That is not a true charge. Calvin did perhaps think of theology as modern men think of a great light-house. He recognized, too, that those who "fill its lamps and trim its wicks" must be skilled workmen. But, in recognizing this, he never forgot that a light-house is constructed, not for the purpose of giving employment to the few who are adjusting its machinery, but primarily for the purpose of lending its signal to the multitude of vessels adrift upon the seas. Calvinism has, therefore, stood for the broadest and soundest training the world has ever known. While many of these very critics have themselves been championing some narrow theory that would limit education to a mere fraction of man's personality, the voice of Calvinism has been heard boldly insisting upon the education of the *whole* man, in the entire circumference of his possibilities, and not simply along lines that will guarantee a larger money value when taken out into the market of professional or mercantile life. It is true that Calvin's plea for education did not rest merely upon the flimsy fact that it contributes to man's capacity for passionate gain-getting. His plea for education rested upon the sterner fact that it may be made to contribute to that richest and most potential asset in the high life of any nation—character and conscience.

"We boast," says Bancroft, "of our common schools. Calvin was the father of popular education—the inventor of the system of free schools." Whether or not that is true, it is an historical fact that Calvin, following Luther, gave a powerful impulse to popular education. It is an historical fact that the stream of influence that flowed from Geneva, through Scotland and Holland, to this country, was by far the strongest factor in establishing the American common school system. It was also the leading force in founding colleges, seminaries and academies of learning for the first two centuries of our national life. Calvin himself made this work the crowning achievement of his large, spacious life. The founding of the Academy of Geneva meant to him "the final step toward the realization of a Christian commonwealth." He held that the best method by which to preserve purity in religion was to enlighten the understanding of men. It is not our present purpose to trace the exact origin or to review the exact history of the great educational movement of Calvin's day. Certainly, high honor is due to Luther, whose name is a synonym of a world-wide revolution in education, and to Melancthon who came to be known as the "preceptor of Germany," to say nothing of Zwingli, Knox and others, who enriched and ennobled the higher life of that day by their devotion to the ideal of sound learning. But it was Calvin who first gave "a local habitation and a name" to this mighty impulse. It was Calvin's genius and sacrifice that first gave to it organization and system. While others were delaying definite action, for lack of funds, and a cold world was exclaiming, then as now, "Silver and gold I have none," Calvin was establishing a great school and summoning his fellowmen "to rise up and walk." It is just here that the work of Calvin stands supreme. It is just here that his great constructive mind and his superb executive genius flowered into full bloom. In establishing a system of education, he did another thing also that will never hinder his reward. He established once for all that view of education which makes God the central sun around which must revolve every system of human thought and every scheme of human training.

We shall now undertake to cite some of the specific things that have determined the influence of Calvin on education, and to assess at its true value the contribution he has made to educational progress.

1. *I submit that the system of doctrine formulated by Calvin has constituted a powerful factor in educational progress.* It may be fairly questioned whether any system of theology has ever made so profound an impression upon thoughtful men. Certainly, none has more insistently involved the logical necessity of mental discipline or more insistently demanded the spread of learning. Calvinism reaffirmed the spirit of the Pauline theology on which it fed and once more proclaimed the fact that religion is not confined to the feeling or to the will. It

laid a profound emphasis of Christian intelligence. It insisted that man must love God, not only with his whole heart, but also *with his whole mind*. Calvin held that "a true faith must be an intelligent faith." He understood that the acceptance and the diffusion of his scheme of doctrine must inevitably depend, not only upon the training of the men who were to expound it, but also upon the intelligence of the great masses of humanity who were to accept it.

The doctrinal scheme of Calvin has historically and habitually created and demanded intellectual manhood. The system itself has been, immediately and directly, a great instrument of intellectual discipline, bringing into requisition all literature, all science and all philosophy. Wherever it has been properly expounded, it has been a mighty factor in stimulating thought and intelligence among the people. But its larger educational influence has been due to the fact that it requires, for its acceptance and diffusion, mental discipline and intellectual culture. This fact pledged not only Calvin himself, but also every man who accepted the system and believed that it embraced divine truth, to the policy of educating the masses of the people. No man can estimate to what extent modern educational progress is the fruit of Calvin's credal statement, even if it has perhaps "smacked of a certain sureness of opinion and passion for its sort of truth."

Such majestic themes as the doctrine of the absolute sovereignty of God, the doctrine of the divine decrees, the doctrine of the total depravity of the human race, and the doctrine of the necessity of the regeneration of the Spirit,—all of them bitterly assailed from Calvin's day to the present time,—invite and summon the best powers of mental discipline and intellectual culture. Calvin understood the logic of the situation. He saw that, if his system was to gain a foot-hold, it was necessary to train the masses. He saw that it would require mental training to master such problems and to trace them out to all that they logically involve.

The church of Calvin, therefore, has been a *teaching* church. It has flourished as intelligence has flourished. It has declined as intelligence has declined. If every system of truth has its educational influence, certainly a system, like that of Calvin, which makes the strongest possible appeal to the human reason, throws its battle lines immeasurably farther into the enemy's territory than a system characterized by less logical clearness of thought and less logical precision of statement. The day has long since passed when any critic of respectable reputation would dare question the fact that Calvin's system of theology has trained a sturdy race of thinkers. Whatever else it has done, it has laid stress on mental discipline. It has been a foe to popular ignorance, and it has given incentive and inspiration to intellectual progress wherever it has gone.

2. *I submit that the system of church polity (and incidentally of civil government) for which Calvin contended, especially in its fully developed Presbyterian form, has exerted a tremendous influence in the spread of popular intelligence and universal education.* Calvin held that the church, under God, is a spiritual republic. In spite of a personal aristocratic bias and a temperamental antagonism to a pure democracy, it still remains that, by the application of his fundamental principle of the equality of all men before God, the logic of his contention was that, in an ideal sense, the will of the people

is the source of authority; that ultimate power rests with the people who are responsible to God alone.

It is easy to infer the inevitable effect of Calvin's contention in these matters upon the education of the masses. Such a contention naturally shook the whole civil, social and religious world to the centre. The logic of his position irresistibly led to popular training. If the people are, under God, sovereign, it is clear that the people, in Calvin's view, must be educated. Otherwise, he was planning to live, and to cause the church to live, under an ignorant sovereign. So also popular liberty, based upon religious liberty, if it means anything at all, means training in the rights and duties of freemen. Thus the church of Calvin, from the beginning, has constituted one of the most effective instruments in the campaign of education. The genius of its polity, as well as the character of its creed, has been one of the foremost factors in inaugurating modern programs for the training of the masses.

We have seen that through Calvin flowed the influence that established the great common-school system of our own country. When the people sit as the court of final appeal, the education of the masses rises above any mere question of philanthropy or of expediency. It becomes a question of law and order. It becomes a question of the vitality and stability of constitutional government, whether in church or in state. It becomes a question of the integrity of democratic rule wherever it is found. The education of the people is the inexorable logic of the Calvinistic program, which has wrought out for the modern world the best features of its educational creed. Education is the weapon with which to arm every warrior who in this conflict would contend for the individual freedom for which Calvin fought. If the people are to rule, let them not be fed on the husks of a shallow discipline, but provide for them "bread enough and to spare" that they may be trained to the high task of self-government. For no government will be better than the people deserve and are able to maintain.

3. *I submit that the form of worship and the system of religious instruction of which Calvin was so stout a champion have fostered popular intelligence and promoted educational progress.* The emphasis upon the didactic feature in church worship and the catachetical method in religious instruction, characteristic of the Calvinistic scheme, have been conspicuous factors in the development of a sturdy and intelligent faith. They have played an important role in the mental discipline of all who have felt the touch of their influence. That sound mental training has resulted from the catachetical method of instruction, for which Calvin contended, is too obvious to require discussion. Of scarcely less importance is the didactic element in church worship. The Calvinistic form of worship is characterized by the utmost simplicity. There is a minimum of ceremony and ritual. From the beginning, it has exalted truth to the place in which art had long been enthroned. Calvin insisted that special emphasis should be laid upon the preaching of the word by trained men. Preaching was to be emphasized as an important part of worship and as an essential agency in the religious training of the people. Calvinism has rigidly stood for a learned ministry by men able to "rightly divide the word of truth." It is an outstanding fact that instruction in the truth has distinguished its pulpits from Calvin's time to the present. It

may here be pertinently remarked that "epochs of great intellectual and moral quickening have almost without exception been epochs marked by great preaching. Such epochs present the sermon as a characteristic form of literature." It would be difficult to form an adequate conception of the educational power of the pulpit. It has been, directly and indirectly, perhaps the most potent single factor in the world's intellectual progress. Calvin has been perhaps its foremost champion. He saw that, through the pulpit and the training school, the great unfinished work of reaching the mind and the heart of the world was to be accomplished. He believed that the truth addressed to the reason is the surest medium by which to awaken the conscience of men. It is this emphasis upon the sermon that has distinguished the church of Calvin, among all other churches, as pre-eminently the church of religious training. This emphasis not only directly induced intellectual discipline, but none the less certainly became a powerful indirect cause of mental culture. The untrained human mind may interest itself in ceremony and ritual; but it is evident that the Calvinistic emphasis upon something more solid than form and ceremony must, in the last analysis, depend for its vitality, if not for its very existence, upon human intelligence and human training.

4. *I submit that the character or quality of training which Calvin emphasized has powerfully influenced educational progress.* There has been widespread misconception of Calvin's views concerning education. It has been charged that his sole interest in education was from the viewpoint of theology. It is charged that his advocacy of the study of the humanities was in the interest of theology alone; that his recognition of the value of

training in language, in history, in philosophy was due to the fact that these branches of study, in a large degree, acknowledge theology as their crown. On the other hand, it has been charged that he was actually hostile to science and to art.

It has, however, been conclusively shown* that Calvinism, so far from being hostile to science and art, has actually fostered and stimulated them; that the principle that underlies Calvinism demands and creates the scientific spirit. It is a familiar fact that Calvinism raises, at the very threshold of all enquiry, the question of the origin, the relation, and the destiny of all that exists. It holds that the universe, so far from being the sport of chance or the passive issue of accident, obeys law and order; that it is under the sway of unity, stability and order, established by God Himself. It proclaims God's decree as the foundation and origin of every natural, moral and spiritual law. It is easy to understand how such a scheme of philosophy gave a new impulse to, and created a new love for, science. It is also true that Calvinism, by means of its dominating principle and its doctrine of "common grace," not only created a new love for science, but actually restored to science its domain,—proclaiming that "there is nothing either in the life of nature, or in human life itself, which does not present itself as an object worthy of scientific investigation." Calvinism, however, did more than merely give a new impulse to science, create a new love for it, and restore to it its domain. It also advanced its indispensable liberty and delivered it from unnatural bonds. It restored the long surrendered right of free enquiry, which Calvin, according to Bancroft, "pushed to its utmost verge." It

---

* Kuyper: *Lectures on Calvinism.*

announced to the world that neither the imperial crown nor the papal tiara would be allowed "to clip its wings or to wring its neck." Finally, it was Calvinism that, having emancipated science, pointed the way to a solution of the unavoidable "scientific conflict"—not the socalled conflict between faith and science, but "the conflict of two scientific systems, proceeding from two kinds of human consciousness, between those who contend that the cosmos, as it exists to-day, is in a normal condition and those who contend that it is in an abnormal condition." It was Calvinism that proclaimed the right and the liberty of each man to build science from the premises of his own consciousness,—yet, at the same time, refusing the scientific name to any man who dares to slip behind his work any whimsical hypothesis of his own making or to draw from it any whimsical conclusion of his own fancy. Calvin saw no conflict between faith and science. There is no such conflict. The fact that a man is not afraid to open his eyes in the presence of nature constitutes no reason in the view of Calvin why he should be ashamed to close them in the presence of God.

Calvinism has stood in a similar friendly relation to art. It has been charged that Calvinism, having no general art-style of its own and depreciating the symbolic form of worship, has not only been unappreciative of art, but actually hostile to it. As a matter of fact, it has fostered art, even though it has refused to embody its religious spirit in monuments of its making. Not only this, but it is a fact that "the highest interpretation of the nature of art flows from the Calvinistic principle." Calvin himself encouraged and commended the lawful use of art. He held that "art reveals to man a higher reality than is offered by this sinful world"; that art originated with God, the sovereign Artist; that it is not simply the product of our own phantasy, nor of our own subjective perception, that, in its highest conception it has an objective existence, being itself the expression of a divine perfection. It was Calvin who, by "releasing art from the guardianship and unjustified tutelage of the church, first recognized the fact that it had reached its majority," and first insisted with emphasis that "all liberal arts are gifts of God," not to the church alone, but by virtue of "common grace" to the unregenerate world as well. It is not enough to say, however, that Calvinism emancipated art; that it demanded for it strength to stand on its own feet, and that it vigorously sought to extend its branches in every direction. It did more than that. As a matter of historical fact, it actually advanced the development of the arts. It is true that Calvinism built no cathedrals, no palaces, and no amphitheatres. But it is also true that, in literature, in painting and in music, Calvinism disclosed to art an entirely new world. One example will suffice. The world knows that, for two centuries, the Calvinistic Dutch school of art "pointed the way to all the nations for new conquests." We are not now discussing the differentiating nature of Calvinistic art. It is sufficient for our present purpose to claim for it that high quality and that original genius which is its due. The point of special emphasis is that, so far from being hostile to art, as has been charged, it has been the patron, the foster-mother, and friend of that which is best, most satisfying, and most uplifting in art and in its highest development.

Having answered thus briefly the charge that Calvinism lacks catholicity in its attitude toward certain realms of knowledge, and claiming for it, not only high service, but also initiative, in the particular directions in which its enemies have charged against it failure and hostility, we are now prepared to say that Calvin's greatest contribution to true educational progress, as we conceive it, lies in another direction. We are prepared to express the conviction that the greatest service which Calvin was permitted to render mankind through education has resulted from his insistence that the *moral and spiritual training of men is entitled to take precedence over other kind of training.* It is just at this point that Calvin's influence has been most pronounced and vital in the past, and it is just at this point that it is most urgently needed in the crisis that confronts the church to-day.

So far from being a matter of reproach, it is to the lasting credit of Calvin that he held that education, rightly conceived, must have in view the elevation of the moral nature of man. This means, of course, that education must stand for character. We know that intellectual discipline does not necessarily involve moral training. This, however, does not mean that the alternative is between a safe ignorance and a hazardous knowledge. Ignorance is never safe, and hazard is no essential of knowledge. Yet, we know that training may not only be instrumental in making a "good man better," but also in making a "bad man worse." We know that there are such things as the honorable instinct of a savage and the atrophied conscience of a prince. Calvin held that sane and balanced training consists not merely in the exercise of the reason, the memory and the imagination. He had sounded the depths of human experience long enough and intelligently enough to know that the man whose soul is sordid and whose conscience is unresponsive had never been led to the "tree of knowledge."

We have fallen upon a time when the mad desire for fame and wealth is apt to blunt, if not destroy, the moral sense of the nation. We need the kind of training that will point a better way. "Be poor and continue poor," wrote a dying mother to her son, "while others around you grow rich by fraud and by disloyalty. Be without place or power, while others beg their way upward. Bear the pain of disappointed hopes, while others attain the accomplishment of theirs by flattery. Wrap yourself in your own virtue. Seek a friend and daily bread. And if in such a course of life you have grown gray with unblenched honor, bless God and die." That type of manhood is the nation's need. It was to supply that need in his own day that Calvin fought and sacrificed in the last years of his life. That was the crowning task to which he set himself. He never lost that vision until his fading life, glorified and strengthened to the end, had pronounced upon it a final benediction.

It is being urged that the sense of honor is waning in this country. Whenever we must plead guilty to this charge, it will mean that we have stacked away, in some unfrequented museum, as a useless relic, the teaching and the ideal of Calvin, who insisted as strenuously as any man could insist that an institution of learning is a place which should train not only the intellect, but also the character and the conscience of men; who recognized as clearly as any man could recognize the fatal blunder of turning out upon the world a great host of college-trained men, to constitute an aristocracy of knaves; who saw as clearly as any man could see that the most brilliant intellect may co-exist with moral turpitude; that the dagger is not less a dagger because of its polished blade and its jeweled hilt; that education without character is abnormal and abortive, and could only be a curse to mankind. "Upon what," exclaimed a great pioneer in American education, "shall be based the training of the American college?" I answer, upon the thesis of John Calvin! For upon that thesis, and that alone, can be constructed an educational fabric that will enable the college graduate to demonstrate to the world which he is expected to fashion and mold that it is not heredity, nor accident, nor intellect, nor circumstance, but character and conscience that constitute the governing force of national and personal life.

Calvin also held that the main thing in all true education, a thing never to be lost sight of, is the spiritual development of man. This theory needs a new emphasis in this day of the apotheosis of mere intellectual culture when vasts multitudes of men are talking the flexible language of the various modern systems of pseudo-religious diplomacy. Intellectual culture may enable a man to "weigh the stars and bridge the ocean." It may give him the power to "foretell the path of the whirlwind" or to "calculate the orbit of the storm." But Calvin knew that no amount of intellectual culture could guarantee that God moves in the texture and the fiber of a human soul. There was no limping in Calvin's logic. That was one of the overwhelming things that made him great.

Calvin doubtless foresaw that the spirit of Pilate would live again in that class of men who are forever asking, "What is the truth?" and forthwith attacking everything that challenges their intellectual vanity. Happily, he did not foresee that these attacks would be justified as a mere exercise of "academic freedom." We witness to-day the strange contention that it is unreasonable to teach the principles of the Christian religion to the youth of our country, and yet that it is perfectly reasonable to teach doctrines of history, science and philosophy, which undermine the Christian faith. That is the kind of "academic freedom" which a certain modern brand of "science" defiantly proclaims. Of course, the votaries of science are at liberty to put nature on the rack, and, having so done, they are at liberty to torture her to the betrayal of her inmost secrets. But it is a different matter, when they "rashly rend the veil," and presume to "enter the Holy of Holies." It is a different matter, when they make bold to say that "God is merely a rotating globe." It is a different matter, when they "think by searching to find out God," or dream of "understanding the Almighty to perfection." It is a different matter when they undertake to apply their tests and solvents to the laws of the spiritual kingdom These are the things that have been hidden from the wise and the foolish and revealed unto babes.

Calvin did a great work when he emancipated science from the unjustified interference of the church. It seems that the church must now emancipate itself from the unjustified interference of "science." A pseudo-science is insiduously seeking to take possession of some of its colleges. It is seeking to nail to their mastheads flags without religious color. It is demanding that there shall be no longer any open and avowed recognition of the Eternal as the most important member of their faculties and as their rightful head. It is asserting that, after all, the Calvinistic program of religious training is "puerile and visionary and narrow and useless." What shall our answer be? Shall we give up the battle? Or shall we join the issue? The church could adopt no course so inconceivably fatuous as to surrender the inmost fortification in the line of her defenses. The church will adopt no such course. It will marshal its forces for this supreme struggle; and to this crusade we may, if we will, hear the clear call of Calvin summoning us to make our last stand for that kind of education which, first and foremost, recognizes God as the supreme motive and the supreme end of every scheme of training.

5. *But, it will be asked, what concrete evidence is there to show that Calvin's influence on education has actually done what has been claimed for it?* Where are the visible signs of this influence, in addition to Calvin's acknowledged contribution to the inauguration of the modern common school system? Granting that the Calvinistic scheme of doctrine and polity and form of worship have, in a general way, caused the spread of popular intelligence, and granting that Calvinism, while friendly to education in all of its phases, stands pre-eminently for that type of moral and spiritual training which is so much needed in modern times— has it, in any definite and special way, succeeded in influencing educational progress? Has the church of Calvin undertaken to educate, apart from the immediate power and influence of its doctrine, its polity, and its form of worship? Has its educating power extended beyond the home, the Bible school, and the pulpit? Has it actually established and maintained schools and colleges?

We have seen that, while Calvinism itself educates, it is also, on the other hand, in a special way, dependent on education. We know that Calvin himself,—one of the best trained men of his day in language, in science, in law, in philosophy, and in theology,—crowned his Genevan work by founding a great school, the Academy of Geneva; that this school, second only to the *Institutes,* became the dynamo that furnished the electric power of the Calvinistic ideal and spirit, first to France and Switzerland, and then to England, to Scotland, to Holland, to Germany, to Italy, and indirectly to our own country. Here was an institution whose earnest spirit might well serve as a model for the colleges of our own day in the fundamental particular that study, and not college life, was made the object of chief concern. Calvin had no theory that the college life should be allowed to swallow up the college curriculum; that the college life should be allowed to become the main circus instead of the sideshow; that the college itself should be allowed to become a kind of country club. His aim was to send out young men who had dreamed dreams and seen visions —young men who had connected themselves with the dynamo and become storage batteries charged with power.

As a matter of fact, from the very beginning, institutions of learning have followed Calvinism wherever it has gone. "Wherever Calvinism gained dominion," says Bancroft, "it invoked intelligence for the people, and in every parish planted the common school." That statement correctly describes the entire spirit of the Calvinistic faith and propaganda. I shall cite one familiar and matchless example of this spirit by recalling to you the world-famous siege of Leyden. To the heroic survivors of that siege, the Prince of Orange, in recognition of their patriotic courage, "offered either a reduction of taxes or the establishment of a school of learning." They chose the school. Their Calvinistic faith put education first, and money second. Thus began the historic University of Leyden. That is the spirit of Calvinism that has caused it to establish schools and colleges throughout the civilized world. We shall not pause to call the roll. Statistics are a despair to a speaker and a terror to an audience. It is a roll of honor and a catalogue of achievement.

But we may be permitted here to say that, in our own country, the number of institutions of all grades founded or controlled or maintained by men of the Calvinistic name and affiliation is vastly in excess of despair to a speaker and a terror to an audience. It is not generally recalled in recent years that the ancient universities of Harvard and Yale, as well as Princeton, were founded by Calvinists. From that early day, through the subsequent period, when the famous "log college" rose into form under Calvinistic influence, until recent years when colleges of almost every name and faith have sprung up throughout the entire nation, the history of the Calvinistic faith and effort in this direction has been characterized by the most honorable and remarkable record of any church in the world. It constitutes an inspiring and brilliant array of achievements which, in spite of certain present discouragements, to which we shall in a moment refer, furnish ground for hope and inspiration to all who believe in Christian training and love the church to whose creed and life Calvin made so large a contribution.

6. *Finally, let us enquire, what are the important lessons and duties which such an educational history and such an educational policy impose upon us in the present time, and especially in this section for which we are so largely responsible?* There is no question that the Calvinistic emphasis upon moral and spiritual training is as sorely needed to-day as ever before in the history of the Christian church. There is also no question that such a type of training, from the viewpoint of the church, has found its most fruitful seed-plot in the Christian college. Unless we are stupidly blind, we must recognize that the Christian college to-day faces a situation that will put to a final test its power to survive in the historic form in which it has hitherto existed. The recent rise and the phenomenal growth of the tax-supported system of higher education brings squarely into the arena an issue that must be met. There is in many quarters a constantly growing sentiment, at times expressing itself in a demand, that the state shall be permitted to do the entire work of training our youth, theology alone being excepted. Enormous and constantly increasing sums of money are being annually appropriated by the state for the maintenance and the expansion of its schools. It would be difficult to find a normal man so blind that he cannot see that many of these schools are destined in the next quarter of a century to witness a development in equipment, in standard of scholarship and in power of achievement that will challenge the wonder of the world.

What does this mean? What relation has it to the problem of Christian education? Is the church ready to surrender the field? These are vital questions that go to the heart of perhaps the most serious problem before the church to-day. If a rigid emphasis upon definite Christian training is essential to the life of the church, is it likely that there will be a less insistent demand for such training in the future? The state is wise in its day. It is doing its duty to education. It is a calumny to charge that a Christian commonwealth is consciously fostering a God-less education. In some of these institutions the Christian religion is a matter of both philosophy and feeling. But the state professedly does not in all cases attempt to guarantee positive Christian training. Certainly, that is the logic of the present-day definition of religious liberty in certain quarters. Thus we see religious training in many localities gradually being forced out of the public schools. Here and there we see teachers of philosophy dynamiting the citadel of orthodox faith, and this situation is by no means confined to the tax-supported college. "If we console ourselves," says Kuyper, "with the thought we may without danger leave secular science in the hands of our opponents, if we only succeed in saving theology, ours will be the tactics of the ostrich. To confine yourself to the saving of the upper room, when the rest of the house is on fire, is foolish indeed." Do we propose to abandon altogether what we believe to be the true theory of education, based upon positive religious training, to a theory of education that cannot, in the nature of the case, guarantee to do this work? Shall we agree to divorce education from religion? Shall we say that Calvin was wrong when he insisted that "religion should never retire from the precinct of the human intellect"? Shall we say that Calvin was wrong when he insisted that the Bible should be enthroned as the true basis of the best culture, as the true foundation of the best individual life, as the true charter of the best national liberty? Shall we say that Calvin was wrong when he insisted that all culture, all individual life, all national liberty, apart from and independent of the Bible, is evanescent, unsatisfying and illusive? To the policy of Christian training, the church of Calvin is, by principle and by conviction, irrevocably pledged.

There has been in this country, especially in the last quarter of a century, a "progressive loosening" of the historic alliance between Christianity and education. It is true that powerful influences from without the church are hastening this tendency. But let me ask a candid reply to this question: Are there not still more powerful negative influences within the church contributing to the same end? Or, to put it in a different way, has there been a sufficiently powerful positive influence within the church to check this movement? I know that it is charged that it is the college, and not the church, that is responsible for this situation. If that is true, let me ask: Why is the college seeking this divorce? Does not the real fault lie, in the final analysis, with the church itself? I have frequently heard it suggested that some of our colleges have not been true to the church. Is it not also fair to ask whether the church has been true to its colleges? It is an easy matter for church courts to censure college trustees and to bring charges of infidelity. But I make bold to say that such college infidelity, if there is such infidelity, would naturally be due to the infidelity of the church itself. The church deserves to have just so many colleges as it will adequately support, and no more.

We need to learn the lesson that church neglect and non-support of its institutions constitutes no necessary or legitimate element of church control. We need to remember that our colleges are, after all, controlled by mere human beings, generally intelligent human beings, who know the needs and the demands of modern education, who recognize that educational efficiency and academic sincerity are, and ought to be, essential to the success of an institution of learning; who cannot fail to see that, in these days of fierce competition, any institution that sails under false academic colors will "go to the wall," and, in fact, ought to go to the wall. Our church colleges may perhaps in some cases be forced to consider whether,—in view of the fact that the church is willing to allow them to languish, to give them a stone when they are asking for bread, to refuse their urgent cry for equipment and to leave them helpless amid increasing demands upon them and amid the fierce and unequal competition with their more powerful tax-supported rivals,—it is not, after all, their real duty to consider actual academic inefficiency and insincerity quite as criminal as technical or theoretical ecclesiastical infidelity, and, in their despair and agony, to sacrifice what has long ago become, in fact, a mere rope of sand. I use the language, "technical or theoretical infidelity," in no loose sense. I mean to say that the breaking of the technical organic bond need not imply the actual loss of the college. For a college can be distinctly Christian without formal ecclesiastical connection. I mean also to say that no college, however closely bound to the church by organic ties, can, by that fact alone, claim to do more efficient Christian service than any other Christian college which differs from it in no other respect than in its legal ownership. It is altogether wrong to assume that a college, in order to be Christian, must be technically "denominational"; and it will be educational and ecclesiastical suicide for our church to be transfixing some of its noblest institutions on such a fallacy. Nothing could be more short-sighted than a policy of neglecting and repudiating and disowning an institution for no other reason than its failure to wear the denominational label.

I hold no brief for any institution that yields to temptation. I do not defend it. But I am here to say that a starving man is apt to waive questions of strict propriety and make a break for bread wherever he finds it. It may be the duty of the college to languish in its organic church connection and to die a martyr to its unhappy fate. I do not attempt to sit in judgment on that high ethical problem. But we are now asking: What of the duty of the church? Whenever a college seems to be drifting from organic control, the church raises its cry of alarm. Perhaps it passes resolutions of censure. It denounces as a crime *the fact* that it seems to be drifting, and the immediate apparent cause of its drifting. But the real cause, and the ultimate cause, *behind the fact,* fails to create a ripple on the surface of its composure save the plaintive cry of some discouraged college president. No college drifts because it wants to drift. Every college would prefer, for a multitude of reasons, not to drift, and no college has ever drifted, or will ever drift, except for cause.

Now I have more than consumed the time allotted to me. I have frankly expressed my views, in good spirit, and, I hope, on large grounds. Certainly, I have had in mind no concrete case. I have tried to discuss the broad principles involved, without thought of any individual institution, certainly without thought of my own institution, which has enjoyed a stable, uniform and consistent policy and method of government since 1782.

I have stressed this matter because I believe that it is vital. I can see no other sure or rational way by which to check this growing tendency to break the organic connection between the church and the college than to create a sentiment in the church that will insist upon church support as equally binding upon the church as college fidelity is upon the college. Then, and not until then, will the college be happy in its alliance with the church, or the church justified in its alliance with the college. If, therefore, our church would rescue higher education, it must seek to imbibe more of the spirit of Calvin, who was willing to sacrifice something for his convictions. If our church de sires to re-establish in a more effective form its historic alliance with higher education and to continue true to its past history, it must study the life of Calvin in the light of the struggles and the sacrifices made by him to inaugurate and to perpetuate a system of education adequate to the great work he had planned.

I have no time to discuss the other educational evils that need to be corrected. I will refer, however, in a word, to the pathetic and needless rivalries that exist between our own church colleges. At best, the struggle is difficult, with the tax-supported schools overwhelming them and the church neglecting them. But, with our own forces divided and needlessly wa ring against each other, the struggle becomes indeed disheartening. I recall the fact that, years ago, I listened to a powerful appeal from a college president of our own church, urging the church to support its colleges. I sympathized with his appeal. But I was surprised to hear, a little later, that the very college over which he presided was engaged in fierce competition, not so much with the tax-supported schools as with other schools of our own church. The pathos of such needless jealousy and inconsistency can only be mentioned as one of those singular symptoms of impending suicide which, I fear, may be more readily deplored than corrected.

I am not to be understood as urging the church to neglect the tax-supported college. Far from it. On the contrary, I am persuaded that the attitude of the church toward some of these institutions, in which there is a religious atmosphere, both sincere and inspiring, has been in the past oftentimes unfriendly, not to say unchristian. Yet in many of these institutions are to be found great groups of students from Christian homes. Our attitude should be friendly and helpful. The church can look after its own in the state school without disloyalty to the church school. It cannot fail to look after its own in any school without disloyalty to itself.

The church of Calvin owes it to its heroic past, so full of educational achievement, to its present, so full of educational need, and to its future, so full of educational opportunity, to re-establish and to re-enforce the alliance between religion and learning. It is time for the church to review the reasons why it is in the educational business at all. It is time for the church to cease regarding its institutions as mere ornaments in its crown, in which it is chiefly interested as objects of selfish pride, of complacent boasting, or of ruinous controversy. It is time for the church to reckon more closely with the economic side of this proposition and to provide for its schools, or to cease to undertake to operate them; to wipe away any possible ground for the increasingly familiar accusation that "denominational" education is a synonym for an "inferior" education; to remember that the world will judge the quality of the religion for which it stands, by the educational efficiency and sincerity of the colleges by which it is represented. It is time for the church-colleges to dismiss any idea that they exist for their own glory, for the fame of their faculties, or for the sentimental interest of their alumni; to cease this internal warfare, this needless rivalry; to get together and not live apart; to enquire whether they have standards, ideals and equipment that justify their academic existence.

Our church is laying great plans and building great hopes. That is the right and proper policy. It is also a sacred duty. But I do not hesitate to say that no plan that we can lay, no hope that we can build, will be abiding, if we neglect the foundation-stone of every plan and of every hope. I come to you from the battle lines. I speak words of soberness when I say that our church needs the conviction, the spirit, the devotion, the sacrifice, and the faith of Calvin to awaken it and to inspire it to do its full duty in this direction. Every form of activity in which we engage as a church —from our great work in the foreign field all the way down the line—will finally and inevitably depend, for its full success, upon the policy we adopt in this matter of Christian education. Calvin understood this. Knox understood it. Shall we of this time, the heirs of so great a past, standing on the threshold of the greatest opportunity, the greatest need and the greatest crisis, which has confronted the church, fail to understand the situation, to grapple with it, and to act upon it? There is no present duty of our church greater or more insistent. There is no present duty that we owe to the memory of Calvin more sacred than this duty of purging ourselves of the blame resting upon us in view of our growing neglect and growing indifference towards a situation, which is to-day both a standing reproach and a standing peril to our church.

CALVIN'S INFLUENCE UPON THE POLITICAL DEVELOPMENT OF THE WORLD.

By Frank T. Glasgow
Lexington, Virginia.

John Calvin died May 27, 1564, in the 55th year of his age; and a quaint writer adds, "He left behind him only $170 in money; but an incalculable fortune in fame and consequential influence."

In this man, we are told by one, "lies the origin and guaranty of our constitutional liberties."

And again: "It is admitted by all scientific students," says Kuyper, "that Calvinism has led public law into new paths; first in Western Europe, then in two continents, and to-day more and more among all civilized nations."

Let us inquire how far these claims are well-founded.

Quoad our subject, or to be more exact, in relation to human government, what is Calvinism?

Fundamental as was the doctrine of Justification by Faith, this we conclude was not Calvin's distinguishing tenet. But going back to a broader generalization, the thoughtful student of Calvin's *Institutes* (said to be one of the most remarkable products of the human mind in any age, and the backbone of the Reformation), cannot fail to recognize the accuracy of the statement, that Calvin's distinctive and dominating principle, in the widest sense manifestly was, *the Sovereignty of the Triune God!* God's sovereignty over his whole creation; in all spheres and kingdoms, visible and invisible. Sovereignty in nature; sovereignty in the state; sovereignty in society; sovereignty in the church, and sovereignty in the individual.

According to Calvin, had not sin entered, God would have remained the sole King of all men, everywhere, and forever.

With sin present, a representative government is the ideal form, that of the Republic.

Calvin's doctrine of sin and depravity has been the greatest of all levellers. "It concludes all men under sin; from the slave in his hovel to the King on his throne." In the light of this tremendous fact, all earthly distinctions disappear; the foundation of the privileges of birth and caste crumbles and the lustre of all earthly grandeur is dulled.

Thus, all men owe to God the same supreme allegiance; and the offer of mercy is made to all men upon the same terms and conditions. If all men are equal before God's law, all men are equal before man's law. Hence emerges clearly to view the fundamental axiom of Modern Democracy, that "all men are created equal, and vested with certain inalienable rights." This great principle, therefore, properly limited, is Calvin's, rather than Jefferson's! . . . It irresistibly follows that "to have placed man on a footing of equality with man, so far as purely human interests are concerned, is the immortal glory which incontestably belongs to Calvin!"

> "And Freedom reared in that August sunrise,
> Her beautiful bold brow."

Sir James Stephen, the eminent English Statesman, churchman, and jurist, and professor of Modern History in the University of Cambridge, in speaking of the organization effected by the General Synod of France in 1559, says: "A great social revolution had thus been effected. Within the centre of the French monarchy, Calvin and his disciples had established a spiritual republic, and had solemnly recognized as the basis of it, four principles, each germinent of results of the highest importance to the political commonwealth.

These principles were:

First. That the will of the people was the one legislative source of the power of their rulers.

Second. That power was most properly delegated by the people to their rulers.

Third. That in ecclesiastical government, the clergy and the laity were entitled to an equal and co-ordinate authority; and,

Fourth. That between the church and the state, no alliance, or mutual dependence, or other definite relation necessarily or properly existed."

Calvin's church organization, Green calls, a "Christian Republic;" a "Christian state, in which the true sovereign was not pope or bishop, but the Christian man."

Calvinism therefore stands throughout for a system of popular government according to law. It provides a true authority, resting humanly speaking on the consent of the governed. By its deep conception of sin it has laid bare the true root of state-life, and has taught us two things:

First, that we should receive with gratitude the institution of the state from God's hand; and at the same time that we must be ever watchful against the danger, which, from human weakness, lurks in the power of the state.

Wm. C. Preston, of South Carolina, wrote: "Certainly it was a most remarkable and singular coincidence that the constitution of the Presbyterian Church should bear such a close and striking resemblance to the political constitution of our country." Dr. Smith, however, in his wonderful book, *"The Creed of Presbyterians,"* a work which, with us I am sure, stands second only to our standards, says: that when "the fathers of our Republic sat down to frame a system of representative government, their task was not so difficult as some have imagined. They had a model to work by. As Chief Justice Tilghman says: "The framers of the Constitution of the United States borrowed very much of the form of our Republic from the constitution of the Presbyterian Church of Scotland.'"

We need not therefore be surprised to find that one of our last and greatest expounders of constitutional law (John Randolph Tucker), in his masterful work on the constitution, gives us concrete Calvinism as applied to the fundamentals of human government, thus:

"Man's title to his liberty is from his Creator. It consists in the selfuse of endowments bestowed on him, under trust responsibility of God. God ordained society as the school of the race; and government, as the organic force, was ordained to preserve social order, and conserve the liberty of man."

These things being conceded, "the related order of these social elements is: Man trustee of his liberty for God; society the Divinely ordained trustee for man; and government the Divinely ordained trustee for society.

Man is the object of all this Divine arrangement. They (government and society), are ordained for him; he not created for them. His good is the *ultimatum* of all their use of power; and their power is only legitimate in title, or in exercise, when it does justice to him in the protection of his right and liberty. Man has not only the right of self-preservation, but God has made it his duty. It is his primal duty therefore to see that the Divine means ordained for his protection shall not be perverted to his injury or destruction."

"To sum up, power and right are correlated; both are divinely ordained. Political power is vested in trust for man; right is vested in man in trust for God. Right is primal, power is ancillary. Right is the end, power and means. Right is the good to be secured, power the minister, the servant of right. The divine constitution is not *jus Divinum regum,* but *jus Divinum hominum.*

"This political philosophy is not the result of social compact; but is the logical consequence of that intense individuality of man, arising out of his sole responsibility to God; to conserve and develop which society and government were divinely ordained."

Let us remember that religious and civil liberty, whilst having no organic connection, yet have a strong natural affinity, the one for the other. And that, "by the side of every religion is to be found a political opinion connected with it by affinity. If the human mind be left to follow its own bent, it will regulate the temporal and spiritual institutions of society in a uniform manner; and a man will endeavor, if I may so speak, to harmonize earth with heaven."

In entering this discussion, we cannot pause even to glance at the early life of this great man; nor to trace his wonderful and chequered career. "The sixteenth century is the greatest century in Christian times; the epoch where (so to speak) everything ends and everything begins. Nothing is paltry, nothing small, not even a little city of 12,000 souls, lying unobserved at the foot of the Alps."

We must content ourselves therefore with concentrating our gaze at once upon this marvelous expounder of Truth, human and divine, as we find him in Geneva; in Geneva, well-styled the "Thermopylae of Protestantism and Freedom!"

"The history of the political emancipation of Geneva is interesting in itself. Liberty, it has been said, has never been common in the world. It has not flourished in all climates; and the periods when a people struggles justly for liberty, are the privileged epochs of history."

Under the heroic, patient and consecrated Farel, God was preparing Geneva for Calvin. At the same time, he had Calvin in the school of preparation for Geneva. The union of these two natures and forces (predestined for each other), could not fail to produce remarkable results in the world.

For years, and even centuries, persistent and perilous efforts had been made at Geneva for a firm establishment of freedom. She had had her martyrs of liberty, and her martyrs of faith. "Her career illustrates the great maxim, that political freedom and Christian truth must advance hand in hand, for the salvation of nations, and salvation of souls." To convert the spark of evangelical fire already in Geneva, into a pure, dazzling light, there was need of an intellect of vast depth, a will of vast energy, and a faith of vast power. God sent the man endowed with these gifts, in the person of John Calvin. In the quiet of due Tillet's library at Agoulême was the forge where the new Vulcan had prepared the bolts, which later he systematized, and finally scattered broadcast on every side from Geneva.

We now fix our eyes on Calvin during the period of his great labors in Geneva, beginning in 1541. He is conducting most remarkable enterprises; as pastor, preacher, teacher, and reformer! We see his wonderful school now firmly established. The teacher is giving full swing to his great and ripe powers. Thousands of pilgrim pupils, from all over Continental Europe and the British Isles, sit at his feet; some fleeing from oppression at home; others fleeing for the hope of the true light set before them. This continues for many years. He prosecutes the great work with tremendous vigor, masterful skill and untiring energy to the end of his life.

Says Bancroft: "More truly benevolent to the human race than Solon, more self-denying than Lycurgus, the genius of Calvin infused enduring elements into the institutions of Geneva, and made it, for the modern world, the impregnable fortress of popular liberty, the fertile deedplot of Democracy."

Had Calvin done nothing more than to make government "of the people, by the people, and for the people" a startling and triumphant reality in the earth, he would have deserved well of mankind.

This achievement marked the opening of a new chapter in the history of humanity.

From Geneva his influence radiated into every corner of Christendom. "Calvin's true home, "Schaff says, "was the Church of God." He broke through all national limitations. "There was scarcely a monarch or statesman or scholar of his age with whom he did not come in contact. Every people of Europe was represented among his disciples. He helped to shape the religious character of churches and nations yet unborn. The Huguenots of France, the Protestants of Holland and Belgium, the Puritans and Independents of England and New England, the Presbyterians of Scotland, and throughout the world, yea, we may say, the whole Anglo-Saxon race, in its prevailing religious character and institution, bear the impress of his genius, and show the power and tenacity of his doctrines and principles of government."

Says Rufus Choate, the great American lawyer: "In the reign of Mary, from 1553 to 1558, a thousand learned Englishmen fled from the stake at home, to the happier states of continental Protestantism. Of these, great numbers—I know not how many—came to Geneva. I ascribe to that five years in Geneva an influence which has changed the face of the world. I seem to myself to trace to it as an influence on English character, a new theology, new politics, another tone of character, the opening of another era of time and liberty. I seem to myself to trace to it the great civil war in England, the Republican constitution framed in the cabin of the Mayflower, the theology of Jonathan Edwards, the battle of Bunker Hill, the Independence of America."

Thus, "the light of Calvin's genius shattered the mask of darkness, which superstition had held for centuries before the brow of religion" and human government.

It is not possible for us here to indicate, much less trace all the channels through which his influence ran, to refresh and water the earth, and to "make glad the city of our God." Calvin played on a harp of a thousand strings; and the music of his playing echoed, wherever heard, in the hearts of untold thousands of brave, God-fearing spirits. We see the fruits of his influence taking shape in France, in the Netherlands, and in Scotland. We see his influence, "under God create the Dutch Republic, and make it the first free nation to put a girdle of empire around the world."

"The one man, who was the principal instrument in the hand of Providence in reforming Scotland, was John Knox. He had learned his theology at the feet of Calvin at Geneva; and had known, as a galley-slave, the tender mercies of Romanism. He was one of the six clerical "Johns" who composed the first General Assembly of Scotland.

His was the voice which taught the peasant of the Lothians that he was a free man; the equal in the sight of the God with the proudest Peer or Prelate that had trampled on his forefathers!" For whilst Calvin's doctrine of sin "abased the pride and humbled the pretensions of the great, his doctrine of predestination exalted the lowly. To the arrogance and pride which went with earthly power, the simple peasant, conscious within himself of his high calling of God in Christ Jesus, could oppose a yet higher pride. 'Though his name did not appear in the Register of Heralds, it was recorded in the Book of Life.' Though unknown among men beyond the limits of his lord's estate, he was known in the councils of Heaven. His name was among those whom the Father from all eternity had given to the Son in an everlasting covenant. He had been bought with a great price, had been saved with a great salvation. For in his stead the Prince of Glory had died upon the tree!"

Marvelous indeed then was the transformation "when the great doctrines learned by Knox from the Bible in Scotland, and more thoroughly at Geneva while sitting at the feet of Calvin, flashed upon the sober mind of Scotland! It was like the sun rising at midnight! Says Carlyle: 'This that Knox did for his nation, we may really call a resurrection as from death.' 'John Knox,' says Froude, 'was the one man without whom Scotland as the modren world has known it, would have had no existence.' Knox made Calvinism the religion of Scotland; and Calvinism made Scotland the moral standard for the world."

" 'Here,' said Melville over the grave of John Knox, 'here lies one who never feared the face of man.' And if Scotland still reverences the memory of the reformer, it is because at that grave her peasant and her trader learned to look in the face of nobles and kings and 'not be ashamed.' He it was that raised the poor commons of his country—into men whom neither king, noble nor priest could force again to submit to tyranny."

Allow me here to pause a moment, to say this much of of the true Scotchman: Wherever we see him in history, he is loyal both to truth, and to liberty. He is also loyal to the faith and traditions of the fatherland. For, whilst solving the world's problems, and extending Anglo-Saxon liberty and Christian civilization around the globe, he ever "carries with him his Confession of Faith, his catechism, Bible and Psalm-book; and from his dwelling or his Kirk, in his native Pentland Hills, or in the Appalatchian wilds; or on the banks of the St. Lawrence, the Ganges or the South Sea Islands, his simple praise ascends to Heaven, in words and music born in the land of the bluebells and the heather."

Later, if we again ask, who brought the final great deliverance to English liberty, we are answered by history. That illustrious Calvinist, William, Prince of Orange, who, as Macaulay says, "found in the strong and sharp logic of the Geneva school something that suited his intellect and his temper; the keystone of whose religion was the doctrine of predestination; and who with his keen logical vision, declared that if he were to abandon the doctrine of predestination, he must abandon with it all his belief in a superintending Providence."

"On two great leaders, William, Prince of Orange, and (second only to him in the great crisis), Marshall Schomberg, a Hollander and a Frenchman, be it said to the everlasting glory of their countries, the liberties of the world were then, under God, depending: the one, William, almost unable to sit on his gray horse from physical weakness and loss of blood; the other, venerable with years and honors, who there, in the Boyne waters, gave his noble life, a sacrifice for the welfare of mankind!"

We see then what element fought the battle of the Boyne. "The very watchword of William's army was 'Westminster'; the word which was before, and has ever since been stamped on the symbol of the Calvinistic churches."

As to the effect of William's victory and reign as William III. of England, Macaulay says: "It has been, of all revolutions, the most beneficent; the highest eulogy that can be pronounced upon it is this, that it was England's best; and that for the authority of law, for the security of property, for the peace of our streets, for the happiness of our homes, our gratitude is due, under Him who raises and pulls down nations at his pleasure, to the Long Parliament, to the Convention and to William of Orange."

"It was the battle of the Boyne (in Ireland in 1690) that decided the fate of Protestantism, not only for Great Britain, but for America; and for the world, indeed; for had William been defeated there, Protestantism could not have found a safe shelter on the face of the earth."

Where learned our ancestors, the immortal principles of the rights of man? Of human liberty, equality, and self-government, on which they based our Republic, and which form to-day the distinctive glory of our American civilization? History here likewise gives answer.

According to D'Aubigne, Luther transformed princes into heroes of faith, but soon settled down at peace with them. The reformation of Calvin, on the other hand, was addressed particularly to the people. It was ever advancing, and ever contending with the rulers of this world. And wherever Calvinism was established, it brought with it not only Truth, but Liberty, and all the great developments which these two fertile principles carry with them.

Says Bancroft: "Calvinism was revolutionary. It taught as a divine revelation the natural equality of man." "It is the essential tendency of Calvinism," says Doyle, the eminent Oxford scholar, "to destroy all distinctions of rank, and all claims to superiority which rest on wealth or political expediency." "Calvinism is essentially Democratic," says Buckle. "A democratic and republican religion," it is called by DeTocqueville, one of the ablest political writers of the century.

"Calvinism, therefore, opposes hereditary monarchy, aristocracy, and bondage." John Richard Green, the author of the greatest history of the English people yet written, belonged to the Anglican church. Yet he says: "It is in Calvinism that the modern world strikes its roots; for it was Calvinism that first revealed the worth and dignity of man. Called of God, heir of heaven, the trader at his counter, and the digger in his field, suddenly rose into equality with the noble and the king." "In that mighty elevation of the masses," he says again, "which was embodied in the Calvinistic doctrines of election and grace, lay the germs of the modern principles of human equality."

And even Castelar, an eloquent unbelieving Spaniard, grudgingly admit, that "Anglo-Saxon democracy is the product of a severe theology learned by a few Christian fugitives in the gloomy cities of Holland and Switzerland, where the morose shade of Calvin still wanders. And that it remains serene in its grandeur, forming the most dignified, most moral, most enlightened and richest portion of the human race."

"Before proving its power in the new world, Calvinism had fought and won the fight for freedom in the old. Not only in Scotland, as we have seen, but also in England and Holland it had challenged and conquered tyranny." To the Puritans, declares Hume (a hater of Calvinism), England owes "the whole freedom of her constitution. . . . The battle that saved England to constitutional liberty was fought and won by Calvinists." Of Holland the same writer says: "The Reformation had entered the Netherlands by the Walloon (Calvinistic) gate."

Seventeen years before Calvin's birth, America was discovered. It waited well nigh two hundred years for important settlements. Europe was not ripe; the hour had not yet struck. By and by, however, the mighty exodus began; and God sent some of his best across the waters first, to lay the foundations for the future. These were Huguenots, Dutch, Puritans, Scotch, and Scotch-Irish! Had there ever before in the world's history been a nation founded by such people as these?

At the time of the Revolution the estimated population of our country was 3,000,000. Of this number 900,000 were of Scotch or Scotch-Irish origin; 600,000 were Puritan English; while over 400,000 were of Dutch, German Reformed, and Huguenot descent. That is to say, two-thirds of our Revolutionary forefathers were trained in the schools of Calvin; embracing the New England colonists, and the Scotch-Irish immigrants, pronounced by the learned author of "American Christianity" the most masterful races on the continent.

According to Bancroft, "The revolution of 1776, as far as it was effected by religion, was a Presbyterian measure. It was the natural outgrowth of the principles which the Presbyterians of the old world planted in her sons, the English Puritans, the Scotch Covenanters, the French Huguenots, the Dutch Calvinists, and the Scotch-Irish Presbyterians of Ulster"; and may I add, in her daughters? For "Calvinism has moulded her own type of womanhood; worth without vanity; self-sacrifice, with self-righteousness; zealous service, without immodesty; strong convictions, without effrontery, and human loveliness, heightened and softened by heavenly-mindedness."

The first Declaration of Independence, certainly the first body of resolutions to that effect, was sent forth by the Mecklenburg Assembly, in session in Charlotte, N. C., composed of twenty-seven staunch Calvinists, of whom nine were ruling elders, and one a Presbyterian preacher.

It strikes us now as strange, that, as late as August, 1775, Thomas Jefferson said: "I would rather be in dependence on Great Britain, properly limited, than on any nation on earth, or than on no nation." And that Washington, in May 1776, said: "When I took command of this army (in June, 1775), I abhorred the idea of independence." These great and brave patriots, however, soon gravitated to the point before reached by the Mecklenburgers, and demanded independence. But the children of the Covenanters were in advance! There is not a doubt, says Bancroft, that the first voice publicly raised in America "to dissolve all connection with Great Britain, came not from the Puritans of New England, nor from the Dutch of New York, nor the Planters of Virginia; but from the Scotch-Irish Presbyterians."

So intense, universal and aggressive was their zeal for liberty, that the struggle of the colonists for independence was spoken of in England as "The Presbyterian Rebellion." An ardent colonial devotee of King George wrote home: "I fix all the blame of these extraordinary proceedings upon the Presbyterians. They have been the chief and principal instruments in all these flaming measures. They always do and ever will act against government, from that restless and turbulent anti-monarchical spirit which has always distinguished them everywhere." And when news of "these extraordinary proceedings" reached England, Horace Walpole said in the English Parliament, "Cousin America has run off with a Presbyterian Parson."

But "the influence of the free spirit of Calvinism in favor of the liberties of the colonies was not confined to the American continent. It was working heroically on the other side of the Atlantic. Two great Scotchmen, David Hume and Adam Smith, were everywhere proclaiming it in their own effective way, and compelling men to hear it. In the House of Commons, also, it was boldly and eloquently upheld by Erin's gifted son, Edmund Burke, as well as by Charles James Fox, of whom Dr. Johnson said, 'Here is a man who has divided a kingdom with Caesar, so that it was a doubt which the nation should be ruled by, the sceptre of George III. or the tongue of Mr. Fox.'"

"The Calvinistic philosophy had also taken a firm hold of the popular mind in Germany, where Kant, imbued with its liberty-loving spirit, was loosening the foundations of despotism, and suffering persecution for his valiant defence of the American cause. France, too, was all aglow with the free, bounding, restless spirit of Calvinism, where Rousseau, in spite of the immorality of his life, and the crudity of his theories, was conducting, through his political science, the same political warfare as that in America. His influence in advocating the rights of man contributed very largely to the forming of the alliance between France and the colonies, and to the unfurling of the royal standard alongside that of the blue flag of the Covenanters, hoisted again in a new form over the

American continent. It was Calvinistic France and Calvinistic America that were going forth in loving unity.to fight on Western soil for the cause of human freedom.

"Thus Calvinism in Europe, and Calvinism in America were leagued together for the promotion of the one great purpose. Their several currents, civil and spiritual, philosophical and religious, had run together and were sweeping on in one great stream, bearing the colonies on to liberty. Out of Calvinistic Protestantism had arisen the great leaders who had issued their rousing calls to the nations for deliverance from mental and political bondage, and had combined their forces for securing the one great object. Rousseau had inflamed the youthful spirit of France with an intense desire for republican simplicity, and Edwards had summed up the political history of America, when he gave Calvinism its political enthusiasm, by declaring virtue to consist in universal love."

In view of all this, can it surprise us when we find D'Aubigne saying: "Calvin was the founder of the greatest republic"? And that the American nation, which we have seen growing so rapidly, "boasts as its father, the humble Reformer on the shores of Lake Leman"? Or when we hear the famous French critic and historian, Taine, declare of the Calvinists: "These men are the true heroes of England. They founded England, in spite of the corruption of the Stuarts, by the exercise of duty, by the practice of justice, by obstinate toil, by vindication of the right, by resistance to oppression, by the conquest of liberty, by the repression of vice. They founded Scotland; they founded the United States, and at this day they are, by their descendants, founding Australia, and colonizing the world."

And so we find that for three and a half centuries now, "Calvinism has been producing in the social conditions of the nations that have received it, transformations unknown to former times. And still at this very day, and now perhaps more than ever, it imparts to the men who accept it, a spirit of power, which makes them chosen instruments, fitted to propagate truth, morality and civilization to the ends of the earth."

May we not, therefore, in concluding, justly claim that this turn in the tide of the world's history, "could not have been brought about, except by the implanting of another principle in the human heart, and by the disclosing of another world of thought to the human mind? That only by Calvinism did the 'Psalm of Liberty' find its way from the troubled conscience to the lips, and that Calvinism has, in fact, captured and guaranteed constitutional liberty to mankind?"

This tree (to adopt the figure of another) may have, to prejudiced eyes, a rought bark, gnarled stem, and boughs twisted often into knotted shapes of ungraceful strength! But, remember, Calvinism is not a willow-wand of yesterday! These boughs have wrestled with the storms of a thousand years; but they hang clad with all that is richest and strongest in the civilization and Christianity of human history. This stem has been wreathed with the red lightning and scarred by the thunderbolt, and all over its rough rind are the marks of the battle axe and the bullet. This old oak has not the pliant grace and silken softness of a greenhouse plant! But it has a majesty above grace, and a grandeur beyond beauty. Its roots may be rugged and strangely contorted; but some of them are rich with the blood of glorious battlefields; some are clasped around the stakes of martyrs; some hidden in solitary cells and lonely libraries, where deep thinkers have mused and prayed, as in some apocalyptic Patmos; while its great tap-root runs back, until it twines in living and loving embrace around the Cross of Calvary!

HOW FAR HAS ORIGINAL CALVINISM BEEN MODIFIED BY TIME?

Rev Samuel A. King, D. D. LL. D.,
Austin Theological Seminary.

This year of grace, 1909, is being made notable by celebrations of the four hundredth anniversary of the birth of John Calvin.

In this session of our Assembly one of the most elaborate of these is being conducted, and not only the members of the body but also great audiences of interested listeners have been edified and delighted by addresses in which the history, the personality, and the work of the great Genevan reformer have been presented by chosen speakers from our own and other lands.

The all but world-wide celebration of this anniversary bears eloquent witness to the greatness and the worthiness of a man whose figure was tall enough to cast his shadow across the space of four eventful centuries, whose influence is recognized in the world to-day, and will be potent in directing the currents of human thought and the movements of men through all coming time until the great consummation, when it shall be announced in a ransomed earth and a rejoicing heaven that the Kingdoms of this world have become the Kingdom of our Lord and of His Christ.

In this our celebration the subject assigned to me is one that does not give occasion for an attractive and popular address; mine is rather a prosaic task which requires the statement, and to some extent the discussion of doctrinal tenets and systems—those things which many have chosen to designate as the "dry bones of theology."

I have been asked to discuss the question, "How far has Original Calvinism Been Modified by Time?"

It is fitting to observe, at the outset, that "Calvinism" did not originate at the period of the Reformation, nor with Calvin, the greatest theologian of the Reformation. It is well known that the specific doctrines which constitute the essence of the system denominated "Calvinism" were elaborately set forth by Augustine, born A. D. 353, more than eleven hundred years before the birth of Calvin, and the system usually styled Calvinistic, is by many, and notably by Dr. Charles Hodge, almost uniformly spoken of as the Augustinian doctrine. Neither did this system originate with the illustrious bishop of Hippo. Every distinctive doctrine of Calvinism is set forth in the inspired writings of Paul, especially in the Epistles to the Romans and the Ephesians. And these were not new doctrines when propounded by the great apostle of the Gentiles. The catchy cry in our times, "Back to Christ," in most cases is an expression of the thought that by going back to the personal teachings of our Lord an escape can be had from the "hard doctrines" of Paul. But when recourse is had to the words of Christ it will be found that the same doctrines concerning God's sovereignty, man's depravity, and efficacious grace, are as plainly taught by Christ Himself in Matt. xi., Luke iv., and John vi., xvii., as in any of the writings of Paul. This much for what is really "Original Calvinism."

To define the phrase in its popular and present day use, it has been suggested by a distinguished theologian that original Calvinism may mean either "the Calvinism of John Calvin himself, as outlined in his *Institutes;* or as contained in the broad concensus of the Reformed Confessions; or the common teaching of the doctors of the "Great Age."

In trying to deal with this subject, I shall consider as "original" the Calvinism of the *Institutes,* and undertake to show that there are "modifications" of two classes.

(1) Those in which there have been advances made in the way of fuller statement, or more precise expression of some of the doctrines, in the Reformed Confessions than is found in the *Institutes;* and

(2) Proposed "Modifications" in which there has been a departure from some of the doctrines, or such a weakening of them as to seriously affect their soundness as part of the system.

Taking up in order the subjects thus outlined, it is well known that the *Institutes* contain a complete system of theology. We find in them all the "departments" which are commonly styled theology proper, anthropology, soteriology, ecclesiology, and eschatology. In regard to some of these the views of Calvin and of Calvinists are virtually in harmony with those held by the great body of evangelical Christians. It is only in some of these departments that we find the doctrines which are essentially and distinctively "Calvinism."

And here I quote a passage from Principal Cunningham, which is pertinent and suggestive: He says: "The more we have studied these subjects the more have we become convinced that the one fundamental principle of Calvinism—that, the admission of which constitutes the real line of demarcation between Calvinists and Anti-Calvinists is, the doctrine of predestination in the more limited sense of the word, or of election, as descriptive of the substance of Scripture with regard to what God has decreed, or proposed from eternity to do, and does or effects in time, for the salvation of those who are saved; and that every man ought to be held by others, and ought to acknowledge himself to be a Calvinist, who believes that God from eternity chose some men—certain persons of the human race—absolutely and unconditionally to salvation through Christ, and that He accomplishes this, or executes this decree in time by effecting and securing the salvation of these men in accordance with the provisions of the Covenant of Grace."

(1) In treating of the "Modifications" of the first class, I would place: *First,* the Sub-lapsarian doctrine of the decrees, as it has developed and formulated since the time of Calvin.

Dr. B. B. Warfield (in New Schaff-Herzog Enc.) names three "varieties of Calvinism," namely, "Supra-lapsarianism, Infra-lapsarianism, and Postredemptionism, all of which take their start from a fundamental agreement in the principles which govern the system. The difference between these various tendencies of thought within the limits of the system turns on the place given by each to the doctrine of election, in the logical ordering of the 'decrees of God.' "

Accepting this classification as correct it may be explained, in brief, that the Supra-lapsarian holds that God elected some and rejected others out of *uncreated* men; that the decree of election preceded (in the order of thought) the decree to create and to permit the fall. The Infra (or Sub) lapsarian holds that out of the mass of men regarded as *created* and *fallen,* God chose some to salvation; while the Postredemptionist holds that out of the race of men regarded as *created, fallen* and *redeemed,* God chose those to whom the universal redemption should be applied.

In this connection the term redemption is employed in the narrower sense of the "impetration of the redemption by Christ."

The extreme Supra-lapsarian scheme implies that God created some men to be saved and others to be "vessels of wrath"—that in the order of thought election and reprobation precede the purpose to create and to permit the fall. This "hard doctrine" is thought by many to be Calvinism, pure and simple, and much of the prejudice against our doctrine is due to this mis-apprehension. The fact is, it was never held by any considerable number of Calvinists. There are no Supra-lapsarian confessions, and while some do not distinctly pronounce against either there is no reformed creed that can be quoted as in favor of Supra-lapsarianism. At the present day it would not be unsafe to say that not one in a hundred of Calvinists is a Supra-lapsarian.

The Sub-lapsarian view is that out of the mass of men, all fallen, guilty, depraved, God chose a great number to be saved through the redeeming work of Christ and the effectual application of its benefits by the Holy Spirit. Dr. Warfield says: "Not only does no confession close the door to Infra-lapsarianism, but a considerable number explicitly teach Infra-lapsarianism, which thus emerges as the typical form of Calvinism."

I have counted this as one of the "modifications" of the Calvinism of the *Institutes* for the reason that it is a disputed question as to which of the two views was held by Calvin himself. I think it fair to conclude that neither Supra nor Sub-lapsarian can claim him or confidently appeal to the *Institutes*. The question had not been raised in his day. His great task was to uphold the doctrine of God's sovereign election of such as are saved, unconditioned by foresight of faith, or good works, or anything in the creature. Hence, with this great thought uppermost in his mind it is not strange that he employed language that could be construed by Supra-lapsarians as favoring their extreme view, while in other cases his words can be plausibly pleaded by those who hold the view now prevalent. Doctrines are more fully apprehended and clearly stated as the result of controversy, and in the fires of controversy waged since Calvin's day have been forged the more exact formulas in which the Sub-lapsarian doctrine and others of the system are now set forth.

In strictly systematic theology the subject just discussed belongs to the department of soteriology, but it is intimately related to an important feature of anthropology, namely, the probation in Adam, the fall, and the effects of Adam's first sin on his posterity.

If the decree of election contemplates men as fallen, as being in "an estate of sin and misery," it is an important inquiry as to how they came into this hapless condition. This estate, in all its elements, is accounted for by the doctrines of the Federal theology. Hence I hold that:

(2) The *Second* of the Modifications of the original Calvinism of the *Institutes* is the view known as the "Federal Scheme" according to which we "sinned in Adam and fell with him," as being not simply the natural but Federal head of the race.

This doctrine, elaborated by Cocceius, born ninety-four years after Calvin, was wrought into the system of theology of the Westminster Assembly, and has been ably expounded by such men as Turretin, and Witsius on the Continent; Chalmers and Cunningham in Scotland; and by the two Hodges, Breckinridge, Thornwell, and Dabney in America.

Dr. A. A. Hodge says: "In Holland, England and Scotland, Calvinism has been *modified* in form by the Federal Scheme, introduced by Cocceius and the Westminster divines."

Dr. Shedd says that "Turretin marks the transition from the *elder* to *later* Calvinism—from the theory of the Adamic Union to the Adamic representation.

I think it manifest that in this Federal Scheme we have a modification of the theology of Calvin, a fuller and clearer view of our relation to Adam, and of the ground of our condemnation as having "sinned in him and fallen with him" as our covenant representative.

I think that Calvin came near to this, but did not clearly perceive and grasp it.

Why should we wonder that he did not see all the truth? He himself modestly said: "God hath never favored His servants with so great a benefit that they were all endued with full and perfect knowledge in everything." The wonder is that he had so much more full and perfect knowledge than any other of his age!

Dr. Thornwell, a great admirerer, in his analysis of Calvin's *Institutes,* says: "Federal representation was not seized as it should be, but rather a mystic realism in place of it."

We find some germs of the doctrine in the *Institutes,* but that is all. In Book II., Chapter I., on the "Fall of

Adam the Cause of the Curse on all Mankind, and the Doctrine of Original Sin," he defines this last as "an hereditary pravity and corruption of our nature, diffused through all the parts of the soul, rendering us obnoxious to the divine wrath, and producing in us those works which the Scripture calls the works of the flesh." In the same chapter he says, "Our ruin must be imputed to the corruption of our nature."

Again he says: "When it is said that the sin of Adam renders us obnoxious to the divine judgment, it is not to be understood as if we, though innocent, were undeservedly loaded with the guilt of his sin, but because we are all subject to a curse in consequence of his transgression, he is therefore said to have involved us in guilt. Nevertheless we derive from him not only the punishment, but also the pollution to which the punishment is justly due."

In Section 7, he says: "The Lord deposited with Adam the ornaments He chose to confer on the human nature, and therefore when he lost the favors he had received he lost them not only for himself but for us all." Later he says, "These ornaments were given, not to one man only, but to the whole human nature." Here, and especially in the last two quotations, we find the germs of the Federal connection, but they are obscured by that predominant idea of the realistic union with Adam which Dr. Thornwell calls a "mystic realism."

Calvin lays the principal stress on the corruption of the nature. He finds here a ground sufficient for the guilt and the punishment in which men are involved. He does not clearly grasp the truth that the sinfulness of our estate consists in the guilt of Adam's first sin, and (as the result of that) the want of original righteousness and the corruption of the whole nature.

The "present truth" which Calvin was zealous to maintain, as against the contentions of his great opponent Pighius, as well as others, was the transmission and universal prevalence of a depraved moral nature; to this he gave special prominence and not to the imputation of Adam's sin which was not then a matter of controversy.

The doctrine of the "immediate imputation" of Adam's sin was not clearly articulated in the time of the reformers. It was brought out later in the discussion of the "Mediate Imputation" theory of Placeus. When the Westminster Confession was written the distinction between immediate and mediate had not emerged, as it did a little later. The statement of doctrine in the Confession, Chapter VI., is not so definite as in the answers to questions 16 and 18 of the Shorter Catechism. In the latter the guilt of Adam's sin is the first element in the sinfulness of our lost estate. Following this (and as a penal consequence of this), are the want of original righteousness, and the corruption of the whole nature. It logically follows that guilt is the cause of depravity—depravity the consequence of guilt.

The fact noted above, that the catechism states more clearly the doctrine of imputation than does the confession may perhaps be accounted for by the fact, to which Principal Cunningham calls attention, that a year intervened between the completion of the Confession and that of the Catechisms. In that time the Westminster divines may have become familiar with the discussions on the Continent over the placean theory of "Mediate Imputation," and hence were led to make a more precise statement in the Catechisms. If this were the case it is another instance in which the formulated statement of a doctrine is modified into a more perfect form as a result of the closer examination brought about by controversy.

In this matter of our relation to Adam and the consequences resulting therefrom we have seen how the "Federal Scheme" enables us to deal with all the facts. This scheme, as found in the Scriptures and wrought into the Westminster Confession, enables us to clearly grasp and arrange into system all the facts and doctrines concerning the ruin in Adam and the redemption in Christ. Two great covenants, the first, that of works; the second, of grace, like the two pillars of Jachin and Boaz, stands at the door of the Temple of Truth, and through these we must pass in order to learn what we are to believe concerning anthropology and soteriology.

The development of Federal theology, and its articulate confessional statement, may be justly esteemed as the most important "modification" of "Original Calvinism" since the days of Calvin.

(3) The *Third* modification, of the first class, we may consider as having been developed in Scotland. This old land is the "Mother Country" of modern Presbyterianism. There have been sharp and protracted controversies regarding doctrine waged by Scottish theologians, and there have resulted therefrom some modifications in the matter and form of particular doctrines of the Calvinistic system.

In the limits I must observe I cannot undertake to treat of these in detail, even were I sufficiently informed to do the subject justice. I shall avail myself of some information furnished by Dr. James Orr, whom we have been privileged to have with us on this occasion, and who has favored us with an able and appreciated address.

In a magazine article in which he had specially in view to give some notes on the doctrinal position of the United Presbyterian Church, he outlines the various controversies that have been waged over doctrinal issues.

He says, "Our controversies move uniformly around two poles—the assertion of the sovereign grace of God in salvation, on one hand (including election to eternal life and the special bearing of the atonement of Christ on the saving of His own); and the assertion of the fulness and freeness of the proclamation of the gospel to sinners, on the other, on the ground of the deed of gift or grant of Christ to mankind—sinners, as such (a universal as well as a special aspect in Christ's atonement). The former side of doctrine comes from the general Calvinistic strain of the Westminster theology; the latter strives to a broader conception of the gospel than the Westminster Standards contain, and ultimately reaches it in the statements of our Declaratory Act of 1879." He adds, "It may be thought by some that the older and more distinctive note in our theology has been altogether left behind. That, we believe, is a mistake. Divested of the forms, and minute, and sometimes hair-splitting, distinctions in which our fathers invested it, the doctrine of sovereign grace in the calling, regeneration, and final salvation of a sinner—moving back, as this must do, on an eternal counsel of God in which it was embraced—is not to be got rid of, or expunged from our theology without serious impoverishment and harm. But even brighter than this in the testimony of our church shines its witness to the full, free, and unrestricted character of Christ's salvation, as based on the all-sufficiency of His atoning sacrifice, and the will of God gifting Him to mankind."

I will only note Dr. Orr's outline of the various stages of the controversy without attempting to embody his luminous statement of particulars under each head.

He says, "The course which controversy has followed as between these two poles of doctrine may be thus indicated:

(1) There was a struggle for the recognition of the freeness of the gospel message as based on the gift of men universally—to "mankind-sinners as such," as the phrase was.

(2) The next stage shows the other pole in the ascendant in the act against Arminian Errors, the object of which was to assert the special suretyship and relation of Christ in His death to His own people—that is to those whom God has given Him, and who are actually saved by His atonement.

(3) The third period is that of attempted adjustment of these two sides, with, again, a special prominence to the universal relation of Christ's work to mankind. This is the period of atonement controversies in the secession church, ending in the separation from the church of the Rev. James Morrison and his sympathizers (1841-3) and in the vindication of Drs. Balmer and Brown.

(4) The last stage is that of the definite triumph of the larger and more Scriptural view in the assertion (from which the church had hitherto held back), in the Declaratory Act of 1879, of the love of God to all mankind, His gift of His Son to be the propitiation for the sins of the whole world, and the free offer of salvation to men without distinction on the ground of Christ's perfect sacrifice. This may, as the article affirms, be in consistency with the church's earlier teaching, but the

truth had certainly (especially as regards the love) never been so fully or unambiguously expressed. The Act contains other adjustments, helping to bring the statements of the creed into fuller harmony with the living faith of the church."

It may be here remarked that controversies in our country have followed much the same lines as those indicated above, and the results have not been widely different. Our ministers, who accept the old Standards without any revision or Declaratory Statement, feel no hesitancy in extending "the free offer of salvation to men without distinction on the ground of Christ's perfect sacrifice," and they feel that they can do this "in consistency with the church's earlier teachings," and in harmony with "the living faith of the church" and of the greatest among Calvinistic theologians.

In years past there were protracted controversies concerning "limited atonement" and "general atonement," but the most staunch advocates of the first were ready to avow that Christ's sacrifice furnished the basis for a universal offer of salvation; while zealous champions of the second were free to admit that in the divine purpose are effectually called. Many of the differences were more verbal than essential. Each party looked too exclusively on *one* side of the shield.

Proceeding now to consider the second class of "modifications"—those which *modify* "original Calvinism," we will notice:

(1) *First,* the views advanced by the French theologians of the Saumur School.

I quote again from Dr. Warfield: "The first important modification of the Calvinistic system which has retained a position within its limits was made in the middle of the seventeenth century by the professors of the French School at Saumur, and is hence called Salmurianism of Amyraldism, or hypothetical universalism." Dr. Warfield has elsewhere remarked that "It is odd that all the modifications of Calvinism—if we include Pajon's views—had their expression at Saumur."

Two of the most noted professors of this school were Placeus and Amyraut. We have already taken note of the Placean theory of Mediate Imputation. Amyraut propounded the theory denominated "Hypothetical Universalism." The leading features of his scheme were that the motive impelling God to redeem men was benevolence, or love to men in general—that He sent His Son to make the salvation of all men possible—that salvation is offered to all men *if* they believe on Christ, and that all men have natural ability to repent and believe—but this ability is counteracted by a moral inability—and that out of the mass of depraved but redeemed men God determined to give efficacious, saving grace, to a certain number of the human race. The advocates of this view belong to the class of post-redemptionists.

Dr. Charles Hodge says of this scheme that, "It was designed to take a middle ground between Augustinianism and Arminianism, but that it is liable to the objections which press on both systems."

He also says that "this theory soon passed away as far as the Reformed Churches in Europe were concerned. Its advocates either returned to the old doctrine, or passed on to the more advanced system of the Arminians. In this country it has been reviewed and extensively adopted."

Dr. Hodge forcibly sets forth the objections to the scheme. Dr. Dabney suggests as a chief objection that

"It represents Christ as not purchasing for His people the grace of effectual calling, by which they are persuaded and enabled to embrace redemption, whereas Scripture represents that this gift, along with all other graces of redemption, is given us in Christ, having been purchased for His people by Him." Dr. Warfield says, "This modification received the condemnation of the contemporary reformed world."

I am treating somewhat at length this Saumurian view of redemption for the reason that "in this country it has been revived and extensively adopted," and that nearly "all the modifications of Calvinism find their expression at Saumur." It has been wrought into the New England and the Cumberland theology, which will later claim out attention.

In this, as in most unsound systems of doctrine, its chief dangerous tendency lies in the element of truth it contains. No system that is totally erroneous is to be feared. In this scheme God's universal benevolence is emphasized, and also the fact that the atoning sacrifice of Christ is sufficient for all the world. Now, God's general benevolence is not questioned by any, and neither Calvin nor any later Calvinist has doubted or denied that the merit of Christ's sacrifice is sufficient for all men, or that the offers of the gospel are to be made to every man. But according to the system under review, while all men are made salvable by the atoning death of Christ, it does not *make certain* the salvation of any. Calvinists of the straitest sect, like Dr. Shedd and Dr. Dabney, hold that Christ's satisfaction is unlimited in its sufficiency, but that its efficacious application is limited to those who are the subjects of "particular redemption." Dr. Dabney well says that "Had God elected all sinners there would have been no necessity to make Christ's atoning sacrifice essentially different. Remember, the limitation is precisely in the decree, and no where else. The vagueness and ambiguity of the term atonement has very much complicated the debate. This word is used sometimes for satisfaction for guilt, sometimes for the reconciliation ensuing therefrom, until men on both sides have forgotten the distinction. The one is cause; the other, effect. The only New Testament sense the word atonement has is that of *reconciliation.* But *expiation* is another idea. Expiation, in itself considered, has no more relation to one man's sin than another. As it is applied in effectual calling, it becomes personal, and receives a limitation. But in itself, limitation is irrelevant to it. Hence, when men use the word atonement, as they often do, in the sense of expiation, the phrases "limited atonement," "particular atonement" have no meaning. Redemption is limited, *i. e.,* to true believers, and is particular. Expiation is not limited."

To the same effect Dr. Shedd says: "*Atonement* must be distinguished from *redemption.* The latter term includes the *application* of the atonement. It is the term 'redemption,' not 'atonement,' which is found in those statements that speak of the work of Christ as limited by the decree of election." "The use of the term redemption is attended with less ambiguity than that of atonement, and it is the term most commonly employed in controversial theology. Atonement is unlimited, and redemption is limited."

These quotations are from the works of great "masters in Israel" who held and taught the Calvinism of the Reformed Confessions. The views they expressed are held in our Presbyterian Church to-day. We do not

Calvin in His Study.

believe, with those who have adopted or absorbed the Saumur theory, that Christ, by His expiatory death, merely made all men salvable, and that He had no special purpose to have any in particular. While we believe that His expiation is sufficient for all, it is efficient for the reconciliation (the at-one-ment) of the people given to Him, who, being the object of God's "everlasting love" have therefore with "loving-kindness" been drawn by efficacious grace to embrace Jesus Christ, freely offered to all men in the Gospel.

Thorough Calvinists, while gladly proclaiming that "whosoever will may come, and take of the water of life freely" do fully accept the doctrine that "the Lord Jesus, by His perfect obedience and sacrifice of Himself, hath fully satisfied the justice of His Father; and purchased not only reconciliation, but an everlasting inheritance in the kingdom of heaven, for all those whom the Father hath given unto Him." He not only makes their salvation possible, but "He *saves* His people from their sins"—not only from the penalty, but from the polution and the power of sin.

(2) The *Second* modification of this class is found in what is styled the New England Theology.

This name is given to theological tenets that have been widely accepted and given shape to the doctrinal views of many Presbyterians and Congregationalists in the United States.

The name is derived from the fact that the men who promulgated these tenets were New England divines.

"The term must be used in a sense sufficiently wide and vague to include different types of doctrine historically associated with various individual divines, and with the Andover, New Haven, and East Windsor (now Hartford) Schools." Many distinguished names are found among the advocates of this theology, among them, Edwards, Bellamy and Hopkins, "the great triumvirate," and in recent times, Leonard Woods, Lyman Beecher, Albert Barnes, N. W. Taylor and Edwards A. Park.

The principal tenets of this type of theology may be summarized as follows:

All the acts of God, even those which seem to be the sternest, are forms of infinite benevolence, and are reducible to a choice of the greatest and highest good of universal being. God is a sovereign, that is, He does what He chooses to do because His choice is infinite benevolence, securing the greatest and highest well-being of the universe.

Holiness and sin are not passive states, but they are acts of the will. They are free acts and imply that the agent's power to render obedience, and avoid disobedience to the moral law, is commensurate with his obligation to render the one and to avoid the other. Man's sinfulness is a consequence of Adam's apostasy. The sin of Adam is not literally "imputed" to us. We are not punished for it, although, on account of it, we suffer evils which represent God's abhorrence of sin, and signify His determination to inflict the legal penalty on those who persist in committing it. We, however, do not suffer a legal penalty for any sin which does not consist in our free choice.

"The term 'original sin' is not a favorite one with the New England theologians. It is entirely disapproved by one class of them, and is variously defined by other classes." As to the Atonement: the sufferings, and especially the death of Christ, were sacrificial; were not the penalty of law, but were equivalent to it; were representative of it, and substituted for it. The demands of the law were not satisfied by it, but the honor of the law was promoted by it as much as by the infliction of the legal penalty on the elect. The distributive justice of God was not satisfied by it, but His general justice was statisfied perfectly.

The atonement was designed for the welfare of all men; to make the salvation of all men possible; to remove all the obstacles which the honor of the law and distributive justice presented against the non-elect, as well as the elect. The atonement is useful on men's account, and in order to furnish new motives to holiness, but it is necessary on God's account to enable Him, as a consistent Ruler, to pardon any, even the smallest sin, and therefore to bestow on sinners any, even the smallest favor.

As to man's natural ability: Not without the *common* influence, but without the *supernatural* influence of God, a man has, in the proper sense of the word, the power to repent of his sin; but it is infallibly certain that he never will use this power in repenting. His natural ability does not lessen his dependence on the special interposition of the Holy Spirit for any, even the smallest degree of holiness.

It will be readily seen that this system is a "modification" of the Calvinism of the Reformed Confessions.

According to these views God did not *"for His own glory* fore-ordain whatsoever comes to pass," but had supreme regard to the "well-being of the universe." "This is the greatest happiness" theory.

In its Anthropology there is a decided slant towards Pelagianism; a denial of the sinfulness of states as well as of acts—a virtual acceptance of the dictum that "all sin consists in sinning," or in personal, voluntary transgression, and obligation is limited by ability.

The imputation of the guilt of Adam's sin is discarded, and it is fairly implied that the "consequences" of his fall come upon his posterity rather as calamities than as penal inflictions visited on us because we sinned in him and fell with him.

In this scheme the atonement is not strictly vicarious—Christ's death did not "fully satisfy the justice of His Father," nor "pay the debt we owe." We have rather the indefinite universalism of Amyraut, the "moral influence" theory of Abelard, and the "governmental theory" of Grotius. In the doctrine of the atonement "the life is in the blood," and the old, old story "satisfies our longings" because Christ "bore our sins in His own body on the tree," and hath "redeemed us to God by His blood."

(3.) The *Third* modification to be noted is in the Cumberland Presbyterian theology. This is invested with special interest because of the recent union of the Cumberland Presbyterian Church with the Presbyterian Church, U. S. A., and the doctrinal basis on which it was effected.

The Cumberland Presbyterian Church began its existence in A. D. 1810, with a single presbytery. A synod consisting of three presbyteries was formed in 1813, and a general assembly in 1829. A Confession of Faith was adopted by the synod in 1814, and this was revised and adopted by the general assembly in

1883. This Confession, as said by Dr. M. B. DeWitt, is "a modification of the Westminster Confession." It was an attempt, as in the case of the Saumur School, to find a middle ground between Calvinism and Arminianism—to introduce a "Medium Theology.' That it did "modify" the old Confession is easily discovered by reference to the teachings concerning the Decrees of God, the Covenant of Grace, the work of Christ, the Mediator, Divine Influence (substituted for Effectual Calling), Repentance, Faith, and Regeneration.

While this was a Presbyterian Church, it was not Calvinistic, as is evidenced not only by its Confession, but also by the testimony of competent men within and without its fold. Dr. A. B. Miller, a distinguished Cumberland Presbyterian minister, wrote: "Nothing that can be said negatively of the doctrinal system of the Cumberland Presbyterian Church is more true or more characteristic of it than that it is un-Calvinistic." Again he says: "The Confession, as adopted in 1829, and still more fully as revised in 1883, is in irreconcilable antagonism to the obvious and historic sense of the Westminster Confession." Dr. W. H. Roberts, in 1889, in a carefully prepared paper, said of the Cumberlanders: "Presbyterians in government they are, but Calvinists in doctrine they are not." In the same paper he designates them as a "distinctly Arminian body," and that "Cumberland revision led inevitably to Arminianism."

Dr. F. R. Beattie said of the Cumberland Presbyterian Church that "It modified the doctrine of the Confession in regard to predestination, so as to become virtually Arminian; while it retains a Presbyterian polity. It is really an Arminian Presbyterian Church."

Dr. B. B. Warfield, in his able discussion of the revision of the Confession, A. D. 1903, speaks of the historically Cumberland view as "the distinctive Arminian view"; and in reference to the "Supplemental Report" of the Cumberland committee he says: "Whatever else this document leaves obscure, or does its best to obscure, this at least it makes clear: that the Cumberland Presbyterian Church is Arminian to the core—that is to say, so far as it is represented by this representative document."

These testimonies as to the unCalvinistic character of the Cumberland Presbyterian Confession are of special interest in view of history that has been made since 1903. Up to that time, in large sections of our country, as in the State in which it has been my lot to labor in the ministry for more than fifty years, the Cumberland and our "old Presbyterian" Churches existed side by side. They, and we, recognized the fact that we did not hold the same beliefs—that our churches were separated by distinct doctrinal lines, marked out in our respective Confessions of Faith. Yet we worked, and preached, and prayed together in Christian fellowship, "agreeing to disagree" in the points which separated us, and "endeavoring to keep the unity of the Spirit in the bond of peace." But we are now confronted with a changed condition. In the year 1903 the Presbyterian Church, U. S. A., adopted a revision of the Confession together with a Declaratory Statement, and two additional chapters. The large and able committee which prepared these, acted under the instruction that "the revision should in no way impair the integrity of the system of doctrine set forth in the Confession, and taught in the Holy Scriptures."

I am one of those who believe that the committee kept within the bounds assigned. While I must say, in candor, that I do not think the revision was needed or helpful, yet I agree with those who have contended that it did not materially "impair the integrity of the system of doctrine set forth in the Confession."

But later developments have given special interest to this revision. In the year of its adoption, 1903, negotiations were set on foot looking to a union of the U. S. A. Church with the Cumberland Presbyterian Church. After full consideration, and observance of all the required preliminaries, the union was effected on a basis mutually agreed upon, and in 1906 the two assemblies formally announced the consummation.

This union was effected on "the doctrinal basis of the Confession of Faith of the Presbyterian Church, U. S. A., as revised in 1903, and of its other doctrinal and ecclesiastical standards," with acknowledgment of the Scriptures as the only infallible rule of faith and practice.

A series of Concurrent Resolutions were also adopted, in the first of which it was declared that "in adopting the Confession, as revised in 1903, it is mutually recognized that such agreement now exists between the systems of doctrine contained in the Confessions of the two churches as to warrant this union— a union honoring alike to both." It was also recognized that liberty of belief exists by virtue of the Declaratory Statement, which is part of the Confession of Faith of the Presbyterian Church, U. S. A., and which states that the ordination vows of ministers, elders, and deacons requires the reception and adoption of the Confession only as containing the system of doctrine taught in the Holy Scriptures. This liberty is specifically secured by the Declaratory Statement as to Chap. III, and Chap. X, Sec. 3, of the Confession. It was also recognized that the doctrinal deliverance contained in the Brief Statement of the Reformed Faith, adopted by the General Assembly, U. S. A., in 1902, reveals a doctrinal agreement favorable to reunion."

In a final deliverance by the assembly in 1906, after reciting the language concerning liberty of subscription, it is asserted that "inasmuch as the two assemblies meeting in 1904 did declare that there was then a sufficient agreement in the systems of doctrine contained in the Confessions of the two churches to warrant the union of the churches, therefore the change of doctrinal Standards resulting from the union involves no change of belief on the part of any who were ministers, ruling elders, or deacons in the Cumberland Presbyterian Church."

I have adduced this record because in treating the subject assigned me I have felt obligated to note the historical facts recited. I feel that it is a delicate task to deal with these matters of such recent date, and in which the parties are contemporary and fellow-laborers with ourselves. The facts involved are these:

(a) The Cumberland Confession, in the judgment of men who accept it and of others, is not Calvinistic.

(b.) The revision by the U. S. A. Presbyterian Church, it was claimed, did not impair the integrity of their system of doctrine;

(c.) Yet, that church and the Cumberland concurred in a declaration that between the two churches such agreement *now* exists as to warrant a union.

(d.) When the union had been effected the Assembly declared that it involved no change of belief on the part of Cumberland Presbyterian ministers, elders, and deacons, and this implies, of course, the liberty to teach and preach the doctrines of the Cumberland Presbyterian Confession, as heretofore.

We are now confronted by this condition: A great number of ministers and churches have been suddenly transformed from Cumberland Presbyterians to U. S. A. Presbyterians; adopting the Westminster Confession, but at liberty to hold and disseminate the teachings of the Confession to which they had formerly subscribed.

It is not my purpose or desire to criticize unkindly the action of the U. S. A. Presbyterian Church in receiving those other brethren into their fold on the basis on which the union was effected, or to discuss the concessions they found themselves willing to make. They had a right to judge of the propriety of the course they thought it best to pursue, and to put their estimate on the Cumberland Standards and to judge of their conformity to their own.

Yet I feel warranted in saying that in my humble judgment. in this recent transaction with the accompanying deliverances, there is one of the most serious and far-reaching modifications of the Calvinistic system of doctrine of which history takes account.

For the people, and the ministry, and the splendid work of the Presbyterian Church, U. S. A., we of the Southern Church have no feeling other than fraternal and cordial esteem. It is a great body of Presbyterians, the largest in the world. Among its trusted leaders there are many men whom we delight to honor.

Dr. Patton and Dr. Warfield are great defenders of the faith, and we count their names worthy to be "writ large" in the same column with those of our own illustrious Thornwell and our colossal Dabney. On this occasion another of their distinguished men, Dr. H. C. Minton, has been one of our guests of honor, and he has favored us with an address which in its grasp of a great theme, displayed the hand of a master; in language and style it was as elegant as Macaulay's, and in delivery superbly eloquent. It is worthy of an honored place among the classic gems of Calvinistic literature.

In speaking of the course pursued by the great Church in which these honored brethren are standard bearers, if I have "nothing extenuated" in the recital of historic facts, I am unconscious of having "set down aught in malice."

And now, Moderator, and brethren, I thank you for the patient attention you have given to this long address. I can only plead in apology for its length that the subject assigned me was exceeding large. It is no light requirement to trace the course of theological thought through a period of four hundred years. At last, my task, however inperfectly, is done.

This Assembly, notable by reason of the Calvin celebration, is nearing its closing session. I trust that we may go hence with hearts inspired by a larger reverence for the great man whose character and work have been kept before us during these busy sessions, and that we will hold with a grip that knows no weakening, the System of doctrine contained in that old Confession which, in these days of change, our Church retains without a revision of its statements or modification of its articles of faith. In no spirit of vain-glory we may assert the claim that this Confessional System of doctrine best agrees with the teachings of Scripture, the dictates of reason, the testimony of consciousness, and the facts of history. It solves more questions, it involves fewer difficulties it gives more solid ground for faith and hope, and it more exalts and glorifies God, than any doctrine which contradicts it. It is the doctrine emblazoned on the banner that has been borne in the forefront of God's Sacramental host in the days of the Church's most glorious history; it has ever strengthened the missionary and sustained the martyr; it has made strong the hands of God's battling heroes and inspired with hope the hearts of His suffering saints.

This doctrinal banner will be the rallying center for an ever-increasing number of the soldiers of the cross, and the song of which it has been the sentiment, will be sung, although mid toils and tears, until the song and the singers become a part of the worship and the worshippers when the host of the redeemed shall, with the voice of a great multitude, and as the voice of many waters, and as the voice of mighty thunderings, sing:

Alleluia: for the Lord God Omnipotent reigneth!

PRESENT DAY ATTITUDE TO CALVINISM.

Rev. Benj. B. Warfied, D. D., LL. D.,
Princeton Theological Seminary.

The subject upon which I am to address you involves the determination of a matter of fact, about which it is not easy to feel fully assured. What is the present-day attitude towards Calvinism? The answer to this question is apt to vary with the point of sight of the observer, or rather with the horizon which his eye surveys.

Our learning to-day is "made in Germany," our culture comes to us largely from England. And the German learning of the day has a sadly rationalistic tendency ; which is superposed, moreover, on a Lutheran foundation that has an odd way of cropping up and protruding itself in unexpected places. Similarly, English culture is not merely shot through, but stained through and through, with an Anglican coloring. Lutheranism was ever intolerant of Calvinism. Anglicanism was certainly never patient of it. Naturalism is its precise contradictory. He who breathes the atmosphere of books, therefore,—whether books of erudition, or books of pure literature—is apt to find it stifling to his Calvinism.

There is, of course, another side of the matter. There are very likely more Calvinists in the world to-day than ever before. Even relatively, the professedly

Calvinistic churches are, no doubt, holding their own. There are important tendencies of modern thought which play into the hands of this or that Calvinistic conception. Above all, there are to be found everywhere humble souls, who, in the quiet of retired lives, have caught a vision of God in his glory, and are cherishing in their hearts that vital flame of complete dependence on him which is the very essence of Calvinism.

On the whole, however, I think we must allow, especially when we are contemplating the trend of current thought, that the fortunes of Calvinism are not at their flood. Those whose heritage it was, have in large numbers drifted away from it. Those who still formerly profess it, do not always illustrate it in life or proclaim it in word. Are there any "Calvinists without reserve" left among the acknowledged leaders, at least, of French-speaking Christendom, blood of whose blood and bone of whose bone Calvin himself was? Outside of the little band of the followers of H. M. Kohlbrügge, are there any left throughout the broad stretches of those German lands in which Calvinism was once able to give so good an account of itself? Even in Scotland, we have been told by Dr. Hastie that, so far as the greater churches are concerned, the race of Calvinists, of strict construction at least, practically died out with William Cunningham and Thomas J. Crawford. Happily in sturdy little Holland, amid wide-spread blight, there is still a fruitful stock, and the Free Churches of the Netherlands especially show yet a vigorous Calvinistic life: they possess to-day, in fact, in Abraham Kuyper and Herman Bavinck, a theologian of genius and a theologian of erudition worthy of the best traditions of Holland's great past. Here in America, the impulse received from the great teachers who illuminated the middle of the nineteenth century—Charles Hodge, Robert J. Breckinridge, James H. Thornwell, Henry Boynton Smith, William G. T. Shedd, Robert L. Dabney, Archibald Alexander Hodge—I enumerate them in chronological order—we are thankful to say is not yet exhausted. There remains, then, undoubtedly a remnant according to the election of grace. But the condition of a remnant, while it may well be a healthful one—bearing in it, as a fruitful seed, the promise and potency of future expansion—is little likely to be a happy one. Unfriendly faces meet it on every side; if doubt and hesitation are not engendered, at least an apologetical attitude is fostered; and an apologetical attitude is not becoming in Calvinists, whose trust is in the Lord God Almighty. In such a situation Calvinism seems shorn of its strength, and is tempted to stand fearful and half ashamed in the marts of men. I have no wish to paint the situation in too dark colors. I fully believe that Calvinism, as it has supplied the sinews of evangelical Christianity in the past, so is its strength in the present, and is its hope for the future. Meanwhile, does it not seem, in large circles at all events, to be thrown very much on the defensive? In the measure in which you feel this to be the case, in that measure you will be prepared to ask with me for the causes and significance of this state of things.

We should begin, I think, by recalling precisely what Calvinism is. It may be fairly summed up, I suppose, in these three propositions: Calvinism is theism come to its rights. Calvinism is religion at the height of its conception. Calvinism is evangelicalism in its purest and most stable expression.

Calvinism, I say, is theism come to its rights. For in what does theism come to its rights but in teleological view of the universe? For, though there be that are called gods, whether in heaven or on earth,—as there are gods many and lords many conceived of men—yet to the theist, there can be but one God, of whom are all things and unto whom are all things. You see, we have already slipped into the Calvinistic formula: The will of God is the cause of things. I do not say, you will observe, that theism and Calvinism have points of affinity, lie close to one another: I say they are identical. I say that the theism which is truly theism, consistently theism, all that theism to be really theism must be, is already in principle Calvinism; that Calvinism in its cosmological aspect is nothing more than theism in its purity. To fall away from Calvinism, is to fall away by just so much from a truly theistic conception of the universe. Of course, then, to fall away in any degree from a pure theism in our conception of things is just by that much to fall away from Calvinism. Wherever, then, in our view of the world an imperfect theism has crept in, there Calvinism has become impossible.

Calvinism, I have said, again, is religion at the height of its conception. For whatever else may enter the conscious religious relation,—a vague feeling of mystery, a struggling reaching out towards the infinite, a deep sentiment of reverence and awe, a keen recognition or dull apprehension of responsibility,—certainly its substance lies in a sense of absolute dependence upon a supreme being. I do not say, you will observe, an absolute feeling of dependence, which in the Schleiermacheran meaning, at least, of a feeling without intellectual content, were an absurdity. What I say is, that religion in its substance is a sense of absolute dependence on God, and reaches the height of its conception only when this sense of absolute dependence is complete and all pervasive, in the thought and feeling and life. But, when this stage is reached, we have just Calvinism. For what is Calvinism but the thetical expression of religion, conceived as absolute dependence on God? Wherever we find religion in its purity, therefore, there Calvinism is implicit. I do not say, observe again, that an approach to Calvinism is traceable there, in less or greater measure. I say, there Calvinism is,—implicitly indeed, but really—present. Religion in its purity is Calvinism in life; and you can fall away from Calvinism only by just in that measure falling away from religion, and you do fall away from Calvinism just in proportion as you fall away from religion in its purity.

It is, however, dreadfully easy to fall away from religion at the height of its conception. We may assume the truly religious attitude of heart and mind for a moment; it is hard to maintain it and give it unbroken dominance in our thought, feeling and action. Our soul's attitude in prayer,—that is the religious attitude at its height. But do we preserve the attitude we assume towards God in prayer when we rise from our knees? Or does our "amen" cut it off at once, and we go on about our affairs in an entirely different mood? Now, Calvinism means just the preservation in all our thinking and feeling and action of that attitude of utter dependence on God which we assume in prayer. It is the mood of religion made determinative of all our thinking and feeling and willing. It is accordingly conterminous with religion in the height of its conception. Wherever, therefore, religion in any measure loses hold of the reins of life and our immanent thought has slipped away from its control,— there Calvinism has become impossible.

I have said again, Calvinism is evangelicalism in its pure and only stable expression. When we say evangelicalism, we say sin and salvation. Evangelicalism is a soteriological conception: it implies sin and salvation from sin. There may be religion without evangelicalism. We may go further: religion might conceivably exist at the height of its conception, and evangelicalism be lacking. But not in sinners. Evangelicalism is religion at the height of its conception as it forms itself in the hearts of sinners. It means utter dependence on God for salvation; it implies, therefore, need of salvation, and a profound sense of this need, along with an equally profound sense of helplessness in the presence of this need, and utter dependence on God for its satisfaction. Its type is found in the publican, who smote his breast and cried, "God be merciful to me a sinner!" No question there of saving himself, of helping God to save him, or of opening the way to God to save him; no question of anything, but, I am a sinner, and all my hope is in God my Saviour! Now this is Calvinism; not, note once more, something like Calvinism or an approach to Calvinism, but just Calvinism in its vital manifestation. Wherever this attitude of heart is found and is given expression in direct and unambiguous terms, there is Calvinism.

Wherever this attitude of mind and heart is fallen away from in however small a measure, there Calvinism has become impossible.

For Calvinism, in this soteriological aspect of it, is just the perception and the thetical expression and defense of the utter dependence of the soul on the free grace of God for salvation. All its so-called hard features—its doctrine of original sin; yes, speak it right out, its doctrine of total depravity and the entire inability of the sinful will to good; its doctrine of election; or, put it in the words everywhere spoken against, its doctrine of predestination and preterition, or reprobation itself—mean just this and nothing more. Calvinism will not play fast and loose with the free grace of God; it is set upon giving to God and to God alone, the glory and all the glory of salvation. There are others than Calvinists, no doubt, who would fain make the same great confession. But they make it with reserves; or they painfully justify the making of it by some tenuous theory which confuses nature and grace. They leave logical pitfalls on this side or that; and the difference between logical pitfalls and other pitfalls is that the wayfarer may fall into the others, but the plain man, just because his is a simple mind, must fall into these. Calvinism will leave no logical pitfalls; and will make no reserves; and will have nothing to do with theories whose function it is to explain away facts. It confesses with a heart full of adoring gratitude that to God and to God alone belongs salvation and the whole of salvation; that he it is and he alone who works salvation in its whole reach. Any falling away in the slightest measure from this great confession is to fall away from Calvinism. Any intrusion of any human merit, or act, or disposition, or power, as ground or cause or occasion, into the process of divine salvation,—whether in the way of capacity to resist or ability to improve grace—of the opening of the way to the reception of grace, or of the employment of grace already received—is a breach with Calvinism. Calvinism is the casting of the soul wholly on the free grace of God alone, to whom alone belongs salvation.

Such is the nature of Calvinism. And such being the nature of Calvinism it seems scarcely necessary to inquire why its fortunes appear from time to time, and now again in our time, to suffer some depression. It can no more perish out of the earth than the sense of sin can pass out of the heart of sinful humanity; than the perception of God can fade out of the minds of dependent creatures; than God himself can perish out of the heavens. Its fortunes are bound up with the fortunes of theism, religion, evangelicalism; for it is just theism, religion, evangelicalism in the purity of their conception and manifestation. In the *purity* of their conception and manifestation! There is the seat of the difficulty. It is proverbially hard to retain, much more to maintain, perfection. And how can precisely these things be maintained at their height? Consider the currents of thought flowing up and down in the world, tending—I do not now say to obliterate the perception of the God of all: atheistic naturalism, materialistic or pantheistic evolutionism—but to blunt or obscure our perception of the divine hand in the sequence of events and the issues of things. Consider the pride of man, his assertion of freedom, his boast of power, his refusal to acknowledge the sway of another's will. Consider the ingrained confidence of the sinner in his own fundamentally good nature and his full ability to perform all that can be justly demanded of him. Is it strange that in this world—in this particular age of this world—it should prove difficult to preserve not only active, but vivid and dominant, the perception of the everywhere determining hand of God, the sense of absolute dependence on him, the conviction of utter inability to do even the least thing to rescue ourselves from sin—at the height of their conception? Is it not enough to account for whatever depression Calvinism may be suffering in the world to-day, to point to the natural difficulty in this materialistic age,—conscious of its newly realized powers over against the forces of nature and filled with the pride of achievement and of material well-being,—of guarding our perception of the governing hand of God in all things in its perfection, maintaining our sense of dependence on a higher power in full force, and preserving our feeling of sin, unworthiness and helplessness in its profundity? Is not the significance of the depression of Calvinism, so far as it is real, then, merely that to our age the vision of God has become somewhat obscured in the midst of abounding material triumphs, the religious emotion has in some measure ceased to be the determining force in life, and the evangelical attitude of complete dependence on God for salvation does not readily commend itself to men who are accustomed to lay forceful hands on everything else they wish and do not quite see why they may not take heaven also by storm?

Such suggestions may seem to you rather general, perhaps even somewhat indefinite. They appear to me nevertheless to embody the true, and the whole, account of whatever depression of fortunes Calvinism may be suffering to-day. In our current philosophies, whether monistic evolutionism or pluralistic pragmatism, theism is far from coming to its rights. In the strenuous activities of our materialized life, religion has little opportunity to assert itself in its purity. In our restless assertion of our personal power and worth evangelicalism easily falls into the background. In an atmosphere created by such a state of things, how could Calvinism thrive? We may, of course, press on to a more specific account of its depressed fortunes. But in attempting to be more specific, what can we do but single out particular aspects of the general situation for special remark? It is possible, indeed, that the singling out of one of these aspects may give clearness and point to the general fact. It may be worth while, therefore, to attend to one of these special aspects for a moment.

Let us observe this, then—that Calvinism is only another name for consistent supernaturalism in religion. The central fact of Calvinism is the vision of God. Its determining principle is zeal for the divine honor. What it sets itself to do is to render to God his rights in every sphere of life-activity. In this it begins and centers and ends. It is this that is said when it is said that it is theism come to its rights, since then everything that comes to pass is viewed as the direct outworking of the divine purpose; that it is religion at the height of its conception, since then God is consciously felt as him in whom we live and move and have our being; that it is evangelicalism in its purity, since then we cast ourselves as sinners, without reserve, wholly on the mercy of the divine grace. It is this sense of God, of God's presence, of God's power, of God's all-pervading activity—most of all in the process of salvation—which constitutes Calvinism. When the Calvinist gazes into the mirror of the world, whether the world of nature or the world of events, his attention is held not by the mirror itself (with the cunning construction of which scientific investigators may no doubt very properly busy themselves) but by the Face of God which he sees reflected therein. When the Calvinist contemplates the religious life, he is less concerned with the psychological nature and relations of the emotions which surge through the soul (with which the votaries of the new science of the psychology of religion are perhaps not wholly unfruitfully engaging themselves) than with the divine source from which they spring, the divine object of which they take hold. When the Calvinist considers the state of his soul and the possibility of its rescue from death and sin, he may not indeed be blind to the responses which it may by the grace of God be enabled to make to the divine grace, but he absorbs himself not in them but in it, and sees in every step of his recovery to good and to God the almighty working of God's grace. The Calvinist in a word is the man who sees God: he has caught sight of the ineffable Vision, and he will not let it fade a moment from his eyes. God in nature, God in history, God in grace; everywhere he sees God in his mighty stepping, everywhere he feels the working of his mighty arm, the throbbing of his mighty heart. The Calvinist is, therefore, by way of eminence the supernaturalist in the world of thought. The world itself is to him a supernatural product; not merely in the sense that somewhere, away back before all time, God made it; but that God is making it now and in every event that falls out, in every modification of what is that takes place, his hand is visible, as through all occurrences his one increasing purpose runs. Man himself is his, created for his glory, and having as the one supreme end of his existence to glorify his Maker, and haply also to enjoy him forever. And salvation in every step and stage of it is of God. Conceived in God's love, wrought out by God's own Son, in a supernatural life and death in this world of sin, and applied by God's Spirit in a series of acts as supernatural as the virgin-birth and the resurrection of the Son of God themselves, it is a supernatural work through and through. To the Calvinist thus the church of God is as direct a creation of God as the first creation itself. In this supernaturalism, the whole thought and feeling and life of the Calvinist is steeped. Without it there can be no Calvinism: for it is just this that is Calvinism.

Now the age in which we live is anything but supernaturalistic. It is distinctly hostile to supernaturalism. Its most striking characteristic is precisely its deeply rooted and wide-reaching naturalism of thought and sentiment. We know the origin of this modern naturalism; we can trace its history. What it is of more importance to observe, however, is that we cannot escape its influence. On its rise in the latter part of the seventeenth century, a new era began, an era in which men have had little thought for the rights of God in their absorption in the rights of man. English deism, French encyclopedism, German illuminism—

these are some of the fruits it has borne in the progress of its development; and now it has at length run to seed in our own day in what arrogates to itself the name of the New Protestantism—that New Protestantism which repudiates Luther and all his fervid ways and turns rather for its spiritual parentage to the religious indifferentism of Erasmus. It has invaded with its solvent every form of thought and every activity of life. It has given us a naturalistic philosophy (in which all being is evaporated into becoming), a naturalistic science (the single-minded zeal of which is to eliminate design from the universe), a naturalistic politics (the first fruits of which was the French Revolution, and its last may well be an atheistic socialism), a naturalistic history (which can scarcely find place for even human personality among the causes of events), and a naturalistic religion which says "Hands off!" to God, if indeed it troubles itself to consider whether there be a God, or if there be a God whether he be a person, or if he be a person, whether he can or will concern himself with men.

You, as ministers of the gospel, have been greatly clogged in the prosecution of your calling by this naturalism of current thought. How many of those to whom you would carry the message of grace, do you find preoccupied with a naturalistic prejudice! Who of your acquaintance really posits God as a factor in the development of the world? How often have you been exhorted to seek a "natural" progress for the course of events in history? Yes, even for the history of redemption. So, even in the region of your own theological science, a new Bible has been given to you; not offered to you merely, but violently thrust upon you as the only Bible a rational man can receive,—a new Bible reconstructed on the principle of natural development, torn to pieces and rearranged under the overmastering impulse to find a "natural" order of sequence for its books, and a "natural" course of development for the religion whose records it preserves. But why stop with the Bible? Your divine Redeemer himself has been reconstructed on the same naturalistic lines. For a century and a half now,—from Reimarus to Wrede—all the resources of an age pre-eminent for scholarship have been bent to the task of giving you a "natural" Jesus. Why talk here of the miracles of the Old Testament or of the New? It is the Miracle of the Old Testament and the New which is really brought into question. Why dispute as to the virgin-birth and the resurrection of Jesus? It is to the elimination of Jesus himself, as aught but a simple man of his day, in nothing, except perhaps an unusually vivid religious experience, differentiated from other Galilæan peasants of his time, that the naturalistic frenzy of our age is set upon. And so furiously has the task been driven on that the choice that is set before us at the end of the day is practically between no Jesus at all, or a fanatic, not to say a paranoiac, Jesus. In this anti-supernaturalistic atmosphere, is it strange that men find the pure supernaturalism of the Calvinistic confession difficult, —that they waver in their firm confidence that it is God who reigns in heaven and on earth, that in him we all live and move and have our being, that it is he and not ourselves who creates in us every impulse to good, and that it is his almighty arm alone that can rescue us from sin and bring to our helpless souls salvation? Is it strange that here too men travel the broad road beaten smooth by many feet, and the Calvinistic gate seems so narrow that few there be that find it, and the Calvinistic way so straitened that few there be who go in thereat?

But let us make no mistake here. For here too Calvinism is just Christianity. The supernaturalism for which Calvinism stands is the very breath of the nostrils of Christianity: without it Christianity cannot exist. And let us not imagine that we can pick and choose with respect to the aspects of this supernaturalism which we acknowledge. That we may, for example, retain supernaturalism, in the origination of Christianity, and forego the supernaturalism with which Calvinism is more immediately concerned,—the supernaturalism of the application of Christianity. Men will not believe that a religion the actual working of which in the world is natural, can have required to be ushered into the world with supernatural pomp and display. These supernaturals stand or fall together. A supernatural Redeemer is not needed for a natural salvation: if we can and do save ourselves, it were grossly incongruous that God should come down from heaven to save us, trailing clouds of glory with him as he came. The logic of the Socinian system gave us at once a human Christ and an autosoteric religion. The same logic will work to-day, and every day till the end of time. It is only for a truly supernatural salvation that a truly supernatural redemption, or a truly supernatural Redeemer is demanded—or can be believed in.

And this reveals to us the real place which Calvinism holds in the controversies of to-day, and the service it is to render in the preservation of Christianity for the future. Only the Calvinist is the consistent supernaturalist: and only consistent supernaturalism can save supernatural religion for the world. The supernatural fact, which is God; the supernatural act, which is miracle; the supernatural book, which is the revealed will of God; the supernatural redemption, which is the divine deed of the divine Christ; the supernatural salvation, which is the divine work of the divine Spirit,—these things form a system, and you cannot draw one item out without shaking the whole. What Calvinism particularly asserts is the supernaturalism of salvation, as the immediate work of God the Holy Spirit in the soul, by virtue of which we are made new creatures in Christ our Redeemer and framed into the sons of God the Father. And it is only he that heartily believes in this supernaturalism of salvation who is not fatally handicapped in meeting the assaults of that anti-supernaturalistic world-view which flaunts itself so triumphantly about us. Conceal it from ourselves as we may, defeat here lies athwart the path of all half-hearted scemes and compromising constructions. This is what was meant by the late Dr. Henry Boynton Smith, when he declared roundly: "One thing is certain,—that infidel science will rout everything excepting thoroughgoing Christian orthodoxy. The fight will be between a stiff thoroughgoing orthodoxy and a stiff thoroughgoing infidelity. It will be, for example, Augustine or Comte, Athanasius or Hegel, Luther or Schopenhauer, J. S. Mill or John Calvin."

This witness is true. We cannot be supernaturalistic in patches of our thinking, and naturalistic in its substance. We cannot be supernaturalistic with regard to the remote facts of history and naturalistic with regard to the intimate events of experience. We cannot be supernaturalistic with regard to what occurred two thousand years ago in Palestine, and simply naturalistic with regard to what occurs to-day in our hearts. No form of Christian supernaturalism can be ultimately maintained, in any department of life or thought, except it carry with it the supernaturalism of salvation, and a consistent supernaturalism of salvation is only another name for Calvinism. Calvinism thus emerges to our sight as nothing more or less than the hope of the world.

HOW MAY THE PRINCIPLES OF CALVINISM BE RENDERED MOST EFFECTIVE UNDER MODERN CONDITIONS?

By A. M. Fraser,
Staunton, Virginia.

The task assigned to me is constructive and practical. It is not explanatory, nor historical, nor apologetic. I am not asked to tell what Calvinism is, nor to relate what it has done, nor to prove that it is true. While I may refer to these themes in the course of my remarks, my main purpose is different. Accepting Calvinism as we find it, assuming that it is true, noting what is peculiar and dominant in modern conditions, forecasting the future as best we may, I am asked to suggest a way by which that system of truth which has wrought mightily in the past may so adjust itself to these modern conditions as to yield the best results.

My diffidence in this undertaking is increased by the thought that in this question the entire Calvin celebration culminates. A mere sentimental celebration of the past is alien to the spirit of Calvinism, which seeks only to glorify God and serve humanity. If, therefore, our review of the past does not yield a substantial contribution to the present, the celebration will so far have failed of its object.

It will aid our efforts to solve this difficult problem if we can get a fuller interpretation of the question proposed, "How May the Principles of Calvinism be Rendered Most Effective Under Modern Conditions?" What are the "Modern Conditions" referred to? What is meant by "the Principles of Calvinism"? What is intended by making them "effective"; or, in other words, what is the "effect" which it is desired that Calvinism shall produce? Let us then, as a preparation for the main question, first consider these three preliminary ones.

I. What are the "Modern Conditions" referred to? What is there in the present attitude of thought and life that distinguishes this age from other ages in which Calvinism has won its victories and done its work?

1. The first of these I would mention is the materialistic tendency of Natural Science. Natural Science proceeds upon the correct principle that it must concern itself only with observed and recorded facts and with those theories which may reasonably be deduced from such facts, and that moreover it must confine itself to those facts which are perceived through the senses. But the phenomena of spirit not being cognizable by the senses, those phenomena are not properly within the purview of Natural Science. Just here two dangers emerge. The exclusive absorption of the attention with material facts leads to the ignoring of those other spiritual facts which are the proper subjects of another science, and so there results a one-sided development of thought. Or else, departing from its own guiding principle to confine itself to its own established facts, Natural Science draws inferences and makes confident assertions concerning spiritual phenomena, which confessedly it does not and cannot observe. Consequently it neglects God and Spirit or denies the existence of either.

This science, not always equally materialistic, but always with a powerful tendency in that direction, holds a commanding and ascending position in the schools. It is fascinating to the young, it colors literature, it controls the practical arts, and in a circle far wider than that in which its facts are known, it causes a feeling of uneasiness lest the foundations of the faith have been shaken.

2. Another factor of the modern situation is the destructive criticism of the Bible. The postulate of a divinely inspired, infallible, sufficient revelation from God is essential to Christianity. The Bible is valuable not merely because it contains a revelation of God, for in a measure natural theology might take the place of that. Nor is it valuable merely because it contains the purest and most correct system of ethics, for in a measure moral philosophy might supply the deficiency there. The Bible is distinguished in that it offers a scheme for the forgiveness of sin, and in that it tells how good morals may be achieved and spiritual life acquired. In this, it is not to be classed with other religious books and flattered as the best of books. Its position is unique and transcendant. It is "the Book."

Modern criticism begins by denying or discrediting the possibility of a supernatural origin for the Bible. Proceeding with a learning that is not always the pledge of wisdom, with an ingenuity that is too often divorced from discretion, and with an industry which "the children of light" would do well to emulate, it subjects every word of the sacred volume to a merciless manipulation and it ransacks the archives of all the ages and the places mentioned in the Bible in the effort to prove a purely natural and human origin for it. Not abashed by its experience in the past, in which similar results, reached by similar methods, have been ignominiously overthrown by fuller knowledge, and in favor of historic Christianity, it continues to proclaim its conclusions with a confidence that intimidates all those who have not equal learning and better judgment, or who have not the inward and incontestable witness of the Spirit.

3. Another obtrusive fact in the confusion of modern conditions is the prevalence and growth of Socialism, whether as an economic, ethical, or religious theory. The goal of Socialism is a state of society in which there shall be something approaching an equal distribution among men of the enjoyment of the world's wealth. Sometimes this is advocated as a policy of statesmanship, and so it is economic in its character. Sometimes it is urged as the dictate of justice, and so is ethical. Sometimes it is claimed to be an inference from the universal brotherhood of man as taught in the Bible, and so it becomes religious. Socialism is fostered, on the one hand, by some of the most generous impulses of the human heart, drawn out into active expression by beautiful visions of self sacrifice and of a universal betterment of humanity. It is fostered, on the other hand, by some of the most powerful and dangerous forces of human nature, the hunger, the nakedness, the suffering, the sense of wrong of an oppressed and intelligent poverty, provoked and aggravated by the surfeiting and waste, the pride and tyranny, the vulgar display and even the religious professions of wealth. There may have been as much poverty in the world before as there is to-day, and as much dense crowding and unhappiness of the poor. There may have been as much arrogance and coldness and cruelty of wealth. But never before

have these conditions been accompanied by such intelligence of the poor, caused by free education, free speech, and marvellously cheapened literature. One result of all this is a startling attitude towards religion—an admiration, amounting almost to reverence, for Jesus of Nazareth, but an envenomed hostility to the church.

4. Another modern movement with which Calvinism must reckon is a nascent civilization in the Far East. In China and Japan and Korea there are kindred races comprising more than one-fourth of the human family. They occupy lands opulent in those natural resources by which great nations may be sustained. They are characterized by a virile personality and an intelligence of the highest order that has lain fallow and has gathered substance through many ages. At a single vault they leap into the arena of the great nations of the world. At once they master all the domain of knowledge which the West had laboriously acquired through centuries. In fifty years, "a cycle of Europe" is acquired by Cathay. They awake to the consciousness of undeveloped power. They not only challenge the prestige of western powers, but, breaking with their own paganism, are ready to embrace Christianity or "modernism," whichever shall first arrest their attention and win their allegiance. If Christianity is embraced, millenial conditions are accelerated, but if they choose modernism, the redemption of the world is indefinitely postponed.

5. Another feature of the modern world which demands the attention of the church, though it is exceptional in this age only in the degree and manner of its self assertion, is sensuality. When we consider the brazen immoralities of that which calls itself "high so-

ciety," and its impudent defiance of most sacred institutions and conventionalities; when we think of the growing pruriency of fiction and of the stage, and the prostitution of marriage to the ends of convenience and of lust; when we see how the same spirit has invaded the very chair of ethics in some of the strongest institutions of learning in the land, and those set to teach morality express doubt as to the reality of virtue; and when we witness the inroads upon the church of those forms of worldliness whose perils lie in the same direction, we see abundant cause for apprehension lest sensuality may have a powerful hold on modern life.

6. Still another condition is the decline of family religion and of the religious instruction of the young in the home. The excellent sermon on this subject preached by the Moderator at the opening of this Assembly leaves nothing more to be said about that at this time.

7. This sketch is not complete but only suggestive, yet it should not be concluded without a glance at the bright side. There is more consecration of wealth and more evangelistic and missionary activity in the church to-day than there has ever been since the days of the early church. There is more systematic study of the Scriptures and of problems of church work than there has ever been. There are as fine examples of Christian conscience in public life as the world has ever seen. There is the strongest sense of the spiritual unity of Christendom.

II. What is meant by "the Principles of Calvinism"? The principles of Calvinism are its essential parts as opposed to its accidental parts. They are that without which Calvinism would cease to be Calvinism. They are the germinal and regulative principles out of which it springs and by which it is moulded. We must distinguish between the principles of Calvinism and that complete system of belief which Calvin himself held. We must distinguish between the principles of Calvinism and any creed held by any Christian organization calling itself Calvinistic, just as we distinguish between the principles of Republican government and any one form of Republican Government. The government may be Republican in its general plan and yet may embody monarchical or other features inconsistent with its central principle. And so Calvinism, powerful, acute, accurate logician as he was, was nevertheless finite and fallible. In the carrying out of his principles he may have been unconsciously influenced to some extent by education and by the circumstances of his life, and so he may have held some views that could not be reconciled with his other opinions. For a stronger reason we conclude that Calvinistic denominations, in the elaboration of their doctrinal formulas, may have produced creeds that were not logically consistent throughout. There may even be some denominations which hold to the radical principles of Calvinism and yet so far fail in the application of those principles in constructing their creeds as to deny some tenets which are characteristic of Calvinism and themselves repudiate the name.

With these general comments, and without pausing to defend my statement, I submit for your approval an outline sketch of the principles of Calvinism. It includes a belief:

1. In an objective personal God, who is infinitely interested in each individual of his creation, and is immediately accessible to each, and to whom each is immediately responsible.

2. The utter wreck of man's spiritual nature by sin, totally disabling him for holiness and alienating him from God.

3. The absolute dependence of ruined man upon the mercy of God for devising, executing, revealing and personally applying whatever scheme of restoration may be possible for man.

4. The granting to the believer of a restoration through the atonement of Christ, so complete that the image of God is regained and every trace of sin is lost, and of such a nature as to be forever indestructible.

5. The establishment of a fellowship between God and the individual redeemed, so free, so unrestrained, that the whole life is fertilized by divine impulses, and all the resources of life are brought under spontaneous contribution to the glory of God.

How deeply do the "five points of Calvinism" enter into this scheme! It enables us to understand what Guizot said of Calvin, that his mind moved in the circle of three chapters of his *Institutes*. The subjects of those chapters are:

1. Man's need of the Bible in order to obtain peace with God.

2. Reason can satisfactorily prove that the Scriptures are a revelation from God.

3. Man's absolute dependence upon the influences of the Holy Spirit in order to understand aright and to appropriate what the Bible contains.

The outline I have drawn perhaps also gives us Dr.

Kuyper's point of view when he says in one place that the distinctive tenet of Calvinism is "The exalted thought that although standing in high majesty above the creature, God enters into immediate fellowship with the creature"; and when he says again, "The persuasion that the whole of a man's life is to be lived as in the divine presence has become the fundamental thought of Calvinism"; and again when he says, "The assurance of eternal Salvation" was the inspiration of the fortitude and the courage of those who suffered martyrdom for the faith and who achieved the victories of Calvinism.

The principles of Calvinism I have given are those which pertain to the doctrines of grace, to which I must be confined this morning. But it should be noted in passing that out of these principles of grace there grow principles of church government sufficient for discipline, and principles of worship, simple, whole-hearted and majestic, and other principles which regulate one's moral and intellectual life, and his domestic, social, industrial and civil relations.

III. What is meant by rendering these principles "effective"? What is the effect we should wish Calvinism to produce?

I submit that the effect we should desire is not to make the gospel popular. Christ did not do that. It is not to adorn religion with artificial attractions, to appeal to the taste or imagination or even the intellect, and so to make it pleasing to the natural heart, for "then is the offense of the Cross ceased." It is not to multiply adherents, admirers, professors and financial supporters. Of what advantage is it that we have plethoric church rolls and houses of worship crowded with enthusiastic listeners if men do not forsake sin and selfishness for

God and service, and if there be in men no power to transform the life and no foretokens of the perfect life of heaven? The effect we should desire is the creation of spiritual life in man. It is the bringing of men by regeneration into the spiritual kingdom of God, and it is the developing in them by santification of a character consonant with the nature of the spiritual kingdom and an anticipation of the heavenly and eternal state. Through individuals so affected we should seek to mold communities and through communities to impress the nation. And thus in ever widening circles we should send out saving influences to the uttermost parts of the earth.

IV. And now we reach the main question. "How May the Principles of Calvinism be Rendered Most Effective Under Modern Conditions?"

In this discussion we must assume that the principles of Calvinism are correct. As a matter of fact we do absolutely believe they are correct. We are Calvinists not from heredity, nor from education, nor from environment, but from individual conviction of the truth of Calvinism. What have we then? Here is a positive, well definied, divine arrangement for the redemption of man and for restoring him to the image, the fellowship, and the service of God. All this is contained in the Bible. We believe it is correctly reproduced in the Calvinistic statement. While then there is no rescinding of this arrangement by divine warrant and no modification of it, while there is no change in the nature of God and no change in the nature of man, we are compelled to act upon the assumption that it is a permanent arrangement adapted to all conditions of humanity in all ages. Inspired revelation is not progressive but fixed. Our understanding of it may increase and become better clarified, but here we have no question as to the substantial correctness of our interpretation. Thus Calvinism contains an economy ordained in the wisdom of the Most High for meeting and controlling all possible developments of human life and thought.

It may be interesting and useful to us to examine the changing phases of human society and ascertain what in them is most congenial with Calvinism, and what Calvinism may use. For instance, the radical principle of Socialism is but the perversion of a principle for which the world is indebted through Calvinism to the Bible. Calvinism teaches us that God is equally accessible to all men and that all men are equally responsible to God. There is then a sort of equality among men which they must recognize. But Socialism goes to the impossible extreme of making that equality absolute, and so obliterates distinctions which the Creator Himself established. Take another illustration. There are more than two hundred million Moslems in the world who believe in fatalism, and there are more than four hundred million Chinese who believe in some form of predestination. These together comprise more than one-third of the human family and more than a half of the unevangelized races, and all this large proportion of the population of the world holds to a more or less perverted form of a doctrine which is distinctive of Calvinism, the sovereignty of God. Or take another illustration. Calvinism, with a better grace than any other religion, can say to Natural Science, You have shown the world more than it has ever known before of the splendor and beauty of creation. You have taught the world more clearly than it has ever known before how the beautiful order of the universe has been wrought out by a plan. Is it not more reasonable to believe that the explanation of this world is the presence of a master intelligence rather than the operation of an unconscious force?"

But after all we must at last confront the fact that we may not depend and need not depend on any natural easy process. Calvinism if it be God's truth has in it a divine energy intended to overcome and fitted to overcome every kind and degree of opposition. The opposition of to-day may differ in form but does not differ in substance from that of other days. That opposition arises from vicious reasoning and a depraved heart. It was a false philosophy and a corrupt society which Calvin confronted and overcame. Guizot says, "The principal and most formidable characteristics of the sixteenth century were its political disturbances, its public immorality and its ardent intellectual outburst, and Calvin was simultaneously resisting all of them." That was a greater task than we have to-day, because the political disturbances, at least, are no longer a feature of the conflict. The proclamation of the truth accompanied by the gracious working of God was ever the means by which the opposition was subdued. Christ said, "Preach the Gospel, and lo, I am with you." On Pentecost Peter narrated the story of Jesus of Nazareth, and the Holy Ghost fell on the multitude and thousands were converted. At Antioch, they preached "the Word" and they preached "the Lord Jesus," and "the hand of the Lord was upon them," and "a great number believed and turned unto the Lord."

A small group of propagandists, with the world against them, with the prestige of heathenism and Judaism in opposition, with the most powerful military government of history actively hostile, clogged by subtle and false philosophies within, nevertheless transfused the Roman empire with Christianity. The teachings of Christ, the sermons recorded in the Acts, the Epistles, which did this work, contain those doctrines which have been formulated in Calvinism. If such is the force of this truth when it is preached "in demonstration of the Spirit and of power," what may it not accomplish?

When the Reformation came in the sixteenth century, both false doctrine and corruption of character were entrenched in the citadel of the church itself. The revolt was not only against corruption. It went deeper and challenged the doctrinal errors which made that corruption possible. The doctrine of the Reformation did not crystallize in Luther. Under God, all honor to Luther for his initiative, his lion-hearted courage, his indefatigable labors, his strongly loving and strongly hating nature and for his sublime leadership. But the doctrine of the Reformation did not come to its crystalline form in Luther, but in Calvin. The believers in Calvinism, strong in their knowledge of the truth, in the presence of God's Spirit, and in their assurance of eternal life, whether they were found in Germany, in the Netherlands, in Switzerland, in France, in Spain, or in Great Britain, blanched not before church or state or any human tribunal. They faltered not for fire or sword, or axe, or rope, or rack or any instrument of torture that man or devil could devise, they feared not to assail sin or error, and again the victory was won against fallacious reasoning and immoral conduct.

Calvinism is the most powerful evangelistic agency ever employed. In the seventeenth, eighteenth and nineteenth centuries, revivals of religion, notable for the intensity of feeling stirred, the number of people affected and the nature and permanency of the results that followed, swept over Great Britain and the United States. The stock of the preaching was Calvinistic.

In local communities, a character for piety, for industry, for integrity, for heroism, for altruism, for initiative has been imparted and transmitted for many generations. Every type of moral character has been reached and regenerated by it. The dissolute, the drunkard, the burglar, the liar, the indifferent, the violently hostile, the ignorant, the highly educated, the moral, the phlegmatic, the emotional, the supercilious, all alike come under conviction of sin and helplessness and cry, "What must I do to be saved"? And all alike being converted cry with Thomas, "My Lord and my God," and with Saul of Tarsus, "Lord, what wilt thou have me to do?"

All of this being true and the question being, "How may the principles of Calvinism be rendered most effective under modern conditions?" the answer is two-fold:

1. Let Calvinism in its integrity be boldly avowed and aggressively pressed. It is not a time for cowardice, "Awake, awake; put on thy strength, O Zion; put on thy beautiful garments, O Jerusalem, the Holy City." Let not the church be afraid of it nor afraid to preach it. As some one has said, "The truth needs no caretakers, it needs only witnesses." Let not the truth be suppressed or concealed. Let it not be compromised nor amended at the dictation of its enemies. Let it not be glossed to please an unbelieving world. It has always done its work in the open field and not in hiding and not by indirection. It has done its work as a whole and

not as a mutilated system. Then let it be proclaimed with confidence.

To say that men will no longer hear doctrinal preaching is a mistake. Only let the preacher himself find a throbbing life in the theme, and let the truth live in his own being, and he will make it live in the lives of his hearers. The street preacher is not afraid of this truth and he has his reward. Thousands turn away from discussions in the pulpit of current events and social topics, and political issues, and merely ethical questions, and try to fill themselves with the husks of occult and puerile philosophies.

Following this suggestion we shall need several things:

1. A ministry thoroughly and boldly in sympathy with Calvinism. Let the emphasis of theological instruction continue to rest upon the chair of systematic theology and increase the emphasis. Let all the learning of the college, the university, and the theological Seminary be focused upon a doctrinal education. Let the doctrine be supported by sound exegesis on the one hand and sound philosophy on the other. Give us a scholarship in the ministry, capable of stating the truth, thoroughly informed as to its history and its bearings on other knowledge and on life, and able to defend the truth at every point of attack. Why should we not have a learning in the pulpit as broad, as deep, as accurate, as highly tempered as any to be found in professors chairs, in the laboratories of science, or in the researches of the field and the forest? If Buckle's observation be correct that the tendency of Arminianism is to produce scholars, and the tendency of Calvinism is to produce thinkers, we need to give special attention to this suggestion.

Yet, far be it from us to disparage personal piety as a requisite for the ministry. As between the minister whose knowledge of the truth and conviction of it are only intellectual, and the man whose "life is hid with Christ in God," evermore give us the man who has obtained his knowledge at first hand, from communion with God and from the Spirit's illumination of the word.

But not only should the minister be in contact with the truth and with God, in order that he may bring the influence of both to bear on human life he must be in sympathetic contact with humanity. The Good Shepherd was responsive to every human impulse and should not the under shepherd know and feel all that is in man? More than in any previous age does the man of God need to be a man among men, acquainted with their conditions and sharing those conditions, loving and being loved, ministering a Christ-like sympathy and help to every kind of man.

In many cases these three phases of ministerial education, the scholastic, the spirtual and the practical, may be united in the same person. The ministry as a whole should be distinguished by all of them.

Then, with the best and most practical men in the pulpit, let the voice of the people and high ideals in Presbytery make it not only possible but imperative that preaching shall be something more than merely emotional, or evangelistic, or hortatory, or ethical and never dryly dogmatic. Let it be all the counsel of God, the word of God "which liveth and abideth forever," the most effective implement of evangelism, the surest ethical foundation.

2. Denominational institutions of learning. By denominational institutions is meant not necessarily those

under ecclesiastical control. A school may be under ecclesiastical control and altogether negative in religious character. A school may not be under ecclesiastical control and yet saturated to the core with the denominational spirit. A school is denominational only when the influence of its instruction and its school life is positively and strongly denominational. Far hence with the thought that a man cannot be an instructor of the highest order because he has decided religious beliefs. Away with the suggestion that Calvinism may not furnish teachers who are the equals of any other teachers. And again let us give no heed to the claim that successful instruction is hindered, when there are parallel efforts made for the spiritual conversion of the student and his sound indoctrination. Let not the Syren voice of money allure us to destruction upon such rocky shores.

Let all the facts of science be fearlessly told, whether of geology, biology, sociology, archaeology or comparative religion. "The truth needs no caretakers." But back of all science place the fact, "In the beginning God created the heavens and the earth," and let the terminus of all science be, "For Thy glory they were and are created." Let Calvin and Calvinism be given their rightful place in history. Why should there be any more sensitiveness about assigning Calvinism its proper place in modern history than there is in discussing the Mecklenburg Declaration or the responsibility for the loss of Gettysburg? Let the science of government be so taught that the contribution of Calvinistic principles to civil liberty and to right theories of government may be clearly seen. Let ethics and political economy acknowledge their indebtedness to it. Let the Bible be taught in all its bearings upon individual life, and marriage, and the family and the state. And let not a pseudo-liberality lead us to suppress the denominational name and intention of our schools. The eloquent Dr. Moses D. Hoge once remarked, "Presbyterians are the only people who make that mistake."

3. A revival of catechetical instruction in the family and in the Sabbath school, and a rebuilding of the family altar. The stream is not apt to rise higher than its source nor to be purer than its fountain head. Not only should the rythmical clauses of the catechism be given to the memory as the molds for future thought, but all explanations of Scripture, all moral lessons, all parental counsel, all wooings of the heart for Christ should be given with a distinct consciousness of the Calvinistic point of view. Then continue to develop the Sunday school along the lines already adopted, until it shall become as effective in its sphere as the public school is in its.

4. Once more, we need with all of this, not less but more catholic spirit, a sincere, generous, loving appreciation of our fellow Christians of whatever denominational name and of whatever creed, because of their service to the truth and because of the souls they have brought to a common Master.

II. The second answer to the principal question is that we should seek, and not cease our seeking till we obtain, copious, deep, wide-spread outpourings of the Holy Spirit. The truth alone without the supernatural grace of God's Spirit has no saving and sanctifying efficacy, whatever natural power it may have. In all the great genuine movements of the church the presence of the Spirit of God has overshadowed all other circumstances. What we need for modern conditions is the almighty supernatural working of God, causing the truth to dispel the darkness, and converting hostility into loving submission and worship. The occasion calls for patience and prayer.

For any distrust of the truth, for any compromise with the world, for any recreancy to duty, "let the ministers of the Lord weep between the porch and the altar, and let them say, Spare thy people, O Lord, and give not thine heritage to reproach." "Then will the Lord be jealous and pity His people. Yea, the Lord will answer and say unto His people, Behold, I will no more make you a reproach among the heathen." When the divine challenge comes, "Awake, awake; put on thy strength, O Zion; put on thy beautiful garments, O Jerusalem, the holy city," let the church say, "Awake, awake, put on strength, O arm of the Lord; awake, as in the ancient days, in the generations of old."

"Let God arise, let His enemies be scattered."

"Give ear, O Shepherd of Israel, Thou that leadest Joseph like a flock; Thou that dwellest between the Cherubims, shine forth.

Before Ephraim and Benjamin and Manasseh stir up thy strength, and come and save us."

"Turn us again, O Lord God of Hosts, cause Thy face to shine and we shall be saved."

JOHN CALVIN—THE MAN AND HIS TIMES.

By Dr. Chas Merle d' Aubigne,
Neuilly-sur-Seine, France.

John Calvin was born on the 10th of July, 1509, in the small town of Noyon, in Picardy. His grandfather was a cooper, and owned a small house on the banks of the river Oise. His father, Gerard Cauvin—the name was later Latinized into Calvinus, Calvin—attained by his perseverance and industry to an honorable situation. He was Secretary to the Bishop of Noyon, and Notary to the Chapter of the Cathedral. His mother, Jeanne Lefranc, was noted as a goodlooking and pious woman. John Calvin had four brothers, and two sisters. Two of them followed him later on to Geneva, and settled down near their more famous kinsman.

Young Calvin showed from his boyhood "a strong mind, a quick and inventive intelligence." He was destined by his father, whose relations with the clergy were constant, to the church, and received, when he was only twelve years of age, the *benefice* or living of the chapel Gesine in the cathedral of Noyon. Such an occurrence was by no means uncommon at a time when John of Lorraine was made Bishop at the age of four, and Odet de Châtillon, Coligny's brother, Cardinal at sixteen.

In 1523, when he was fourteen, young John was sent to Paris as a companion to some youths of the noble family of Montmor. He and his friends were received into the college of La Marche and, a few months later, into that of Montaigu, whose principal was the celebrated Beda, later on one of the fiercest opponents of the dawning Reformation.

In that college the fare was meagre, the discipline severe the work unremitting and the dirt indescribable. From 4 o'clock in the morning till 9 at night, lessons went on almost uninterruptedly, with half an hour's break twice a day, to partake of a hasty meal.

But the scanty diet was made up by abundant flogging. In that college they whipped for yes, and they whipped for no. The whip was the great means of education. "It was administered," says Erasmus, who was also a pupil of the school, "with all the ferocity which one can expect from the hand of the executioner."

As to cleanliness, I cannot enter into details. Let me only mention the fact that it was forbidden in Montaigu to the pupils to put their hands to their heads during meals—for fear of what might fall therefrom!

How did young Calvin fare in that unpropitious school-house? The order does not seem to have disagreed with his temperament, and no doubt he trained himself there to the austere discipline, and ceaseless work which were his rule all through life. He was ardent in his studies, marvellously quick to learn, unflinchingly severe with himself and others. It was no doubt for that reason that he was given by his comrades the nickname of "Accusative."

However, Calvin's student years in Paris would have been barren indeed had it not been for his meeting, in the College of La Marche, a master who was to be to him more than a teacher, a friend, and finally, curious to state, a disciple. Mathurin Cordier was not only one of the best Latin linguists of his time, the reformer of the study of that language, but a pedagogue of keen insight, and what is better still, a pious heart and earnest Christian. Speaking of the continual flogging, which was the habit of his time, he says: "Why do you constrain, beat and torture. If you want to instruct easily? Begin by God and heavenly things. . . . The name of Jesus Christ—pour it drop by drop into your pupil's heart. Inculcate into them the word of God, that they may be touched by some spark of the divine love. Remove the pack of rods, and approach the brand and little flames of piety."

Such was the teaching which Calvin imbibed in the college of La Marche for many a month. We cannot doubt that it was received into well prepared ground. The reformer never forgot what he owed his old master. Years later he dedicated to him one of his commentaries, and called him to be the master of the school which he had founded in Geneva.

In 1528, he was then nineteen, Calvin has finished his course in arts, and, instead of preparing for the church, we find him for five years studying laws, and then literature in the universities of Orléans, Bourges and Paris.

At the time when the young and promising student betook himself to the *Alma Mater* on the banks of the Loire, the University of Orléans was in the full bloom of its prosperity. There Erasmus had taught Latin, Aleander Greek, and the German Reuchlin Hebrew. There the famous lawyer, Pierre de l'Etoile, "The Prince of Laws," as he was called, lectured to the crowd of students attracted to the fair city from all parts of the world. It was a motley crowd, composed of princes, dukes, and counts, as well as of the sons of the rich burghers of the city. It was also a joyous crowd. The students went by the name of "The Dancers of Orléans," and "there were," says a chronicler, "more than forty games of ball where the Prince of Orléans, later King Louis XII., played with the citizens, the Doctors with their pupils." "And as to breaking their heads with study," adds the famous Rabelais, "they did not do much of that, for fear of injuring their sight."

It needs scarcely be said that young Calvin had less consideration for his eyes. On the contrary, he appears to us, at that early age, that tremendous worker, that indefatigable student he remained all his life. "He often worked till midnight," says his biographer, Theodore Beza—and let it be remembered that the time for rising then was four or five in the morning. He ate little at supper to be free in his mind, and in the morning, as soon as he awoke, he was used to sit in bed, recalling what he had studied the night before." "There can be no doubt," Beza adds, "that such sleepless nights gravely injured his health, and occasioned that weakness of the bowels which after causing him several illnesses, brought about his premature death." "He possessed," says the same biographer, "an incredible memory, which retained every point, and forgot nothing. He could remember the most insignificant details of what had taken place years before. Later on, when he taught, or preached, he never had before him the slightest manuscript, and, when interrupted while dictating a letter or a commentary, he could begin again straight way, without being told where he had left off."

With such readiness and such toil, Calvin progressed rapidly. "Under Pierre de l'Etoile," says Beza again, "Calvin profited so well and in such a short time, that they did not hold him a scholar, but one of the ordinary doctors, and in fact, he was more often a teacher than a listener."

Three years later, in 1531, when Calvin was twenty-two, these laborious studies culminated in a work which placed him, at the very outset of his career, in the front ranks of the humanists of his time. It was a commentary on the "De Clementia" of Seneca. Whether there was in the choice of such a subject, a sort of protest against the persecution which was then raging, and a disguised appeal to the magninimity of the King, is uncertain. Calvin shows himself in the book, a perfect master of the Latin language, a singularly elegant, mature and searching writer, and a scholar of almost incredible erudition. He quotes no less than fifty-five Latin authors, and some of them almost unknown.

Such constant study would not seem to have left Calvin, during his student days, much time for relaxation and social intercourse. He was, so he says himself, "of a shy and retiring disposition," but it would be a great mistake—a mistake that has been often made—to see in him a sombre and lonesome hermit, a hater of his fellowmen, and of their society. On the contrary, we find him in Orleans, in Bourges and in Paris, the center of most interesting groups of young men. He entertained with them the closest relations, and with some the friendship continued intimate and warm to the end of his life.

* * * * * *

But already, Calvin was something more than a hard working student, than an elegant and learned humanist. If you go to the quaint old town of Bourges, they will show you, almost under the shade of the old Cathedral—one of the marvels of architecture—on a little square, "la Pierre de Calvin" Calvin's stone. From there, the future reformer is supposed to have preached to the people assembled in the market place. A little further, you will see a sort of bow-window jutting out from the wall of an old convent, that is "la Chaire de Calvin," Calvin's pulpit. And in the immediate neighborhood of the town, a rickety old stone bridge over a small stream retains to this day the name of Calvin's bridge, "le Pont de Calvin."

Now I will not vouch for the perfect trustworthiness of every one of these local traditions—yet it seems absolutely certain that Calvin did preach the gospel at Bourges, even in his student days, and probably near that very bridge, to the villagers of the neighboring hamlets. Liquières, Asnières, whose descendents trace back to him their Protestant faith. What was it then that brought about the great change, which made of the former candidate to Holy Orders and of the classical scholar a preacher of God's word, and the great reformer of French speaking and of many other countries? The question of Calvin's conversion is not an easy one to solve. He was somewhat shy in speaking of his inner life, and we do not have from others trustworthy records of his change of mind. Yet when we consider the time in which he lived, and the men with whom he associated, it is not difficult to make out under what influences took place that momentous evolution.

The year young Calvin arrived in Paris, 1523, is the very one in which the great movement produced by the Biblical studies of Lefèvre and by the events taking place in Germany, was becoming irresistible.

On the throne of France was Francis I., the gallant and handsome King. His beauty, his intelligence, his bravery, made him the most chivalrous prince of his time. None could surpass him in the art of riding a stallion, or of weilding a lance in a tournament. Courageous, and even foolhardy on the field of battle, he was an intense lover of art, the promoter of learning and of literature, and the builder of the most exquisite gems of Renaissance architecture. Francis was no friend of the Monks. Their ignorance and coarseness repelled him, and gladly would he have welcomed a reformation in the church, had he not discerned in the Protestants an austerity which was a rebuke to his licentiousness, and a love of freedom which would have been a check on his immoderate thirst for domination.

Next to Francis, not on the throne, but very near it, was his sister, the charming and graceful Marguerite de Valois, duchess of Alencon, and later on Queen of Navarre. To her natural beauty, she added a quick intelligence, a great taste for letters—she was a good poet— and what is better still, a real tenderness and earnestness of soul. In a court noted for its levity, she set the example of a pure life, and if all her writings are not irreproachable, her private conduct never gave rise to the slightest suspicion.

It was under Marguerite's protection that old Lefèvre d'Etaples, doctor of the University of Paris—a man who, though he never formally joined the Reformed Church, yet can in truth be called "The Father of French Protestantism"—that Lefèvre published his famous commentary on the Epistles of St. Paul. In that book, Lefèvre affirmed in 1512—note the date, five years before the posting up of Luther's theses in Wittenberg—over against the traditions of the Roman Church the sovereign authority of the word of God, and absolute inefficacy of good works and merit for salvation. In the following years, Lefèvre followed up that courageous act by publishing in French a translation of Holy Scripture, in 1521 the gospels, in 1524 the other books of the New, and in 1528 the whole of the Old Testament. Briconnet, Bishop of Meaux, the friend of Marguerite de Valois, sedulously propagated at his own expense, those books in his diocese, and many of them penetrated into Paris.

The effect of the reading of the Bible in the vulgar tongue was extraordinary and very rapid. "Such a desire," says a chronicler, "was begotten in the hearts of many to know the way of salvation, that the artisan, woolcarders, combers and others had no other thought, while working with their hands, than to confer about the word of God, and to seek it in their consolation."

Very soon a host of distinguished men assembled around the old teacher. Michel d'Avande Marguerite's private chaplain, Gèrard Roussel, the preacher, Leclercq, the pastor of the little congregation at Meaux, the noble Louis de Berquin, as learned as he was courageous, and above all, William Farel, from Gap in Dauphine.

All these men, and we can add women, were not only Calvin's contemporaries, living in Paris at the very time when he was persuing his studies, but many of them became his friends and correspondents. Can you wonder that a young man of that independence, culture and earnestness of purpose, thrown into the company of such men, should have opened his mind to the ideas they were advocating with such courage and intensity.

But very soon a formidable opposition breaks out.

against the innovators. Not only are Lefèvre's commentaries censured and all translations of the Bible condemned to be burned, but the reformers themselves are ruthlessly persecuted. Lefèvre and Farel flee from Paris to save their lives. Fourteen members of the congregation of Meaux are arrested and burned, after having had their tongues cut off. Their pastor, Jean Leclercq, has his fist hewn away, his nose torn with red hot pincers, his arms and breast lacerated, and then he is led to the stable to be burned. Suddenly a cry is heard in the crowd: "Vive Jesus Christ et ses enseignes." "Hurrah for Christ and His marks!" It is Leclercq's own mother rejoicing over her son's death for his Master. John Calvin was in Paris at the very time of Leclercq's and his friends' martyrdoms. We can readily imagine what impression they made upon the young man whose faith in the church of his birth was already more than shaken. Add to that, Calvin's intimate friendship with Pierre Robert Olivetan, the translator of the French Bible, who first of all introduced him into the study of Holy Scripture, and the influence of the German Melchior Wolmar, Professor in Bourges, a decided Lutheran, that is a Protestant, who taught him Greek, the Greek of the New Testament, and you have, humanly speaking, a sufficient explanation of his change of mind. "Search the Scriptures," Olivetan used to say to this young friend; "give yourself up entirely to the study of God's word."

God's Holy Word! The French as well as the German and Swiss, and every other Reformation has no other origin, and it is on that anvil that were forged the arms which were soon after to overthrow the power of the Roman Church, and open the kingdom of God to thousands of believers.

So decidedly is Calvin on the side of the new evangelical ideas, that on his return to Paris in 1531, he mixes with no others than with the little persecuted flock. Very soon Calvin is known in the congregation, he is consulted, he preaches to them, he defends them against certain enthusiasts who would, if they were allowed free course, ruin the cause. He gradually comes to the front rank, which is his, and is recognized as the ablest exponent of a religion founded, not upon tradition, but on the authority of the Scriptures.

On the first of November, 1533, the rector of the University of Paris, Nicholas Copp, had to deliver a discourse for All Saints' Day. He took for his subject a rather unusual topic for a doctor of medicine: "Christian Philosophy." In this discourse, the orator opposes the gospel of the law and to the merit, speaks of "the immense good will of God towards us men," of "the assurance of salvation based on the promise of Christ alone, and ends by declaring those blessed "who are persecuted for justice sake and are called heretics, imposters, seducers and accused." The allusion was too direct, and the proclamation too hardy. The Sarbonne did not mistake the purpose, and trembled with rage. The prisons were immediately filled with Lutherans, ready to be sent to the stake.

And who was the author of that masterpiece of eloquence as well as of courage? It was our reformer himself. The fact is certain to-day, the manuscript, or rather the first page of it, has been found in Geneva, written in Calvin's own hand. The Rector Copp, little accustomed to handle theological subjects, but sharing the new evangelical ideas, had asked his young friend to compose the address for him. Responsible for that daring act, he had to flee from Paris, and Calvin himself barely escaped the Inquisitor's hands. He was let down, they say, by his friends in a basket from the window, while the baliff Morin was walking up the staircase.

Then began for Calvin a wandering life, which lasted three years, and ended only when he settled in Geneva. At the end of 1533 he is in Angoulême in the South West with Canon du Tillet, who became for a time his intimate friend. Shortly after, we find him visiting old Lefèvre at Nèvac, and preaching to a few peasants in a cave near Poitiers. Then again he is in Basel and in Strasburg. Then again he is in Italy, at the court of the Duke of Fevare. There he had the satisfaction of winning over to the reformed faith the Duchess herself, of the Royal house of France, sister-in-law to the King, one of the most remarkable women of that remarkable time.

But those three years were not only spent in journeying, and in friendly intercourse with the humble and the great. From the day in which he had found himself before the little assembly of worshippers in Paris, in the home of the pious merchant, Etienne de la Forge, Calvin had felt the need of the hour; a complete and systematic exposition of Christian doctrine such as he had found it in the Scriptures. And through all his journeyings, he kept his object well in view and worked at it perseveringly.

In 1535, while Calvin was in Basel, the King of France who needed for his fight against the Emperor Charles, the help of the German princes, mostly favorable, as you know, to the Reformation, sedulously propagated the notion that the Protestants, whom he was at the time bitterly persecuting, were nothing, as he said, but a pack of enthusiasts, enemies of public order, furious madmen, excited by the father of lies." That was too much for the man, who in Paris, and elsewhere, had been witness of the ardent faith, blameless conduct, and heroic deaths of the French believers. He rapidly put the finishing stroke to the great work he had been preparing, and seizing his pen, which by this time, had become that of a master, he wrote that famous preface to his *Institutes,* which begins in this strain:

"It is your office, Sire, to turn away neither your ears nor your heart from such a just defense, principally when the matter is about such a great cause as the glory of God. How it shall be maintained on earth, how His truth shall retain honor and integrity, how the reign of Christ shall remain supreme. O matter most worthy of your ears and of your royal throne! For that alone makes the real king, if he deems himself the servant of God in the government of his kingdom."

Did the lighthearted and futile king ever read Calvin's eloquent and impassionate address? After all, it is of little consequence. Those words, burning with the love of the oppressed and with jealousy for the glory of God, reached over the king's head all the thinking world, and that was what Calvin wished to attain. They carried the young man's fame to the most remote regions, and dubbed him a master in theology and a leader of men.

Such is the man, who at the age of twenty-six—it is hardly credible—wrote the *Institutes.* He is as well prepared to play his part on the scene of the world as a man can be. Brought up in the very bosom of the church, he has known from his youth its weakness and abuses. All the light that human intelligence can shed, has been poured into his mind. Unlike Luther, shut up in his convent, he has been placed in contact with the greatest men of his age. He has mixed in their society, and absorbed their learning.

A prodigious worker, a rigorous ascete, he is full of youthful buoyancy, fluent in conversation, ardent in discussion, quick in lively and often witty repartee, he astonishes every one by the enormous quantity of knowledge he has stored up in his mind. Of a rather retiring disposition he has a magnetic attraction for all who meet him, so that those who have seen him once, want to see him again. Above all, by the experiences of his own life, by witnessing the faith of the new believers, by his study of the word of God, he has obtained a full grasp of the truth such as it is in Christ, and he is burning to communicate it to others.

In a word, by this time Calvin is thoroughly equipped, ready for the task that God had prepared for him. How he came by that task, and how he accomplished it, is what remains for us to see.

* * * * * *

In 1536, Calvin arrived in Geneva. Geneva, "the fair city by the blue lake and the rushing Rhône, on which Mont Blanc, the giant of the Alps, looks down through all the centuries from his dome of everlasting snow," is a little town hedged in between the mighty empires of France, Germany, Italy and Spain. It is under the suzerainty of its powerful neighbor, the Duke of Savoy, represented by the Bishop, but, for almost a century, its citizens have striven to shake off that yoke, and to obtain complete freedom. At the same time, thanks to the influence of its allies, the Swiss, the reformation has been introduced into the town and the citizens have not been slow to see that the break with the Bishop and with Rome would be the strongest guarantee of their political independence.

In 1532, William Farel, the fiery Farel, the disciple of Lefèvre, and his friend Viret, arrive in Geneva and begin to preach. Three years later, a crowd of people invade the Cathedral, pull down the images of the Saints, and expel the priests from their stronghold. In 1536, the reformation of the church is solemnly voted by all the citizens assembled in council. "It is decided," so run the minutes, "and by a general show of hands concluded, promised and sworn that we will all unanimously, with the help of God, live in this Holy evangelical law and word of God, as it is announced to us, casting off all masses, ceremonies, papal abuses, images, idols and the like, and that we will live in union and righteous obedience."

The victory seemed complete for the cause of the gospel in the little town; but those who knew the actual state of things, were not buoyant as to the future. Many of those who had acclaimed the change, had done so more for political reasons than from religious conviction, and besides, the scandalous living of the clergy had for years propagated among the people a license and immorality which were incompatible with the profession of the gospel. Farel, himself, inimitable as he was as a preacher of the reformation, and irresistable in his condemnation of the errors of Rome, did not possess those qualities of organization, of wise and prudent statesmanship which were necessary at this point. He felt it, and looked about him for a helper.

It was at this juncture that one day of July, 1536, the rumor went abroad that a young French doctor, already famous for his writings, had arrived in the city. Calvin, on his return from Italy, was on his way to Basel. His intention was to spend only one night in the city. But, Farel, having heard of his arrival, saw that he was the providential man to organize the reformation in Geneva. He instantly betook himself to the inn where Calvin was staying, unfolded to him the situation of the church, and asked him to remain. Calvin was very reluctant to consent. He pleaded his plans, his studies, his taste for quiet and retirement. The more Farel presses him the more he is terrified at the prospect which opens up before him. "Then," says Calvin himself, "Farel, trembling with a holy wrath, stands up, and with his thundering voice, said: 'In the name of the Almighty God if you allege your studies, and refuse to give yourself up with us to this work of the Lord, I declare it unto you, God will curse you, for you are seeking yourself rather than Christ.'" "And that word," adds Calvin, "so disturbed and terrified me that I desisted from my journey, as if God, Himself, from above, had stretched out his hand to arrest me."

It was thus Calvin was given to Geneva, and Geneva to Calvin. Henceforward the man and the city, the city and the man are one.

His entrance on his new sphere of work was in a way dramatic, but it was far from sensational. Strange to say, the minutes of the Town Council do not as much as mention the reformer's name. On the 5th of September of the same year, we find the following item: "Master William Farel exposes the necessity there is of the lectures begun in the Cathedral by that Frenchman, 'ille Gallus,' and asks that he be retained and fed." The good councillors were evidently not greatly impressed by the arrival of "that Frenchman," or by the honor done to their city thereby, for five months later we find again in the same minutes the following: "Here is spoken of Calvinus, who as yet has received nothing, and is decide that he be given six crowns (about as many dollars). Six dollars for five months' work! I do not know whether many of the fathers and brethren here present would be content with such a salary. . . . And Calvin has been accused of riotous and expensive living!

Calvin's immediate task was to apply the principles of the Reformation to every day life of the citizens of Geneva. "When I first came," he wrote later, "sermons were preached, the idols had been sought out and burned, but there was no other reformation." It appeared to him there was no great advantage in throwing off the bondage of Rome, if men did not accept the law of Christ and become a holy people. During the first years of the Reformation, and up to Calvin's arrival, no discipline had been applied to admission to the Lord's table. Every man and woman, whether believer or not, sinner or saint, approached it as he or she felt inclined to do, and without even the preparation that was required in former times by the confessional. Calvin insisted that the church should have the power to exclude the undeserving and that its censures and excommunications should be upheld and enforced by the arm of the state.

Another object which Calvin aimed at with all the perseverance and tenacity which were in his nature was to obtain in the small city that perfect unity of faith on which alone it seemed to him possible to build up a republic worthy of God. For that reason a confession of faith was drawn up, the different councils were first asked to adhere, and then all the citizens by batches of ten, were invited to follow their lead.

That was, as we see to-day, going decidedly too far. The church has not the right to enforce religious faith on all the citizens of a community, and the state has not the right to use its power to carry into effect the censures of the church. But if Calvin erred, he erred for conscience sake. His ideal of a community in which all should be members of the church and of a church in which all should be saints, was an impossible one to realize and especially by the enactments of the law. But it was a high ideal, and we can only thank God, and bless Calvin's memory for having placed it once at least before our eyes.

For the present, the carrying out of the program, proved to be above the powers even of such a man as he. It would have been difficult under any circumstances and in any community. Among such a stiff-necked people as the Genevese (I can only say so, since I am one of them) and considering the licentiousness which had prevailed in the city for years, it was an utter impossibility. The opposition to the reformers and to their regulations waxed stronger and stronger, and on the 23rd of April, 1538, two years only after he had arrived there, Calvin and his friend Farel, for he also had remained in Geneva, were banished from the town. "Well," they exclaimed, on hearing the sentence, "so much the better! If we had served men, we should have had a sorry recompense, but we serve a greater Master, and He will give us our reward."

* * * * * *

In the old German town of Strassburg, whither the Reformer betook himself, he found, it must be owned, a more congenial atmosphere than on the shores of the blue Leman. Strassburg was earnest, God-fearing and studious city. Around the Church of St. Thomas nestled a group of men who were among the most remarkable of their time. Bucer and Capito, the two great and learned reformers, Matthew Zell, the popular preacher, Jacob Sturm, the eminent statesman, and John Sturm, the renowned pedagogue. Truly a unique group of men! Moderate, intelligent, full of faith but also prudence, they led their people on progressively and without break from the darkness of Rome to the full light of the Gospel.

In Strassburg, Calvin was at the same time, pastor and professor. The salary was small—one florin a week—and at one time Calvin was so poor, that he was obliged to sell all his books; but the opportunities for intercourse as well as for study were incomparable, and Calvin, we may be sure, made good use of them.

In the meantime, things had not been going on well in Geneva. The pastors who had succeeded Calvin were decidedly inferior to their task, and several had to be dismissed. Of the four magistrates who had deposed him, three went wrong, and one was beheaded. Every one felt that Calvin alone was strong enough to re-establish order and decency, and he was unanimously recalled.

"For the next twenty-three years," says one of his biographers, "Calvin was the dominating soul of that little city. He had many and hard battles still to fight, but his influence grew stronger and stronger, until he bore down all opposition, moulded Geneva in most things after the pattern of his own heart, and raised it at last to the dignity of becoming a model for the other Reformed Churches, as well as the mother-city of them all. John Knox has described it as "the most perfect school of Christ that ever was on earth, since the days of the Apostles." "In other places," he adds, "I confess Christ to be truly preached, but manners and religion to be so sincerely reformed, I have not yet seen in any other place beside."

Now for his contests with the Libertines of Geneva, as well as with the divers heretics he had to do with, Calvin is accused of a great many things. He is held up for his high-handed dealing and for his tyranous disposition, he is accused of having been unduly sensitive, and jealous of his authority. Now, I admit that he did sometimes overstep the mark. I grant that he allowed himself to be carried away by his nervously overstrung and passionate temper,—let him who has never been ruffled in his life cast the first stone. But when I remember how he was constantly provoked by the vilest gang of calumniators, when I consider that his health was the most miserable that one can imagine, and that at a certain period of his life he was overcome by four illnesses at the same time, "I rather wonder," to quote Prof. Doumergué's words, "at the spirit of moderation and conciliation which he manifested in the midst of these crises of pain, and how he possessed his soul by a patience, which showed all the more the power of divine grace, that it could be less attributed to his human nature."

And as to the burning of Michel Servetus, with which he has been so much reproached, let it be remembered that the Spanish anti-trinitarian was condemned, not by Calvin alone, but by the Council of Geneva, composed at that time of men by no means subject to the Reformer's influence, and that that condemnation was approved of by all the leading reformers previously consulted. Far from urging the judges to excessive severity, Calvin, it is well known, pleaded for a milder form of punishment. If, therefore, Servetus' death was an error, and we think it was, it was not Calvin's error alone, but that of his generation, and it is as unjust to brand him as a bloodthirsty tyrant, as it is to judge him from our own standpoint of liberty and toleration, which is the result of centuries of evolution.

* * * * * *

However, to know the real Calvin, and admire him as he deserves to be admired, we must look away from this phase of his life, and consider him as the pastor, preacher and teacher of men. In that respect, he was incomparable. Not only did he preside weekly at the Consistory and the Pastor's meeting, visit the citizens in their houses, and especially the sick, preach daily every second week, inspect the famous school and academy which he had founded, lecture to the students, but he carried on his strong shoulders the care of all the churches. His sermons,—we have three thousand of them,—were immediately taken down by fast writers, published and translated into many languages. So were his Commentaries on almost every Book of the Bible, which he dictated at home to his secretaries. And if you remember that besides all this, Calvin found time, in his spare hours to carry on an immense correspondence with the leading men and churches of the times,—the complete collection of all his writings, published in our days, fills 58 folio volumes,—you feel giddy at the thought of what that man accomplished and you can only praise God that he raised up such an admirable defender of our faith.

Who can say what ardor, what perseverance, what indomitable energy and what tenderness of heart he displayed in that immense religious propaganda whose very life and soul he was up to his last breath? What a wonderful apostolate that was, for more than a quarter of a century among the princes and the peasants, the learned and the ignorant. In France alone, more than 2,000 churches were organized by his care, in England he advises King Edward and the Duke of Somerset, in Scotland he inspires John Knox, in Poland he opposes the anti-trinitarians, and he is in touch with all the heads of the German Reformation, working perseveringly for the great object he had at heart: the union of all true believers.

In Geneva, very soon after the founding of the academy, hundreds of students flocked together from all parts of the world, attracted by the fame of that institution, and by him who was its leading spirit. After having listened to his sermons, and imbibed his teachings, these men returned to their several countries inflamed with faith and zeal, and set to their work of preaching the Gospel with the ardor and courage of martyrs. To him, these pastors and confessors looked for council and encouragement, and it was a letter from him they expected to strengthen them when tortured, in prison, or marching to the stake. They loved and respected him as a father, and we can understand his proud answer to those who upbraided him for having no children of his own: "Children," he said, "I have them by the thousand in all the Christian world!"

* * * * * *

But such constant care and ceaseless toil soon told upon his already enfeebled constitution. Calvin was never a strong man, and during ten years of his life, in order to retain the clearness of his mind, he never ate more than one meal a day. During the later years, he was a constant sufferer. The doctors have ascribed to him, as has just been said, four serious illnesses at the same time; pleurisy, consumption, nephritic pains and gout, besides countless minor ailments. "He had," says his contemporary and friend, Theodore Beza, "such a feeble body, so weakened by watches and too great sobriety, that no one who saw him could think that he could live at all." And yet all that feebleness and pain did not prevent him from working for others to the very last weeks of his life.

In the beginning of 1564, his friends felt that the end was near. On the 6th of February, while he was preaching, he was taken with such a violent fit of hemorrhage, that he was obliged to stop several times during the sermon. On the 27th of April, the Council having heard that he "was pressed by illness even unto death," decided that they would go to his house to hear what he would have to say to them. Calvin, receiving this official visit, thanked the members of the Council for having supported him in his too vehement affections and in his vices, but protested before God that he had always announced to them the word of the Lord. Finally he exhorted them to honor God more and more, for it is He alone, he added, who maintains the state. The next day, his leave-taking from his colleagues, the other ministers, was even more touching. "I have had many infirmities," he said, "which you have had to bear, and even all that I have done was worth nothing. The wicked will lay hold of this word, but I repeat it: all that I have done was worth nothing. I am a miserable creature. But I can say that I had the will to do good, and my faults have always displeased me, and the root of the fear of God has been in my heart."

A few days later, old Farel, aged 75, came on foot all the way from Neuchâtel, to take leave of his friend. From that time up to the day of his death he prayed continually. In the fits of acute sufferings, he was heard to murmur: "O Lord, Thou bruisest, but I will suffer in patience, for it is Thy hand that has done it."

On the 27th of May, 1564, at about eight in the evening, so quietly that up to the last moment he was able to converse with those around him, Calvin passed away. "And that was how," writes Beza, "the greatest light in the church went out at the time when the sun ceased to illumine the earth."

The next day his body was carried to the common cemetery without any pomp or ceremony whatever. According to his own wish, no monument, not even a stone, marked the place of his tomb; only on the minutes of the Consistory was marked the following item: *"On the 27th of May of the present year Calvin went to God."*. That was the only eulogy pronounced at the death of that mighty man of God, let us rather say, of that faithful servant of the Lord.

Such is the man whose birth, 400 years ago, we are celebrating and whose powerful mind moulded the faith and discipline of Presbyterian churches all over the world. A character of wonderful complexity, varied, many-sided, and therefore very difficult to fathom and thoroughly comprehend.

He is constantly pre-occupied with his work, bent upon his duty, "The man," says a writer, "of his task, the man of the Church, the man of the Christian world." And yet he is not opposed to relaxation and repose. He is tender in his affections, a good and loving husband, true to his friends.

At times, we find him austere and grave; we should like to see him more genial, more open to the delight of art, to the enjoyment of the beautiful. But when we penetrate below that rugged and apparently unartistic surface, we are delighted to discover, here and there, in his writings, a very delicate taste and a high appreciation of the beauties in nature and in the arts of man, and we understand what he says of himself that he was "of a temperament inclined to poetry."

He is conscious of his power and, in a measure, jealous of his authority, but Calvin is very far from being the despot some have made him out to be. He is ready to avow his mistakes and faults, he is generous and large-hearted towards his opponents, provided they make the slightest concession, and he, the master of masters, the man before whom the greatest avow their inferiority, he is humble. That is recognized even by such a man as the French writer, Ferdinand Buisson, who is by no means one of his admirers.

Before everything, Calvin is the man of one idea, and of one book. The book is the Holy Scriptures, the idea the glory of God. It is told of him, that often, in the middle of a conversation or of a discussion, he would pause one moment, take off with one hand his black cap, and with the other, point to heaven, saying: "All for the glory of God." In that gesture, Calvin is entirely. Absolutely disinterested, he lives and dies a poor man, and all that he left behind him, including all his books, did not amount to $300. "The power of that man," used to say Pope Pius IV., "is that money is nothing to him."

But what was something to him, what was all in his life, that was the glory of his Divine Master. Calvin never did what he wished, one can say that he always did the contrary of what he felt inclined to do. In Basel, when he published his *Institutes*, in Geneva when Farel forces him to take up the reins of ecclesiastical government, later on when the Genevese want him back to their town, and every sense within him rebels against the very idea, he was not seeking his own will. "I know them," he exclaimed, speaking of the citizens of Geneva, "they are insupportable to me and I to them. I shudder at the very thought of seeing them again."

To drive him out of that retired life and make of him an actor in the great tragedy of the world, it required more than human intervention. "It needed," as Michelet puts it, "an evident moral necessity, the violence of conscience and of heaven, the tyranny of God." "*Cor mactatum in Sacrificium offero*," "I offer my heart in sacrifice," he said, on returning to Geneva, and that was what he placed on his coat of arms: a hand holding out a heart and presenting it to God.

An instrument in the hand of the Almighty,—he may have erred at times,—no one is infallible,—he may sometimes have mistaken the instrument for Him who alone must wield it; but without doubt, that persuasion that he was an instrument in God's hands, made of Calvin what he was, and enabled him to accomplish, not in Geneva, or in France alone, but in the world, that tremendous task, for which we cannot be too thankful.

Other Solid Ground Titles

Solid Ground Christian Books is honored to present the following titles, many for the first time in more than a century:

COLLECTED WORKS of James Henley Thornwell (4 vols.)
CALVINISM IN HISTORY *by Nathaniel S. McFetridge*
OPENING SCRIPTURE: *Hermeneutical Manual by Patrick Fairbairn*
THE ASSURANCE OF FAITH *by Louis Berkhof*
THE PASTOR IN THE SICK ROOM *by John D. Wells*
THE BUNYAN OF BROOKLYN: *Life & Sermons of I.S. Spencer*
THE NATIONAL PREACHER: *Sermons from 2nd Great Awakening*
FIRST THINGS: *First Lessons God Taught Mankind Gardiner Spring*
BIBLICAL & THEOLOGICAL STUDIES *by 1912 Faculty of Princeton*
THE POWER OF GOD UNTO SALVATION *by B.B. Warfield*
THE LORD OF GLORY *by B.B. Warfield*
A GENTLEMAN & A SCHOLAR: *Memoir of J.P. Boyce by J. Broadus*
SERMONS TO THE NATURAL MAN *by W.G.T. Shedd*
SERMONS TO THE SPIRITUAL MAN *by W.G.T. Shedd*
HOMILETICS AND PASTORAL THEOLOGY *by W.G.T. Shedd*
A PASTOR'S SKETCHES 1 & 2 *by Ichabod S. Spencer*
THE PREACHER AND HIS MODELS *by James Stalker*
IMAGO CHRISTI *by James Stalker*
A HISTORY OF PREACHING *by Edwin C. Dargan*
LECTURES ON THE HISTORY OF PREACHING *by J. A. Broadus*
THE SCOTTISH PULPIT *by William Taylor*
THE SHORTER CATECHISM ILLUSTRATED *by John Whitecross*
THE CHURCH MEMBER'S GUIDE *by John Angell James*
THE SUNDAY SCHOOL TEACHER'S GUIDE *by John A. James*
CHRIST IN SONG: *Hymns of Immanuel from All Ages by Philip Schaff*
COME YE APART: *Daily Words from the Four Gospels by J.R. Miller*
DEVOTIONAL LIFE OF THE S.S. TEACHER *by J.R. Miller*

Call us Toll Free at 1-866-789-7423
Send us an e-mail at sgcb@charter.net
Visit us on line at solid-ground-books.com
Uncovering Buried Treasure to the Glory of God